THE PEOPLE'S MONEY

HOW VOTERS WILL BALANCE THE BUDGET
AND ELIMINATE THE FEDERAL DEBT

SCOTT RASMUSSEN

THRESHOLD EDITIONS

New York   London   Toronto   Sydney   New Delhi

Threshold Editions
A Division of Simon & Schuster, Inc.
1230 Avenue of the Americas
New York, NY 10020

First Threshold Editions hardcover edition February 2012

THRESHOLD EDITIONS and colophon are trademarks of Simon & Schuster, Inc.

For information about special discounts for bulk purchases, please contact Simon & Schuster Special Sales at 1-866-506-1949 or business@simonandschuster.com.

The Simon & Schuster Speakers Bureau can bring authors to your live event. For more information or to book an event, contact the Simon & Schuster Speakers Bureau at 1-866-248-3049 or visit our website at www.simonspeakers.com.

Designed by Joy O'Meara

Manufactured in the United States of America

10 9 8 7 6 5 4 3 2 1

Library of Congress Cataloging-in-Publication Data

Rasmussen, Scott W.
   The people's money : how voters will balance the budget and eliminate the federal debt / Scott Rasmussen.—1st hbk. ed.
      p.   cm.
   1. Budget deficits—United States.   2. Bailouts (Government policy)—United States.   3. Debts, Public—United States.   4. Government spending policy—United States.   I. Title.
   HJ2051.R37   2012
   336.73—dc23   2011044990
ISBN 978-1-4516-6610-6
ISBN 978-1-4516-6612-0 (ebook)

This book is dedicated to the memory of my mother,
Lois (Mickey) Rasmussen (1934–2011).
She loved books, her family, and her country.

CONTENTS

———•◆•———

INTRODUCTION

What the Bailouts Unleashed

———•◆•———

Events that change history get lost in legend.

It's impossible for us today to really appreciate what it was like when the Shot Heard 'Round the World was fired in 1775, when the first woman entered Congress in 1917, when the Japanese bombed Pearl Harbor in 1941, or when Rosa Parks refused to give up her seat on a bus in 1955. Myths take over, times change, and powerful, passionate reality becomes nothing more than a simple story with dates to memorize. That will someday happen to the events we're living through right now. But the most recent history-changing catalyst is still fresh enough that the passions can be stirred just by rereading the news accounts.

On September 18, 2008, the *New York Times* reported, "The head of the Treasury and the Federal Reserve began discussions on Thursday with Congressional leaders on what could become the biggest bailout in United States history." [1] The plan had support from Republican president George W. Bush and the Democrat who would soon succeed him. Then-senator Barack Obama was so supportive that he offered to call wavering House members to seek their vote. Wall Street's reaction was enthusiastic as stock prices surged on the news.

But a Rasmussen Reports survey found one group that wasn't on board—the American people. Just 24 percent of voters nationwide sup-

---

1. Edmund L. Andrews, "Vast Bailout by US Proposed in Bid to Stem Financial Crisis," Sep. 2008.

ported the plan.[2] Within a week, protests were held in over a hundred cities around the country. One protester said the plan was "just taking advantage of a crisis in order to frighten the American people into submission."[3] Half the nation shared that view and thought the politicians were more interested in gaining additional power than in fixing the economy.[4]

The *Los Angeles Times* reported, "As congressional leaders struggled to craft a bailout plan for the nation's troubled financial system Thursday, angry protesters mobbed Wall Street, telephones rang off the hook in House and Senate offices and a group of prominent economists sent off e-mail blasts critiquing the proposal."[5]

The paper quoted a young homeowner's perspective: "I find it a very hard pill to swallow that I have to work my butt off to pay my mortgage and other people get bailed out."[6]

Wall Street and Washington liked the plan, but the American people did not. Apparently, the public didn't matter. Within a week or so of the protests, voters were ignored and the bailout legislation was approved by a Democratic Congress and signed by a Republican president. Within months, politicians would further ignore and infuriate the voters by expanding the bailouts to the auto industry and the insurance industry.

That would eventually lead to the creation of the Tea Party movement, an authentic grassroots movement that no one in Washington could figure out. The Tea Partiers played a major role in 2010, beginning just a few months after the bailouts, when they forced Arlen Specter out of the Republican Party (and eventually out of the Senate).

But while the Tea Party was visible and vocal during 2010, it was only one part of a much larger rejection of the status quo. At various points during the year, between 15 and 25 percent of Americans considered

2. Rasmussen Reports, "Support for Bailout Plan Now Down to 24%," Sep. 2008.
3. Real News Network, "Bailout Sparks Anger." Sep. 2008.
4. Rasmussen Reports, "51% Say Bailout Plan Is a Power Grab," Sep. 2008.
5. Ken Bensinger and Carolyn Cole, "Masses Aren't Buying Bailout: Indignant Americans Stage Protests, Deluge Congressional Offices," Sep. 2008.
6. Ibid.

themselves part of the Tea Party movement.[7] That loud and visible new-comer on the political scene was strongest when it aligned with majority opinions such as opposition to the bailouts. Solid majorities consistently thought it would be better for the nation if all incumbent members of Congress were defeated.[8] Through it all, the nation's Political Class simply acted as if the opinion of the voters didn't count.

By 2011, anger at the bailouts spawned another protest group: Occupy Wall Street. While most Americans favored a different set of solutions from those of the Wall Street protesters, 79 percent agreed with their chant "The big banks got bailed out, we got left behind."[9]

Most political leaders and pundits still don't get it. The *Washington Post* wrote an editorial bemoaning the defeat of several incumbents just for supporting the bailouts.[10] To this day, they don't recognize what caused all the anger and why people are still angry. It wasn't just the money, although $700 billion is a lot of money. What seemed normal and necessary in Washington and on Wall Street seemed wrong, immoral, and un-American to everybody else.

It was partly that the money was requested and "needed" so fast. When making the initial pitch, the Treasury secretary sounded like a used-car salesman promising a better deal if you signed before leaving the lot. There wasn't even time to draft proper legislation saying how the money would be used. For many Americans, it was hard to trust a government that suddenly needed $700 billion right away, but didn't have the competence to see it coming.

On top of that, most of the money seemed to go to the people who created the problem. Without knowing all the details, people sensed that a cozy relationship between politicians, regulators, and financiers created a mess that ended up giving $700 billion to financiers for politicians to regulate.

---

7. Rasmussen Reports, "48% Say Their Views Closer to Tea Party Than to Congress," Apr. 2011.
8. Rasmussen Reports, "65% Say Country Better Off If Most in Congress Defeated This November," July 2010.
9. Rasmussen Reports, "Public Divided on Occupy Wall Street Protestors," Oct. 2011.
10. *Washington Post*, "The Political Price of Backing Invaluable TARP," July 2010.

Perhaps most fundamentally, the bailouts were, and are, massively unpopular due to the taint of official corruption. Americans believe in and support free market competition where everybody plays by the same rules. If you provide a valuable service to customers and make a lot of money, you get to keep the profit. That's fine.

If you don't, you either lose money or go out of business. That's fine, too.

The bailouts seemed to change the rules and completely eliminate accountability for politically connected corporations. Under the new rules, those who have friends in government could keep the profits during good times and get bailed out by taxpayers when they messed up. For the seven out of ten voters who believe that big government and big business generally work together against the rest of us, the bailouts simply confirmed their worst fears.[11]

At the same time financial corporations were being bailed out, homeowners were struggling. Barely half believed that their own homes were worth more than the mortgage.[12] In a nation where people were taught to buy a home as the cornerstone of their personal financial well-being, this wasn't supposed to happen. By the middle of 2011, only 13 percent of homeowners thought their home would increase in value over the coming year.[13]

But the rules had changed in ways that helped the well-connected corporations while hurting middle-class homeowners. Those who had played by the old rules, who had bought a home and paid their mortgage on time, got burned. That's a sure formula to spark populist outrage. Again, it wasn't easy to understand all the details, but there certainly was a problem with the relationship between Congress, regulators, and pet corporations such as Fannie Mae and Freddie Mac.

The Political Class response to all this, showing once again how out

11. Rasmussen Reports, "68% Believe Government and Big Business Work Together Against the Rest of Us," Feb. 2011.
12. Rasmussen Reports, "Just 49% Say Home Is Worth More Than Mortgage," July 2011.
13. Rasmussen Reports, "Homeowners Remain Pessimistic About Home Values over Next Year," July 2011.

of touch they were, was to add a homeowners' bailout to the wish list. Most voters, including most homeowners, disagreed. They believed that solving the housing crisis required fixing the economy rather than coming up with more bailouts.[14] Voters wanted a lasting solution while politicians proposed a short-term Band-Aid.

Within half a year, just 53 percent of Americans believed that capitalism was better than socialism. Among those under thirty, one-third said capitalism was better, one-third said socialism, and one-third weren't sure.[15] Yet, at the same time, Americans young and old overwhelmingly believed that a free market economy was better than a government-managed economy.[16]

When an economist I know heard those figures, he said it showed how little the American people understood about economics. In his mind, capitalism and free markets were one and the same. But what the data really showed was how little the economist understood the American people. Voters have come to believe that capitalism as practiced in America is Crony Capitalism, a corrupt system where the government picks winners and losers. Sweetheart deals for well-connected companies such as Solyndra; nothing for those who simply offer a better product, a better service, or a better price. Americans prefer free markets where everyone plays by the same rules—those who provide a better service win and those who don't lose.

The Political Class hates that approach because it leaves them out of the loop. The politicians would rather be in a position to pick winners and losers while handing out favors to their friends. That's the way it used to work for the king of England, whose favored friends included the East India Tea Company. Americans didn't like that sort of arrangement in the 1770s and they don't like it today.

When all was said and done, the Political Class may have convinced themselves that voters would eventually come around and support the

14. Rasmussen Reports, "61% Say Government Should Keep out of Housing Market," Feb. 2010.
15. Rasmussen Reports, "Just 53% Say Capitalism Better Than Socialism," Apr. 2009.
16. Rasmussen Reports, "Voters Champion Free Market but Want More Regulation," Dec. 2009.

$700 billion scheme. Or, they may have decided it was too important to let voter opposition get in the way. Whatever their rationale, the bailouts remain the most hated piece of legislation in recent American history. More than two years after the fact, just 25 percent of American voters thought they were a good idea.[17]

In terms of their political impact, the bailouts made clear just how wide the gap had grown between the Political Class and Mainstream America. Highlighting this gap ignited the frustration about government spending that had been building for decades and energized voters to demand fundamental change. To really understand the impact of this historic catalyst, it's necessary to first understand the underlying frustration that had been building for decades.

Taking the long-term view begins with the recognition that the last time government spending in America went down from one year to the next was long before most Americans alive today were even born. It didn't happen in the Clinton era or the Reagan era. It didn't happen when Jimmy Carter was in the White House or during the presidencies of Gerald Ford, Richard Nixon, Lyndon Johnson, or John F. Kennedy.

The last time government spending went down in America was during Dwight D. Eisenhower's first term in office. It was 1954, a time when an average new house cost just over $10,000 and Hank Aaron was a rookie with the Milwaukee Braves.

Think about that.

For more than half a century, American voters kept electing candidates who promised lower spending and taxes. The most recent example was Barack Obama, who promised tax cuts for 95 percent of all Americans during his campaign for the White House. Ronald Reagan, Bill Clinton, and both Bushes made similar pitches during their campaigns. Jimmy Carter made it clear he was a fiscally conservative Democrat, and even Richard Nixon appeared less spendthrift than his opponents, Hubert Humphrey and George McGovern.

Despite that clear message from voters, total government spending

---

17.   Rasmussen Reports, "Bailouts Remain Popular with Just 25% of Voters," May 2011.

has kept going up every year since Bill Haley was topping the charts with "Rock Around the Clock" and a young singer named Elvis Presley made his first commercial recording. To keep the game going, politicians even invented gimmicks that let them claim to vote for budget cuts while spending kept going higher and higher.

With a track record like that, it is easy to see why voters are angry.

It's important to note that from 1954 to 2010, Republicans controlled the White House for thirty-four years and Democrats for twenty-two. Democrats controlled Congress for forty-four years and the Republicans for twelve. This long-lasting spending spree was enabled on a completely bipartisan basis. The result is that roughly eight out of ten Americans living today have never been alive in a year when government spending went down.

Some may say I'm not being fair to the politicians. After all, the argument goes, we have to at least adjust for inflation and population growth. Some might even say government spending should grow at a faster rate, perhaps as fast as the economy itself. That highlights one of the problems in discussing the budget. The politicians have all sorts of numbers they can use to hide the growth of spending.

Yes, at times in a budget process it's appropriate to consider the impact of inflation and population growth. At times it's best to look at how much of the overall budget is consumed by a particular program. Politicians also use many different spending baselines to conceal the problem. Sometimes politicians talk of uncontrollable spending and discretionary spending, sometimes the focus is off-budget or on-budget, sometimes it's total government spending, sometimes it's inflation-adjusted spending, and sometimes it's just federal or state or local spending.

With so many different numbers to use, and because politicians will use them in whatever way helps make their case, it's especially important to keep an eye on the actual spending totals. That's the ultimate protection against the games politicians play.

Remember, even as spending has gone up every year for more than half a century, the traditional media stories have been filled with references to budget cuts and belt-tightening. So, if a reporter writes a story on the budget, look for the actual spending totals. How much was spent last year, how much will be spent this year, and how much do you expect to spend next year? If the story says that spending is being cut, but the actual spending is going up, demand an explanation.

The bigger challenge, of course, is to avoid getting hung up on individual numbers and to get a sense of what they are telling us. For example, most Americans would be quite comfortable letting government spending go up enough every year to keep pace with population growth and inflation.[18] It makes sense at a visceral level. If there are more people, there's probably a need for more services (and more of us to cover the cost). Inflation is also a fact of life that we all have to address.

During the 1950s, federal spending grew faster than population growth plus inflation five times and slower than that rate five times. That seems intuitively reasonable and sustainable. Certainly, if that pattern had continued, voters would not be as angry today.

However, things have changed dramatically since the 1950s. Federal spending alone has increased faster than population growth and inflation thirty-five times in the last forty years.

When you add in state and local governments, the numbers are even more depressing. Since 1965, total government spending in America has grown faster than population growth plus inflation in every year but one.

That trend began the year the Beatles played Shea Stadium in the first-ever stadium rock concert. Nineteen sixty-five was also the year miniskirts first unnerved parents of teenaged girls, an American astronaut first walked in space, and health warnings were first required on cigarette packages. Americans learned all of this by watching one of three television network newscasts, and most watched in black and white.

That's how long government spending has been out of control in America. It's not something that happened in the last few years or even the last decade. The price of gasoline jumped from 31 cents a gallon in 1965 to where it is today, the population grew from 194 million to more

---

18.   Rasmussen Reports, "56% Favor Spending Cap Tied to Population Growth and Inflation," May 2011.

than 300 million, and still government spending outpaced that growth in forty-four out of forty-five years.

And, again, it's not as if voters weren't voicing concerns during all this time. The ongoing growth of spending took place in a political environment that included the tax revolt of the late 1970s, the Reagan era, the Perot movement, and President Bill Clinton's declaration that the "era of big government is over."[19]

Those events served as both an early-warning sign and a bit of a safety valve to let off steam just as the British withdrawal of the Stamp Act bought a little time for the British king in the 1760s. Unfortunately, like King George, America's Political Class never took the time to really listen to what the American people were saying. There was plenty of time to avoid the current crisis, but America's politicians failed to lead.

As a result, the underlying discontent continued until it boiled over with the bailouts in the fall of 2008. The impact of all that spending can be seen in the graph on page 10.

The lower line on the graph shows what would have happened if, since 1954, government spending had grown just enough to keep up with the population and inflation. If that path had been followed, government spending would have totaled approximately $1.2 trillion in 2010.

The top line shows the actual history of spending since 1954. You can see that the two lines weren't far apart in the 1950s and early 1960s. Then, starting during the administrations of Lyndon Johnson and Richard Nixon, government spending began to grow faster and faster. Both those presidents made short-term, politically expedient decisions during their time in office that are still creating headaches for us nearly half a century later.

As a result, rather than spending $1.2 trillion in 2010, governments in America spent four times that amount—$5.2 trillion.

America's elected politicians should have been drawing attention to these unsustainable budget realities for decades. Instead, they took part

---

19.   William Jefferson Clinton, "1996 State of the Union Address," Jan. 1996.

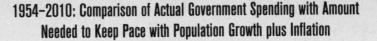

1954–2010: Comparison of Actual Government Spending with Amount Needed to Keep Pace with Population Growth plus Inflation

All Figures in Millions of Dollars

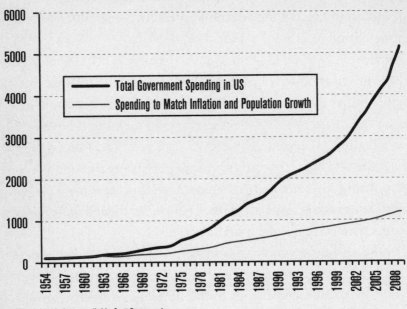

(data from 2011 federal budget, compiled by Scott Rasmussen)

in a bipartisan cover-up. Rather than leveling with the American people, politicians used budget gimmicks and creative accounting to hide the growth of government spending.

In some ways, the Republicans are more to blame than Democrats. The Democratic Party has, after all, been fairly open about its desire to see federal spending grow. It formally advocates a larger role for government, and it would make tactical sense for the Democrats to downplay the cost side of their agenda. A good salesman always wants the product to seem less expensive than it really is.

DC Republicans, on the other hand, have spent decades claiming to favor fiscal restraint, but have failed to act that way. They, too, chose to hide behind accounting gimmicks rather than educating voters about the underlying spending trends. That's one reason 72 percent of Republican voters around the country continue to believe congressional Republicans are out of touch with the party base.[20]

But far more important than to assign partisan blame for past failures is to realize that the government's spending problems are much deeper than decisions made in the past few years by Congress. This systemic problem has been building for decades. It requires a long-term substantive solution rather than short-term Band-Aids and budgetary gimmicks.

The American people instinctively understand this. When President Barack Obama gave his 2010 State of the Union address, voters supported his call for a freeze on discretionary spending. However, at the same time, only 9 percent thought the freeze would reduce the deficit significantly.[21]

A year later, when congressional Republicans tried to trim the budget by up to $100 billion, only 26 percent of voters believed that effort would significantly reduce spending and deficits.[22]

In both cases, the voters were right.

This awareness that the proposals from both sides of the political aisle fall short only adds to the high level of frustration in the nation today. Most Americans aren't sure what it will take to gain control of spending, but they sense that politicians from both parties are ducking reality. A majority doubt that President Obama will even present a serious proposal to address the problem. Most have the same doubts about congressional Republicans.[23]

Again, the voters are right.

A serious approach to budgetary issues would begin with a look at where the money goes. It's not difficult to find or define, but most politi-

---

20. Rasmussen Reports, "72% of GOP Voters Say Republicans in Congress out of Touch with Their Base," June 2010.

21. Rasmussen Reports, "9% Expect Obama's Spending Freeze to Have Big Impact on Deficit," Jan. 2010.

22. Rasmussen Reports, "53% Say Even GOP Spending Cuts Won't Dent the Deficit," Apr. 2011.

23. Rasmussen Reports, "65% Say Significant Long-Term Spending Cuts Unlikely Before 2012 Elections," Apr. 2011.

cians would prefer to avoid the subject entirely. The majority of all federal spending is consumed by just three budget items—national security, Social Security, and Medicare. Those items plus interest on the federal debt account for more than two-thirds of all federal spending.[24] The latest projections show that this handful of items will grow faster than the economy and the rest of the budget over the next five years. By the end of that time, they will account for 77 percent of all federal spending.[25]

Not surprisingly, therefore, the growth in overall government spending has been driven by the growth of national security spending, Social Security, and Medicare. In 1954, these items plus interest on the federal debt consumed 89 percent of all federal tax revenue. By 2010 the cost of these same items was slightly more than the total of all federal tax revenue. No matter how you measure it, this is where the money goes.

Spending on national security and veterans' affairs totaled $54 billion in 1954 and $844 billion in 2010. Social Security costs grew from $3 billion to $721 billion. Medicare didn't exist in 1954 but cost $457 billion in 2010.

While national defense grew a bit more slowly than the others from 1954 to the present, that's partly because it started from a higher base. In 1940, on the eve of World War II, defense spending had totaled just $2.2 billion. Fourteen years later, by 1954, it was twenty-six times that amount.[26] Regardless of which program grew faster than another, these programs are the driving force of federal spending growth. Anybody who is serious about cutting spending must be willing to intelligently and significantly reduce the cost of these essential programs.

This perspective is not an ideological preference, it's a numerical reality. The good news is that twenty-first-century American voters are quite willing to make the needed changes. They are ready to support strategic changes in military strategy that will save hundreds of billions of dollars annually (chapter 3). They are ready to let people select their

---

24.   *Budget of the United States Government, Fiscal Year 2012.*
25.   Ibid.
26.   Historical Tables, *Budget of the United States Government, Fiscal Year 2012.*

own retirement age and embrace other reforms that will make Social Security work better for a new generation while dramatically reducing the nation's long-term liabilities (chapter 4). On Medicare, the challenges are tougher, but can be addressed by following the commonsense wisdom of the American people (chapter 5).

The changes supported by voters are generally more thoughtful and offer more lasting solutions than those suggested by politicians. They also involve a lot of common sense, which may be another reason that those in the ideologically driven world of professional politics can't see the forest for the trees.

The willingness of voters to tackle the big issues means that the only thing standing in the way of solving the budget crisis is a Political Class committed to defending the status quo.

That will be the real political battle of the coming decade.

PART ONE

——— •◆• ———

The Political Class

1

———•———

What the Political Class
Thinks Voters Think

America's Political Class wants to govern like it's 1775, a time when kings were kings and consent of the governed was irrelevant. This collection of elected officials, lobbyists, political staffers, activists, and their allies on Wall Street has grown in influence over the past half century as the federal government has grown in size and power. They have pursued their own self-interest, used taxpayer money to help their friends, and succeeded in making Washington, DC, the wealthiest metropolitan area in the United States.

While holding a variety of ideological and partisan views, this elite group shares a common belief that the federal government is the source of all legitimate authority in the nation. Rather than acknowledging the American people as the true sovereign authority of the land, the Political Class displays a growing contempt for those they are supposed to serve.

Fifty-nine percent of political insiders told the *National Journal* that the public doesn't "know enough about the issues facing Washington to form wise opinions about what should be done."[1]

The *Politico*, another publication that chronicles the world as seen by

---

1. James A. Barnes, "Six of Ten Political Insiders Believe Public Is Ill-Informed," Mar. 2011.

DC insiders, reported that a major policy debate would be determined "less by the intelligence of advocates on any side than by the ignorance of most Americans."[2] Peter Orszag, a former director of the Office of Management and Budget, wrote an article explaining why he believes that "we need less democracy." Orszag says that the way to fix our political institutions is "by making them a bit less democratic."[3]

These comments and scores of others like them sound suspiciously like rationalizations to justify ignoring the voters. The governor of North Carolina went so far as to suggest that "we ought to suspend, perhaps, elections for Congress for two years and just tell them we won't hold it against them, whatever decisions they make, to just let them help this country recover."[4] As a public-opinion pollster, and as an American citizen, I find this attitude offensive, misguided, and wrong. It is an affront to the very notion of a self-governing society.

It's true that the public does not know the details of every petty partisan and ideological talking point that Washington insiders consider important, but most of those details aren't worth knowing. Common sense, pragmatism, a sense of fair play, and a firm grip on reality are much more important. That's why I'm with the 73 percent of voters nationwide who trust the American people more than America's political leaders.[5] It's also why I'm confident that our nation can find a way out of the fiscal-policy challenges we are facing today. All we have to do is follow the collective wisdom of the American people.

A careful and comprehensive review of history, budgetary documents, and public-opinion data shows that voters are far more willing than their politicians to make the hard choices needed to reduce federal spending. The American people are ready to do what it takes to balance the budget, completely eliminate the federal debt, and prepare the nation for the twenty-first century.

But, while ready to face hard choices, voters are not willing to let

---

2.   Victoria McGrane and Lisa Lerer, "Is Health Care Bill Too Complex to Grasp?" July 2009.

3.   Peter Orszag, "Too Much of a Good Thing: Why We Need Less Democracy," Sep. 2011.

4.   Ben Smith, "Perdue: Cancel Congressional Elections," Sep. 2011.

5.   Rasmussen Reports, "73% Trust Judgment of People More Than Politicians," Feb. 2009.

politicians make those choices. Americans simply don't trust their political leaders. For this reason, Americans overwhelmingly believe that any proposed changes in Social Security or Medicare must be submitted to the American people for approval before they can go into effect. They want a similar chance to approve any tax hikes proposed by Congress.[6]

With these protections in place, a solid majority of voters are prepared to embrace thoughtful, fair, and strategic changes in major government programs including the three categories that make up the bulk of all federal spending—national security, Social Security, and Medicare. In fact, voters are prepared to take steps that will reduce government spending far more than any politician in Washington has yet proposed.

I recognize that such a statement of confidence in the American people will be greeted with snickers by those in the Political Class. Their perception, summarized by the *New York Times*, is that "Americans overwhelmingly say that in general they prefer cutting government spending to paying higher taxes." However, their preference for spending cuts "dissolves when they are presented with specific options." To bolster this claim, the paper cites "several bipartisan and academic panels" suggesting that the required spending cuts "would be deeper than anything the public would accept."[7]

The *New York Times* and the conventional wisdom are wrong.

I say this with confidence even after reviewing a constant stream of media polls claiming to back up the insiders' condescending opinion of voters. The Pew Center, for example, has asked several times over the years about eighteen categories of spending and always found majority opposition to cutting any of them.[8] It didn't matter whether the spending was for defense, education, the environment, or anything else, most respondents were opposed to cutting whatever the pollsters asked about.

Rasmussen Reports polling finds the exact same type of response. In one poll, 54 percent said the federal government "needs" to spend more

6. Rasmussen Reports, "Voters Say Congress Should Ask Permission Before Changing Social Security, Raising Taxes," Sep. 2010.
7. Jackie Calmes and Dalia Sussman, "Poll Finds Wariness About Cutting Entitlements," Jan. 2010.
8. Pew Research Center, "Section 3: The Deficit and Government Spending," Feb. 2011.

money on infrastructure projects such as roads, bridges, and trains.[9] That's consistent with the Pew results and many other polls. On the surface, this seems to support the conventional wisdom.

But the Rasmussen Reports poll also dug a bit deeper and found that just 33 percent of likely voters think the government should continue providing subsidies and grants to Amtrak. Fifty-three percent want the subsidies to end.[10] Other Rasmussen Reports polling showed that a majority wants the government to go even further and sell Amtrak to private investors.[11] So, while voters are willing to go on record in generic support of infrastructure spending, they are quite willing to support cuts in specific programs.

The same pattern can be found on every other broad category of government spending. Consider military spending and national security. Less than one-third of voters say we should cut defense spending.[12] After all, who would want to suggest putting the nation at risk just to make the ledgers balance? But, while opposing unspecified cuts, most are quite willing to consider removing troops from Western Europe and other strategic changes that would end up saving substantial amounts of money every year.[13]

These examples and plenty of others make the point that asking about broad categories of spending is not the same as asking about cuts in specific programs. Asking generically about spending more on education or protecting the environment is like asking about support for mom and apple pie. Polls that measure the mom and apple pie value of various spending categories make politicians happy because they show support for the status quo. Polls that ask about specific and thoughtful changes show that the American people are ready to prepare the nation for the twenty-first century.

---

9. Rasmussen Reports, "Just 33% Want Amtrak Subsidies to Continue," Feb. 2011.
10. Ibid.
11. Rasmussen Reports, "Most Want Government to Sell Amtrak, GM, and Chrysler," Oct. 2009.
12. Rasmussen Reports, "Voters Underestimate How Much US Spends on Defense," Feb. 2011.
13. Rasmussen Reports, "Half Want Troops out of Europe, Japan, but South Korea's Another Story," Jan. 2011.

Of course, some spending cuts that get talked about aren't very thoughtful. Not surprisingly, Americans overwhelmingly oppose mindless and harsh short-term spending cuts such as eliminating Medicare or getting rid of school lunch programs and playgrounds. Nobody wants to deny schoolchildren a good lunch or a place to play. Nobody supports throwing retirees on the street or taking away their doctors. Voters recognize the budget debate is about far more than simply slashing spending and respond accordingly.

Imagine, for example, that someone in Congress noticed the all-volunteer army is more expensive than an army of draftees. If that legislator proposed reducing the military budget by reinstituting the draft and cutting military pay, the polls would instantly show it to be massively unpopular. Americans overwhelmingly oppose the military draft[14] largely because it conflicts with our belief in individual freedom and self-governance. Additionally, an all-volunteer army is actually an army of professional soldiers who keep the nation safer than an army of unwilling draftees. Finally, of course, there is the sheer indecency of cutting the pay for those who are defending our freedom.

It should surprise no one that such a proposal would be unpopular. Unfortunately, the spin in Washington wouldn't be all that surprising either. With polls in hand showing massive opposition to a draft and military pay-cut plan, the Political Class would add this to their body of evidence showing that people say they want spending cuts, but don't really mean it. They would be drawing a false conclusion that is not supported by the data. That voters oppose some spending cuts does not mean they are opposed to all spending cuts. It just means that the politicians have failed to come up with more credible options for the voters to consider and the pollsters to test.

The lack of polls showing support for specific spending cuts says more about the Political Class than it does about public opinion. There are only two possible explanations, and both are pretty discouraging. The

---

14.   Rasmussen Reports, "18% Favor Military Draft, 30% Support Required Year of Public Service," July 2011.

first possibility is that our elected politicians simply don't know what to do. They may be so focused on their partisan and ideological games that they honestly can't see a way out of the mess they've created. The other possibility is that they know what the voters might embrace but don't want the nation to head in that direction.

Regardless of the reason, the nation's current leadership has failed to develop reasonable options for voters to consider. Instead, government officials have put their energy into developing creative accounting techniques and gimmicks to hide their failure. Sixty-two percent of voters have caught on to one of the gimmicks and now recognize that when politicians talk of spending cuts, they really mean just a slower rate of spending growth.[15] As will be discussed in chapter 2, that's just the tip of the iceberg.

To get a sense of scale, consider that the president's 2012 budget projected a $1.65 trillion deficit.[16] That staggering number is obviously unnerving to ordinary Americans who try to live within their own family budget. Unfortunately, the way that official Washington calculates deficits dramatically understates the magnitude of the problem. The current approach was devised by President Lyndon Johnson to hide the cost of his Great Society programs and the Vietnam War. If the government used the same Generally Accepted Accounting Principles it requires companies to use, the annual deficit is actually about $5 trillion a year.[17] That's three times higher than the official figure and means the government is consuming a much larger share of our national income than anybody wants to think about.

While this will be discussed in detail later, most of the difference between the official figures and the real deficit comes from acknowledging the unfunded liabilities for Social Security, Medicare, veterans' benefits, and other retirement programs.

The gap between official government figures and reality is especially

15. Rasmussen Reports, "62% Understand That Spending Cuts Really Means Slowing Pace of Spending," Aug. 2011.

16. *Budget of the United States Government, Fiscal Year 2012.*

17. *The 2010 Financial Report of the United States Government.*

noticeable once you move beyond annual deficits and take a look at the total debt. Every year or so, an interesting political tussle breaks out when Congress is required to raise the official debt ceiling. That's the total amount of money the government is formally allowed to borrow.

In the summer of 2011, following a high level of partisan bickering and theatrics that made everyone involved look bad, the debt ceiling was raised a couple of trillion dollars from $14 trillion to $16 trillion. While those are big numbers, the actual total debt of the US government is up to eight times higher—somewhere between $60 and $120 trillion.[18]

For a variety of reasons to be discussed in the next chapter, precise numbers are difficult to estimate, but it's important to understand the magnitude of the problem. As former Congressional Budget Office director Douglas Holtz-Eakin explained to me, "The debt from the past is a problem, but the future potential debt is a crisis. Left unchanged, federal programs are on track to spend so much money that there will be no way to either tax or grow ourselves out of the problem. We will explode from borrowing fifty-five thousand dollars *every second* to two or three times that."

As with the difference between the stated annual deficit of $1.65 trillion and the actual deficit of roughly $5 trillion, the difference between the official debt totals and the actual debt obligations comes primarily from commitments for future retirement benefits that have been made by the government but are not included in the official debt figures.

The reality is that the politicians spent a whole summer arguing about a $2 trillion increase in the formal debt ceiling without even acknowledging that it's but a tiny fraction of a much bigger problem. It's truly scary that our elected officials have deliberately chosen to hide up to 80 percent of the total debt burden rather than fessing up. Such behavior from a corporation would land the CEO in jail.

If our political leaders had been honest with the American people about federal finances over the past four or five decades, voters would have forced changes on the system long ago and we would not be in the

---

18.   Michael Tanner, "Bankrupt: Entitlements and the Federal Budget," Mar. 2011.

mess we're in today, but that's not where the Political Class wanted to take the nation. Rather than respecting voters as the sovereign power in the land, political insiders have acted like a gambler who keeps losing money but hasn't told his wife. The gambler always hopes or believes that the next bet will come up big enough to cover all the losses and avoid an unpleasant discussion.

Politicians have for decades placed their bet on the belief that they could someday convince voters to support tax increases big enough to fund the Political Class view of the world, but it hasn't happened yet and it's not going to happen anytime soon. Instead, voters have expressed growing frustration with the federal government. For three consecutive elections in 2006, 2008, and 2010, Americans voted against the party in power. It didn't matter whether Republicans or Democrats were in power, they just voted against the team in charge.

This continued and accelerated a trend that has been growing since 1992, the year Bill Clinton was elected president. He came to power with a Democratic majority in Congress, but his party lost control of Congress during his tenure in the White House. He was followed by George W. Bush, who was elected president along with a Republican majority in Congress. His party also lost control of Congress during his time in office. That had never before happened in back-to-back administrations in American history.

But it didn't stop there.

President Barack Obama was elected with huge majorities in both the House and the Senate. Two years later, in 2010, his team lost control of the House of Representatives in the biggest GOP victory since the 1940s. This pattern reflects a fundamental rejection of both political parties, and the trend even continues between elections.

In 2009, President Barack Obama proposed a freeze on discretionary spending. Voters liked it, but few thought it would have any significant impact on the deficit.[19] In 2011, newly empowered House Republicans

---

19.   Rasmussen Reports, "9% Expect Obama's Spending Freeze to Have Big Impact on Debt," Jan. 2010.

proposed $61 billion in spending cuts. Again, voters liked it but few thought it would have any significant impact on the deficit.[20]

In early 2011, President Barack Obama unveiled his budget plan based upon a vision of "living within our means." Republican congressman Paul Ryan introduced his alternative budgetary plan and focused more on spending cuts, but a majority of voters said neither President Obama nor the congressional Republicans were likely to propose a serious plan to address the nation's fiscal problems. Two-thirds said nothing significant would be accomplished before the next presidential election.[21]

The loud and clear message is that voters don't think either side is making any sense, but those in power don't see it that way.

The Political Class view of recent elections may best have been summarized by a political science professor who is frequently quoted as an expert on public opinion. Charles Franklin said, "I'm not endorsing the American voter. They're pretty damn stupid."[22]

Unfortunately, I've run into this attitude directly more times than I care to remember.

Once, I spoke to a trade association and said that the American people don't want to be governed from the left, the right, or even the center. They want to govern themselves. For most Americans, this is little more than common sense. The speaker following me, however, was less than sympathetic. A man whose résumé put him high up in the Political Class ranks said simply, "All that talk about self-governance is fine. The only problem is that the American people are too stupid to do it."

A *Washington Post* blog also directly challenged my assessment by asking, "Do Americans really want to govern themselves?" To answer, they cited a study suggesting "the public would rather have other

20. Rasmussen Reports, "53% Say Even GOP Spending Cuts Won't Dent the Deficit," Mar. 2011.
21. Rasmussen Reports, "65% Say Significant Long-Term Spending Cuts Unlikely Before 2012 Elections," Apr. 2011.
22. Alicia Yager, "Pundits Ponder Wisconsin Election Results at Society for Professional Journalists Forum," Nov. 2010.

people make the decisions, so long as those people are 'empathetic, non-self-interested decision makers.'"[23]

The Founding Fathers long ago addressed the fantasy that such wise and impartial rulers could be found. The fifty-first *Federalist Paper* stated succinctly, "If men were angels, no government would be necessary. If angels were to govern men, neither external nor internal controls on government would be necessary." But the reality is that we have "a government which is to be administered by men over men."[24] No angels are involved in government today, just politicians.

Perhaps the DC crowd see themselves as "empathetic, non-self-interested decision makers," but hardly anybody else does. Polling consistently shows that Americans trust a used-car salesman more than a member of Congress. Only 27 percent think their own representative is the best person for the job. No matter how bad something is, voters overwhelmingly believe that Congress could always make it worse.[25] Those things are true regardless of which party is in charge.

To be fair, an excess of cynicism may sometimes be expressed by voters, but it's the attitude of the Political Class that is truly dangerous. Their view that the American people are stupid, ignorant, and want somebody else to make decisions for them is a direct assault on the founding ideals of our nation.

The Political Class's desire to govern as if it were 1775 is also the root cause of our fiscal crisis. It's no coincidence that congressional turnover fell to single digits for the first time in 1968 and that federal spending was pushed to unsustainable levels in the same decade.[26] In the decades since, voters were consistently ignored while government spending kept growing and trust in government kept falling.

Today, while deficits grab the headlines, the deeper problem has

---

23.   John Sides, "Do Americans Really Want to Govern Themselves?" Aug. 2010.
24.   James Madison, "The Structure of Government Must Furnish the Proper Checks and Balances Between the Different Departments," Feb. 1788.
25.   Rasmussen Reports, "Voters Continue to Believe Congress Can Always Make Things Worse," Jan. 2011.
26.   Historical Tables, *Budget of the United States Government, Fiscal Year 2012.*

reached the point where only 17 percent of voters believe that the government has the "consent of the governed."[27] In a nation founded on the belief that governments derive their only just authority from such consent, that's a devastating assessment.

The gap between Americans who want to govern themselves and politicians who want to rule over them may now be as big as the gap between the colonies and England during the eighteenth century. In revolutionary times, a rallying cry for the colonists demanded, "No taxation without representation!" Today, 79 percent of Mainstream voters think Americans are overtaxed; 87 percent of those who support the Political Class disagree.[28]

Only 10 percent of voters now trust the judgment of the nation's political leaders more than the collective wisdom of the American people. Only 9 percent of all voters can be considered supporters of the Political Class worldview.[29] That's less support than historians believe the king of England enjoyed in the colonies during the American Revolution.[30]

That gap exists today because just about every budget-cutting proposal favored by the American people involves shifting decision-making authority, money, and/or power away from official Washington. Most of the proposals embraced by voters shift power away from government altogether and give individuals more control over their own lives. Many other changes shift power to some other level of government where competition can give individuals more control.

At the other extreme is the Political Class dream of even more power, authority, and money flowing into Washington. That's why our nation's fiscal crisis is, at its core, a political crisis.

While painful for voters to live through, this gap between voters and politicians is a recurring theme in American history. As this effort has

27. Rasmussen Reports, "New Low: 17% Say US Government Has Consent of the Governed," Aug. 2011.

28. Rasmussen Reports, "64% Say Americans Are Overtaxed, Political Class Disagrees," Apr. 2011.

29. Rasmussen Reports, "10% Trust America's Political Leaders More Than Public on Key Issues," Sep. 2011.

30. USHistory.org, "Loyalists, Fence-Sitters, and Patriots."

played itself out over the centuries, politicians always lag behind the public. When voters recognize that change is needed, elected politicians become the primary defenders of the status quo. Then, when the change becomes impossible to resist anymore, the politicians ratify the changes that have already taken place.

This happens because individual Americans live in a dynamic world and are constantly adjusting their views and attitudes based upon encounters with reality. The Political Class lives in a more static, bureaucratic world and encounters politics more than reality. Elected politicians are more likely to hear complaints about change from donors and lobbyists than they are to hear from entrepreneurs about the benefits of change. In the short term, the politicians can protect the status quo, but eventually voters figure out a way to bring the politicians back in line with reality. Such trends get lost in the short-term political world of sound bites, petty partisan agendas, ideological posturing, and the 24-7 news cycle. Rather than focusing on all the yelling and blogging, it is useful to look at the larger context of history to see how public opinion leads in America and politicians follow.

The sound-bite version of 1775 history says that the American Revolution began in Lexington and Concord with the Shot Heard 'Round the World. Looked at in isolation, it's hard to understand how a relatively minor showdown on Lexington Green sparked a war that eventually led to the defeat of what was then the world's mightiest military power.

The underlying reality is that public opinion in the colonies had been shifting for decades. Even those who considered themselves loyal to the king of England recognized important differences between the colonies and the mother country. The decade leading up to the April morning when Captain John Parker mustered the Minutemen in Lexington had been marred by growing friction over the Stamp Act, the Intolerable Acts, the Boston Massacre, the Boston Tea Party, and more.

It's important to remember that all this took place before Thomas Jefferson penned the Declaration of Independence. Jefferson's words did not spark the revolution, they merely articulated the attitudes that had been growing among colonists over a long time. Jeffersonian eloquence didn't convince Americans that we were "endowed by our Creator with certain unalienable rights," the American colonists already knew that. He just gave voice to those deeply held beliefs.

It's also important to remember that more than a decade passed after the war began before a constitution was drafted and ratified. The political actions simply confirmed and codified what public opinion had determined long before. John Adams put the entire era into perspective: "The Revolution was effected before the war commenced. The Revolution was in the minds and hearts of the people."[31]

The public attitudes and frustration bubbling beneath the surface for decades led to the American Revolution. The events at Lexington and Concord merely served as a catalyst. The political acts to ratify the changes came later. This was not a unique event in American history. It was merely the first act in a drama whose core theme was to be repeated again and again to this day. Public opinion leads and eventually the politicians catch up.

That's the way women got the right to vote in America. In 1869, long before Congress was ready to consider the suffrage amendment, women were first allowed to vote in Wyoming. Over the next half century, through periods of ups and downs, women won the right to vote in several local and county elections. On a statewide level, women had a hard time getting the vote from state legislators, but male voters were more supportive and women won the right to vote in several Western states with a series of referendum victories. In fact, surprise wins in California and Washington elections brought the issue back to Congress.

If a catalyst was needed to shake up the Congress, Jeannette Rankin provided it. She was the first woman elected to Congress and was sent to Washington from Montana in 1916. That was before the rest of Congress thought her gender deserved the right to vote. The amendment giving women the right to vote wasn't ratified until 1920, four years after Rankin was first elected. It must have been a sight to see when she first walked onto the floor of the House of Representatives.

---

31.   John Adams. "John Adams to H. Niles," Feb. 1818.

It wasn't just the presence of a woman in Congress that persuaded the others to act. It was simple math. By the time Congress approved the suffrage amendment, more than 40 percent of Congress was elected with the votes of women. More states were following the trend, and even the staunchest defender of the status quo could see that a majority of Congress would soon have to court the female vote to keep their jobs.[32] Somehow, voting against suffrage didn't seem like a good campaign slogan anymore. The bottom line is that Congress did not give women the right to vote. It acted under duress to ratify a decision that had long since been made by the American people.

The sound-bite version of history also tells us that Americans were isolationists determined to stay out of World War II on December 6, 1941, and instantly flipped their views following the Japanese attack on Pearl Harbor. Actually, Americans had long applauded a growing role for their nation in world affairs dating at least back to the time when Teddy Roosevelt led the Rough Riders up San Juan Hill in the late nineteenth century. Following the devastation of World War I, most Americans wanted the nation to play a bigger role in world affairs. They were even prepared to join some sort of international League of Nations if Woodrow Wilson had shown a hint of pragmatism in his plan. Long before the "day of infamy," Americans embraced support for the Western allies, instituted a military draft, and raised an army of almost 2 million men. Far from being isolationists, 62 percent of Americans at the time held the view "that defeating Germany is more important than staying out of the war." A year before the Japanese attacked, 89 percent said the implementation of a peacetime military draft was a "good thing."[33] That 1940 support for a military draft is simply unimaginable in today's world.

The bottom line is that public opinion on America's role in the world had shifted long before December 7, 1941. The attack on Pearl Harbor served as a catalyst converting that changed attitude into an "arsenal of

32.   Mary M. Huth, "US Suffrage Movement Timeline, 1792–Present," 2006.
33.   Gallup Poll, "Timeline of Polling History: Events That Shaped the United States, and the World," 2011.

democracy" capable of defeating both Japan and Hitler's Germany. The underlying change in public opinion also laid the groundwork for the long Cold War struggle needed to prevent communism from plunging the world into darkness.

A similar phenomenon took place in 1955 when a young woman refused to give up her seat on a bus in Montgomery, Alabama. Sound-bite history tells us that Rosa Parks launched a civil rights movement. Dr. Martin Luther King Jr., however, knew that the movement began with "the magnificent words of the Constitution and the Declaration of Independence," which promised "that all men, yes, black men as well as white men, would be guaranteed the unalienable rights of life, liberty, and the pursuit of happiness."

King said that his famous dream was "deeply rooted in the American dream." His dream was that America would "rise up and live out the true meaning of its creed: 'We hold these truths to be self-evident: that all men are created equal.'"[34]

Still, after Parks served as a catalyst for challenging our nation to live up to its ideals, it took more than a decade before Congress enacted the Civil Rights Acts of 1964 and 1965. As always, Congress simply ratified the changes already felt in the hearts and minds of the American people. By the time Congress got around to considering the 1964 Civil Rights Act, 61 percent of Americans supported it (70 percent outside the South). Support for integrated schools was at 62 percent, and integrated neighborhoods were supported by 64 percent. Both figures had roughly doubled in a generation.[35] Where the public led, the politicians eventually followed, but it took a lot of work to get the legislators to climb on the bandwagon.

Rosa Parks's actions and Martin Luther King's words did not create the civil rights movement any more than the Shot Heard 'Round the World and Thomas Jefferson's words created the American Revolution. In both cases, the actions served as a catalyst to spark a movement based

---

34.   Martin Luther King Jr., "I Have a Dream," Aug. 1963.
35.   Steven F. Hayward, *The Age of Reason: The Fall of the Old Liberal Order* (Aug. 2001).

upon an immensely popular and powerful idea. In both cases, remarkable men gave eloquent voice to public opinion that had been developed long before. And in both cases, as with other great events in American history, the attitudes of Americans changed first and the actions of the politicians lagged behind.

Today, as we enter the second decade of the twenty-first century, America's politicians are once again lagging far behind public opinion. The Political Class is now isolated in a fantasy world where it thinks the credible policy options run from defending the status quo to increasing the role of government and government spending. The big question from the Political Class perspective is when the American people will finally realize they need to pay more in taxes.

American public opinion has solidified around an entirely different perspective. After bubbling beneath the surface for half a century, general frustration with government and government spending has now become energized and deeply committed to reducing the size, scope, and cost of government at all levels. This attitude is consistent with America's long-held skepticism about government and politics and a belief in freedom and self-governance. It also reflects a deeply held belief that we should not be passing on a burden to future generations. The newly energized desire for spending cuts has been reinforced by a growing belief that politicians have ignored voters for too long and don't really care what their constituents think.[36]

If historical patterns hold, this energized public opinion will not be content with a onetime effort to balance the budget and a return to politics as usual. The depth of public opinion will relentlessly challenge the defenders of the status quo for decades, not years. It will focus not just on reducing spending, but also on increasing the accountability of elected politicians, strengthening the economy, and increasing freedom for all Americans.

The budget debate is really a debate about how to pass on a brighter

---

36. Rasmussen Reports, "New Low 17% Say US Government Has Consent of the Governed," Aug. 2011.

future for the next generation and the generation after that. The Political Class is content to pass on a burden to future generations. The American people are not.

The history of our nation tells us that we shouldn't find it surprising that politicians are so far behind the curve. It's happened before and will likely happen again and again. It also shouldn't surprise us that the gap between the Political Class and the rest of us is creating real tensions and policy dilemmas. The good news is that same history also gives us hope that the American people have a pretty decent chance of defeating the Political Class agenda. But it also tells us that the road ahead is likely to be more than a little bumpy.

2

———•———

How the Political
Class Deceives

The simplest way to get people to make bad decisions is to give them bad information. That's how con men work, and that's how America's Political Class led America into a fiscal crisis. For several decades, the federal government has consistently and systematically misled the American people about federal spending, deficits, and the federal debt.

To be fair, most of today's politicians are blissfully unaware that they are doing this. Those who go to Washington and play for their political team prefer to spend their time and energy on things that are more interesting than budgets and accounting. When the numbers are presented, they simply go along with something that started long ago; they have no clue how misleading the government's financial reporting has become. That also means they have no clue as to how official misinformation distorts decision making and damages the nation.

While today's politicians may just be going along with the status quo, some of the things they go along with today were specifically created to mislead the public. In 1968 Lyndon Johnson was desperately trying to hide the costs of the Vietnam War and his Great Society programs. One of the changes he implemented was to shift a sleepy federal agency known as Fannie Mae off the federal books.[1] It had been established in the New Deal to provide liquidity for the housing market and appeared to have functioned adequately. The agency owed huge amounts of debt at a time when Johnson was trying to reduce the amount of debt on the federal balance sheet.

To address his political needs, Johnson shifted Fannie Mae from its status as a federal agency to a nominally private company, albeit one that enjoyed a "special relationship" with the government. This corrupt arrangement was documented and described in an aptly titled and important book, *Reckless Endangerment*. For decades, official Washington pretended Fannie Mae was a totally private company and that the federal government no longer owed the money it guaranteed. Government officials knew of the risks, and many reports were written about the dangers that Fannie Mae posed to taxpayers, but nothing was done, largely because the company aggressively bought political protection from both sides of the partisan aisle.

Fannie Mae grew over time to become a cancer eating away at our economy, and it played a key role in destroying the housing market and the financial industry. Along the way, it became a classic example of corruption, a case study in how government and big business work together against the rest of us. Fannie Mae took government subsidies and used them to help favored politicians and to enrich and support those with friends and relatives on the right political committees. They also, of course, took a bit off the top for company officers and investors.

While the accounting details are enough to make anybody's eyes glaze over, the result is easy to understand. The government spent four decades pretending the taxpayers had no liabilities related to Fannie Mae. Despite that, when the company finally collapsed, taxpayers got stuck with the tab of at least $317 billion.[2] That's more than $1,000 for

1. Gretchen Morgenson and Joshua Rosner, *Reckless Endangerment: How Outsized Ambition, Greed, and Corruption Led to Economic Endangerment* (May 2011).

2. Deborah Lucas, "The Budgetary Cost of Fannie Mae and Freddie Mac and Options for the Future Federal Role in the Secondary Mortgage Market," June 2011.

each and every living American, a pretty stiff tab for a liability that supposedly didn't exist. Shockingly, the $317 billion price tag is only part of the problem. It wreaked financial devastation on millions of low-income homeowners, the very people Fannie Mae claimed it was serving.[3]

The Fannie Mae story is far from unique. Many other phony accounting techniques led to real and outrageous debts for taxpayers to absorb. All of the misleading information distorts the policy process, and all of the gimmicks are based upon a common approach—word games. Words that mean one thing in the real world are given an entirely different meaning in the political world. The way that America's politicians have distorted the plain meaning of words is even more brazen than anything George Orwell ever imagined.

If America's Political Class wanted to communicate effectively and meaningfully with the American people, it could do so. It has enough media and message consultants available to get credible information into the public dialogue. But it doesn't. Instead it uses terms that have a very real meaning for most Americans and uses them in ways that are nothing like the common understanding of the words. When official Washington uses terms such as *balanced budgets*, *trust funds*, and *spending cuts* (or *spending increases*), their meaning is twisted beyond recognition. It gets away with this because, as with the case of the Fannie Mae scam, the accounting details are boring enough to make people lose interest, but the real world impact is even bigger than the $317 billion bailout of Fannie Mae.

Consider what it means to balance a budget. That's a concept deeply rooted in common sense that implies paying bills on time, not going further into debt, and not draining savings or retirement accounts. Ideally, when things are going well, a family balanced budget even sets aside a little money for a vacation, retirement savings, or a rainy-day fund. Most Americans believe that if a family must balance its budget, the government should do the same.

Like most commonsense ideals, this wisdom forms a sound basis for

---

3.   Ibid.

public policy because it rests upon a deep and practical understanding of reality. Balancing the family budget implies a sense of accountability and limits—you can't spend more than you take in. When income is down, people have to cut back a bit on spending.

Unfortunately, in the bizarre world of Washington word games, the official measures of balanced budgets bear no resemblance to that commonsense ideal. For example, using the government wording, the federal deficit was about $1.6 trillion in 2010, but the government really went about $5 trillion further in debt.[4] Even if the federal budget were officially "balanced" in 2010 using Washington terminology, the government would actually have fallen another $3 trillion further in debt. That's the kind of balance only a politician could love! It has absolutely nothing to do with what voters are trying to accomplish and does nothing to provide accountability or fiscal discipline. Needless to say, if a so-called balanced budget lets you go that much further in debt, it doesn't provide any sense of accountability or limits. That's one reason official Washington is in no rush to change the rules of the game.

This craziness is possible because the political world has also distorted the commonsense meaning of the words *trust fund*. Just as with the liabilities for Fannie Mae, government accounting simply pretends the trust fund liabilities don't exist. To most Americans, a trust fund is where money is set aside for one purpose and only that purpose. A trust fund can be set up by parents or grandparents to provide future income for children and grandchildren. Churches and nonprofit groups raise money that is set aside to be used only for a specific purpose. In these cases and others, the money in a trust fund is disbursed according to strict and legally binding guidelines that were established in advance. It is, in the end, something you can trust.

Franklin D. Roosevelt played upon that popular understanding in the 1930s to sell the American people his plan for Social Security. He always referred to the Social Security taxes as "contributions" and said the program "must be financed by contributions, not taxes." He was clear

---

4.   2010 *Financial Report of the United States Government.*

that Social Security "should be self-sustaining in the sense that funds for the payment of insurance benefits should not come from the proceeds of general taxation."[5]

It was a simple and understandable concept: workers would pay a small portion of their income into a trust fund, the payments would be matched by their employers, and the money would be set aside to earn interest and pay future retirement benefits. American voters at the time overwhelmingly endorsed and supported that concept. They still do today.[6] The idea of government trust funds has been used to win support for many other programs over the years.

A Highway Trust Fund was set up during the Eisenhower administration in 1956 to pay for a new interstate highway system.[7] The concept was for those who used the highways to pay their own way, something that voters can feel good about. In this case, motorists would pay gasoline taxes into a trust fund that provided two-way protections. One form of protection was for the motorists who paid the taxes. They were assured that the tax they paid at the pump would be set aside to build and maintain the highway system and could not be diverted to pay for other government programs. The other side of the protection was to assure all taxpayers that the cost of the highway system would not be subsidized by other taxes. Those who drove the most would pay the most. As with the underlying premise of Social Security funding, American voters accept this approach as reasonable and appropriate.

Lyndon B. Johnson used the same story line when he put together the Medicare program as an extension of Social Security in 1965. Medicare was implemented as a reform of the Social Security Act and included two trust funds, one for hospital coverage and one for supplementary coverage. The head of the Social Security Administration at that time had explained the concept for funding Medicare a few years earlier, and it sounded a lot like the pitch for Social Security: "Under social insur-

---

5. Franklin D. Roosevelt, "Message to Congress on Social Security," 1935.

6. Rasmussen Reports, "30% Favor Tax Hikes to Keep Social Security, Medicare Solvent," June 2011.

7. Federal Highway Administration, "The Highway Trust Fund," Apr. 2011.

ance practically all of the people could provide for their health insurance protection in retirement by paying toward it during their working lives, just as they pay now toward cash benefits. When they are older they would have the health insurance protection without having to pay additional amounts out of reduced incomes. This is the basic reasoning behind the President's proposal."[8]

In all these cases and others, the public was told one thing but the government did something else. Here's what it says in the president's 2012 budget: "The Federal Government uses the term 'trust fund' very differently from the private sector. The beneficiary of a private trust owns the trust's income and may own the trust's assets." However, "the Federal Government owns and manages the assets and earnings of most federal trust funds." As if that wasn't enough, the government "can unilaterally change the law to raise or lower future trust fund collections and payments or change the purpose for which collections are used."[9]

You read that right.

The government owns all the trust fund money and has the right to "unilaterally" change the purpose for which those funds are used. The US Supreme Court has even given its blessing to this interpretation.[10] The money in government trust funds can be diverted to pay for anything the politicians want to spend it on. That's true for Social Security, Medicare, unemployment funds, government employee pension funds, highway funds, and every other government trust fund. The government treats all the money as if it's in a single pot that can be spent on anything according to the whims of Congress.

What all this means is that many major programs were sold to the public on the basis of money being set aside for a specific purpose. Once enacted, however, the government simply disregarded those commitments. In the real world, such a bait-and-switch technique would be called fraud and result in jail time for all involved. In the political

---

8.   Robert M. Ball, "The Role of Social Insurance in Preventing Economic Dependency," Oct. 1961.

9.   *Budget of the United States Government, Fiscal Year 2012.*

10.   *Flemming v. Nestor*, 363 U.S. 603, Supreme Court of the US, 1960.

world, there's no jail time because those who committed the fraud get to write the rules. Their rules say that the people who misled us about trust funds think we should just trust the government.

Only 6 percent of voters are willing to do so. Eighty-two percent would feel far more secure about their retirement and other programs if there were real money in a trust fund somewhere rather than a nonbinding promise from the federal government.[11]

A government committed to our nation's founding principles of self-governance would never display such blatant disregard for voters. If our politicians were genuinely committed to seeking the consent of the governed, they would provide information in terms meaningful to voters rather than seeking to deceive them. At the least, that would mean using terms such as *balanced budgets* and *trust funds* to mean what voters think they mean.

As I write this, I recognize that many DC-based policy wonks will grimace at the notion that they should adjust their cherished terminology in an effort to communicate effectively with their boss, the American people. In their view, voters are the problem because they choose to believe that the trust funds are real.

I recently had a conversation with a conservative policy analyst who despaired about how hard it was to convince people that there really are no trust funds. When I suggested he had it backward and that maybe the politicians should do what they promised and treat the trust funds on the basis that they were sold to the American people, he was stunned. That attitude has been around for a long time in official Washington. Three decades ago, a formal study exploring the actuarial status of Social Security declared that the provisions in the original law about reserves being established in "accordance with accepted actuarial principles" were mere "window dressing." It went on to state, "Unfortunately, many people believe that this window-dressing language meant that the origi-

---

11.   Rasmussen Reports, "Just 10% Know Government Can Spend Social Security Money Any Way It Wants," Oct. 2011.

nal program was intended to be on a full-actuarial reserve basis, just as private pensions should be." [12]

In other words, the way the program was sold to the public was misleading and it's unfortunate that the American people believed it! That's the kind of arrogance that makes people so incredibly skeptical and suspicious of official Washington. Once again, it displays the Political Class desire to take us back to 1775 rather than acknowledge the sovereignty of the American people.

If the government stopped playing word games and used terms such as *balanced budget* and *trust fund* in the way they are commonly understood, it would fundamentally change the budget debate. While it would ultimately make it easier for voters to hold politicians accountable and address the long-term fiscal imbalance, the initial impact would be to show that the situation is even worse than just about anybody wants to believe.

For example, the Obama administration projects that the federal deficit will fall to $649 billion in 2016. But, the real operating budget deficit will actually be, according to the administration figures, $888 billion. The difference exists because the trust funds are projected to take in $239 billion. [13] For those who are ready to scream at the current president about this unseemly practice, it's important to point out that it's been done this way since the late 1960s. Every president has used the extra cash in the trust funds to reduce the reported deficit.

No president has acknowledged the other half of the problem—that unfunded liabilities are growing at the rate of about $3 trillion a year. [14] Learning that the deficit is worse than imagined may make the possibility of a balanced budget look even more difficult to achieve, but dealing with the reality of the situation is an essential first step toward solving it.

That's why it's important to recognize that the nation's largest trust

---

12. Dwight K. Bartlett III, "Measures of Actuarial Status for Social Security: Retrospect and Prospect," 1983.

13. Historical Tables, *Budget of the United States Government, Fiscal Year 2012.*

14. *2010 Financial Report of the United States Government.*

funds are woefully underfunded and the federal debt is much higher than reported. That the government has never really set up trust funds but has commingled all the money it receives is just part of the problem. Even if there were real trust funds in place today, the promises made by politicians greatly exceed the revenue dedicated to cover them. The disinformation gap now totals more than $100 trillion. Calculations by Michael Tanner of the Cato Institute show that if government officials were required to follow the same disclosure and accounting rules as private companies, the total debt would be approximately $120 trillion, not $15 trillion.[15] That works out to a debt of nearly $400,000 owed by every man, woman, and child in the nation.

As with most things in the federal budget, you can find the numbers if you look hard enough (and know where to look). But the pieces are scattered in many different places throughout a large number of documents. Tanner found that the Social Security trustees reported an unfunded liability of $16 trillion. That's nothing compared to the Medicare trustees, who showed unfunded liabilities totaling $89 trillion in 2009. Add this to the officially recognized debt that the politicians talk about and the total is $120 trillion.

It is difficult to precisely measure the long-term unfunded liability partly because slightly different assumptions lead to vastly different results. For example, the Obama administration assumed that the health care law passed in 2010 would reduce the cost of medical care so much that the unfunded liability would drop from $89 trillion to $27 trillion. Tanner notes, "There is reason to be skeptical about that revised figure. The Centers for Medicare and Medicaid Services, for example, believes that the spending reductions projected under health care reform are unrealistic."[16]

What this means is that if the Obama administration's optimistic projections of health care savings are right, the federal government debt is "only" about $60 trillion. If the health care reform does nothing to

---

15.   Michael Tanner, "Bankrupt: Entitlements and the Federal Budget," Mar. 2011.

16.   Ibid.

increase or reduce health care costs, the debt totals $120 trillion. You don't even want to think about what the debt might be if, as most voters expect, the president's health care reform law will increase the cost of care.

Regardless of the specific numbers, these projections highlight that the government has promised future benefits far, far in excess of the revenue set aside to pay for them. The specific numbers may be hard to precisely estimate, but the numbers do give a great sense of scale and draw attention to the problem. Even worse, these promises have been made for important and popular programs, which makes the disinformation even more morally reprehensible.

To get a sense of scale, the table below shows the total wealth held by all millionaires in the United States side by side with the official debt owed by the US government along with the total debt including unfunded liabilities.

Before Social Security was enacted, Franklin Roosevelt warned about

Combined Wealth of US Millionaires vs. US Debt

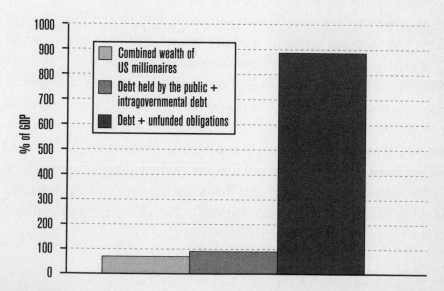

Source: Cato Institute

how "organizations promoting fantastic schemes have aroused hopes which cannot possibly be fulfilled."[17]

In Roosevelt's time, those "organizations" were further to the left than the president and were promoting a number of retirement and pension schemes that promised enormous benefits without any credible way of paying for them. Now, the federal government itself has done what FDR feared from outside groups in 1934. In reality, none of us can comprehend numbers such as $15 trillion or $120 trillion or even the difference between millions, billions, and trillions. At some point, they're all just numbers on a spreadsheet. The purpose of highlighting the government's deceptive budget practices is not to come up with a bigger and scarier number or to make the accountants happy. It's to highlight the deceptions themselves.

The deceptions matter because there's no way voters would knowingly have approved of policies to plunge the nation $120 trillion into debt. During the 1960s, an intentionally deceptive budget process let politicians get credit for increasing benefits in the short term while passing on the burden of paying for those benefits to future generations. We are the generation that got stuck with the bill. For better or worse, it is now our responsibility to fix the process.

Poll after poll has shown that Americans today do not want to pass an even bigger bill on to the next generation. Even though an honest look at the budget deficit and total debt shows that things are far worse than anybody wants to believe, the American people are ready, willing, and able to solve the problem. Specific policy changes that could enjoy popular support and eliminate the government's debt burden will be discussed in subsequent chapters, but first it's appropriate to take a quick look at how a bad budget process in the 1960s led to a fiscal policy crisis in the early twenty-first century, and, it must be emphasized, how the same flawed budget process is standing in the way of rational solutions today.

---

17.   Franklin D. Roosevelt, "Address to Advisory Council of the Committee on Economic Security on the Problems of Economic and Social Security," Nov. 1934.

As President Lyndon Johnson tried to hide the cost of his Great Society programs and the Vietnam War, he created a "unified budget."[18] This basically meant throwing all the money from the various trust funds and operating funds into a single pot. It made no logical or ethical sense to consider money that was supposed to be in a trust fund the same as money in the operating budget, but this technique made the reported deficit look smaller. That was a political advantage the president considered worthwhile. Johnson's approach did fit with prevailing economic views of his day, which added at least some credibility to his scheme. Government economists of that era believed they could "fine-tune" the economy by controlling deficits and other fiscal policy levers. These economists were advocates for the theories of John Maynard Keynes that placed the government as the central player and prime mover of a national economy. If the economy was slowing down, you applied a little stimulus. If it was heating up, you applied a little restraint. Only 11 percent of voters agree with that approach today, but the sixties were just different.[19] In the Keynesian world, government mattered and entrepreneurs didn't. No wonder politicians wanted to believe in it.

With Keynesian economics as the guiding light, the most important budget figure for the fine-tuning was measuring the cash flowing in and out of the federal treasury during any single year. For the economists involved, these were heady times. Managing the economy was the task at hand, and it mattered more than balancing the budget or avoiding long-term liabilities. In fact, long-term obligations were apparently to be dealt with by applying another Keynesian perspective — "In the long run, we're all dead."

Today, after decades of witnessing just how disastrous government management of the economy can be, just 28 percent of voters believe that managing the economy is a more important policy goal than protecting individual rights.[20] Polling on whether the nation should return to the

18.   Larry DeWitt, "Research Note #20: The Social Security Trust Funds and the Federal Budget," 2007.

19.   Rasmussen Reports, "Americans Reject Keynesian Economics," Feb. 2010.

20.   Rasmussen Reports, "53% View Government as Threat to Individual Rights," May 2011.

gold standard highlighted the distrust of politicians running the economy. Initially, people had mixed views on whether the gold standard was a good idea. Given that it's rarely discussed around kitchen tables, only 24 percent held strong opinions about the concept. However, when told that a return to the gold standard would "dramatically reduce the power of central bankers and political leaders to steer the economy," 57 percent favored the idea and only 19 percent were opposed.[21] With such attitudes, it makes no sense to use a budget process that is attuned to the needs of central bankers and political leaders who want to steer the economy.

In the 1950s and '60s, however, the government was also just coming to grips with the reality of having a Social Security trust fund. The government had never before dealt with anything where it was entrusted with funds paid early in workers' careers with the expectation that they would get them back as a pension decades later. Some analysts were concerned about the problem of accumulating a trust fund surplus that was too big.[22] That was probably not anywhere on a list of voter concerns, but it filled government reports. Closer to the mark were some voices as early as 1958 suggesting that the problem might be too little funding for Social Security rather than too big a surplus.[23]

Others thought the whole idea of a trust fund was a mistake to begin with and argued that the entire system should be funded entirely by general revenues of the federal government. If FDR had proposed that approach, Social Security would never have been so widely accepted by the American people. In discussions with one advocate of eliminating the trust fund approach, Roosevelt explained, "We put those payroll contributions there so as to give the contributors a legal, moral, and political right to collect their pensions and their unemployment benefits. With those taxes in there, no damn politician can ever scrap my social security program." FDR also made it clear that the payroll taxes had a

---

21.   Rasmussen Reports, "Public Has Mixed Views of Return to Gold Standard," Oct. 2011.

22.   Dwight K. Bartlett III, "Measures of Actuarial Status for Social Security: Retrospect and Prospect," 1983.

23.   1957–59 Advisory Council on Social Security, *Misunderstandings of Social Security Financing*.

psychological effect by separating Social Security payments from being on the dole.

Advocates of eliminating the trust funds shifted gears and argued that the trust funds should be modified to run on a pay-as-you-go basis. In that model, whatever came in from taxes in any one year should be roughly the same as the amount paid out that year. The words would be the same as what voters had bought into, but the meaning was entirely different. Eventually, among the political insiders, the pay-as-you-go model won out. Government economists would set tax and spend parameters so that the costs were covered in the short term, and it was assumed the long-term obligations would somehow take care of themselves. However, nothing was done to inform the American people of the change. Polls consistently show that voters would have greatly preferred to stick with the plan they bought from FDR, a plan that included building up a trust fund surplus to cover the cost of future benefits.[24] But voters weren't all that important to those fine-tuning our economy.

The pay-as-you-go mind-set enabled President Johnson to win support from seniors with a much desired Medicare plan without the bother of having taxpayers know how much it would eventually cost. In the short term, the gang in Washington could make the numbers work. The hospital insurance portion of the program cost the government $3 billion in 1966. At the time, projections suggested that the cost would grow to $12 billion by 1990.[25] Those making the projections said they involved "very conservative assumptions with respect to all foreseeable factors." In reality, the program was wildly more expensive than anticipated, and the actual cost was more than five times as much as projected—$67 billion.[26]

The *pay as you go* terminology was just another example of politi-

---

24. Rasmussen Reports, "Just 10% Know Government Can Spend Social Security Money Any Way It Wants," Oct. 2011.

25. Robert J. Myers and Francisco Bayo, "Hospital Insurance, Supplementary Medical Insurance, and Old-Age, Survivors, and Disability Insurance: Financing Basis Under the 1965 Amendments," Feb. 1968.

26. Historical Tables, *Budget of the United States Government, Fiscal Year 2012.*

cians using words differently from the rest of us. For most Americans, *pay as you go* conjures up images of buying only what you can afford when you can afford it. It suggests a reluctance to take on debt. That's not at all what *pay as you go* meant in the political context of the 1960s. Instead, it meant that the trust funds only had to worry about paying benefits to those who were already retired and not worry about the promises being made to the next generation of retirees.

Once the Democratic Johnson left the White House, Republican Richard Nixon proved he could play the same game just as well. Nixon was elected in 1968, and his obsession with winning reelection in 1972 eventually led to Watergate and his resignation in disgrace, but his handling of Social Security to support his reelection bid may be an even more troubling legacy for the nation.

During Nixon's first term, the Advisory Council on Social Security "recommended full acceptance of the philosophy of pay-as-you-go financing." It also questioned "how much importance should be attached to the long-range cost projections."[27] This paved the way for the president to sign two pieces of Social Security legislation in the months leading up to Election Day 1972.

In a blatant ploy that would never pass muster in the Internet era, Nixon's plan provided an immediate 20 percent increase in Social Security benefits that went into effect just two months before Election Day.[28] He also enacted a much-needed plan to provide automatic cost-of-living adjustments for seniors. The formula did more than help seniors keep up with inflation; it let benefits grow at twice the rate of inflation without a corresponding increase in long-term financing (the formula was corrected after Nixon left office). Since the COLAs first went into effect more than three decades ago, benefits have grown 80 percent more than inflation.

Because the government had officially adopted the pay-as-you-go

---

27.   Dwight K. Bartlett III, "Measures of Actuarial Status for Social Security: Retrospect and Prospect," 1983.

28.   Richard M. Nixon, "Statement of Signing the Social Security Amendments of 1972," Oct. 1972.

approach, the legislative summary reported the following: "Consistent with past policy of maintaining the social security program on a sound financial basis, provision is made for meeting the cost of the expanded program."[29]

In the way the Political Class had redefined the trust fund, it was true. In the way that voters understood things, it was not. The Nixon plan tinkered with the tax structure just enough to insure that cash flow was covered through the first half of the 1970s, but there was nowhere near enough funding to keep the system going. Just a decade later, tax-cutting president Ronald Reagan was forced to raise Social Security taxes to help cover the cost of Nixon's promises. Even today, the system remains underfunded largely because of the faulty budget process developed in the 1960s that allowed Nixon to reap the short-term rewards while letting others worry about the long-term costs.

It's especially noteworthy that the decision to abandon long-term planning was made just as the baby boom generation was coming of age. Clearly, all involved knew that the number of retirees and retirement costs would dramatically escalate when the boomers began to hit age sixty-five. Instead of making any provision to deal with it by protecting the trust funds, the political leaders simply chose to hide their head in the sand.[30] By taking that approach, the decisions made by Lyndon Johnson and Richard Nixon in the 1960s have created a fiscal crisis for those of us living in the twenty-first century.

One other lesson that Nixon gave the nation is that the cover-up is often worse than the crime itself. That's certainly true of budgetary history in recent decades. For the last several decades, voters have consistently elected politicians who promised to cut taxes and spending. But, spending has continued to increase and consume an ever larger share of the nation's economy. In every year but one since 1965, government spending in America has grown faster than the combined total of population growth plus inflation.

---

29.   Robert M. Ball, *Social Security Amendment of 1972: Summary and Legislative History*.
30.   Ibid.

Since dealing with the problem would require telling voters the truth about the unsustainable commitments made by Richard Nixon and Lyndon Johnson, politicians from both parties began to engage in a cover-up. Needing to appease voters, politicians quickly defined some spending as "uncontrollable" and other spending as "discretionary." That way, they could claim to hold the line or make cuts on all discretionary spending and try to convince voters that was enough.

Voters eventually caught on and more help was needed, so the Political Class invented a language that let it claim spending was being cut even while it was going up. The basic tool was deceptively simple: the Current Services Budget.[31] Rather than report changes in actual government spending from one year to the next, the Congressional Budget Office, using this technique, reported changes from projected spending. If spending for a particular program was expected to increase by 10 percent, but it only increased by 5 percent, that would be reported as a spending cut. As noted earlier, 62 percent of voters are now aware of this approach, but four decades of damage has already been done.

In fairness to the policy wonks, this technique actually *can* be a pretty useful indicator when wielded properly. It projects what a certain program would cost under current law and provides a baseline to measure any policy changes against. But, while useful in narrow applications, in the hands of a politician it becomes a weapon of mass deception that has cost the American people trillions of dollars.

To see how this works, consider what happened when House Republicans and President Obama agreed in early 2011 to what they both described as serious spending cuts. Nobody—from either political party—mentioned that total federal spending would end up about $400 billion higher than it was the year before.[32] Why mess up a good story on fiscal discipline with facts?

The president's 2012 budget shows just how far the language of of-

31.   Analytical Perspectives, *Budget of the United States Government, Fiscal Year 2012.*
32.   Historical Tables, *Budget of the United States Government, Fiscal Year 2012.*

ficial Washington has drifted from the language spoken in the rest of the nation. The numbers in the budget show that spending for 2012 would be $362 billion higher than it was the year before. Even using optimistic assumptions, the president's budget projected that federal spending would be $649 billion higher five years down the road.[33]

To most Americans, growth in spending from $3.4 trillion in 2011 to $4.4 trillion in 2016 might seem like a pretty big increase, but that's no challenge for a skilled politician. Somehow, those figures showing the reality of a trillion-dollar increase in spending never made it to the president's budget message. Instead, he talked of how his budget "lays out a path for how we can pay down these debts and free the American economy from their burden."[34]

How did he reach this conclusion? The president touted a "five-year freeze on all discretionary spending outside of security." He said, "Over a decade, this freeze will save more than four hundred billion dollars."[35] Now, in normal usage, a spending freeze would mean no increase or decrease. But in the language of politicians, a freeze saves $400 billion. He never mentions the trillion-dollar growth in annual federal spending.

According to the president, "This budget also includes many terminations and reductions to programs across the entire federal government." He claimed, "We have put forward more than two hundred terminations and reductions for over thirty billion dollars in savings."[36] That certainly conveys an aura of fiscal restraint, and there were some modest cutbacks, but it doesn't explain why the government keeps spending more money.

What President Obama is doing is not doing anything differently from other presidents. That's the real problem. Because they speak in a language unique to Washington, DC, politicians have spent the last several decades talking about how they've cut the budget when they haven't.

It's more complicated to say that the budget will increase by $600 bil-

---

33. Ibid.
34. *Congressional Record*, Feb. 2011.
35. Ibid.
36. Ibid.

lion over the next five years and that some programs had to be trimmed just to keep spending at that level, but the more complicated explanation has the virtue of being true. It's important for politicians to use truth and to present the budget in terms the voters can recognize from their day-to-day life. If that kind of discussion had been held over the past forty years, we wouldn't be in the mess we're in today.

Unfortunately, the story of America's descent into a nightmare of deficits and debt has been led by politicians who consistently provided voters with faulty information. Some knew the information was faulty, some were simply going along, but the result is a government more than $100 trillion in debt.

So what can we do?

Yes, the problem is worse than we thought. Fixing that mess will be painful, but it can be done. A necessary first step is for the Political Class to come clean and level with the American people. The exclusive and deceptive language of official Washington must be put away so that the budget debate can move forward on a more honest footing. That means using words in Washington the same way they are used in the rest of the country. No more word games for the Political Class.

In practical terms, this means fixing the way that official Washington defines balanced budgets, trust funds, and spending changes.

1. The federal budget should be considered "balanced" only when the government is not going further into debt. The operating budget must be balanced on its own, without appropriating trust fund surpluses. Someday, balancing the budget will even include a provision for making regular payments to reduce the existing federal debt.

2. Trust funds should be respected, protected, and actuarially balanced over an appropriate time frame. It's easy to recognize that the flows of the Social Security trust fund follow a different rhythm from the flows for unemployment insurance. For some of the long-term trust funds, the challenge will be to make them real, rather than just a series of promises from the government.

3. Spending changes should be measured in terms of real dollar amounts rather than in comparison to anticipated spending or any other measure. Every budget document should state plainly what the top-line numbers are—how much was spent last year, how much is being spent this year, and how much will be spent next year. Details can follow, but voters need to know how much spending is going up each year. Then, they can learn the reasons why.

America's voters can handle the truth, and they deserve it.

These changes will make it possible to have a healthier budget debate. It would put the official measure of a balanced budget in line with popular expectations. The trust fund changes will provide a vehicle for focusing on long-term changes rather than short-term fixes. And the need to plainly state spending changes will help educate both the Political Class and Mainstream voters about the forces driving up federal spending. To give a sense of why this is important, the Congressional Budget Office (CBO) recently published projections of how the federal budget would look after the $2.5 trillion in budget "cutting" promised by Congress as part of the debt-ceiling deal. After including all the promised budget "cuts," spending still grows from $3.6 trillion in 2012 to $5.8 trillion in 2021.

A healthier process will make it possible for voters to clean up the mess that the politicians have made. But, ultimately, policy changes must be made to ratify the will of the American people.

PART TWO

——•——

How Voters Would Spend the People's Money

3

---·---

How Voters Would Fix Defense

Nothing undermines efforts to reduce federal spending more than conservatives who demand federal spending cuts in every program except the military. Every time a conservative makes such a call, liberals find it easy (and justifiable) to claim hypocrisy. Not surprisingly, only 35 percent of voters nationwide share the view of cutting everything but defense.[1]

It's ridiculous for anybody to claim that we need to make major spending cuts on everything except for their favorite issue. That attitude helped create the mess we're in today; it certainly doesn't point toward any solutions. Unlike the politicians who created the mess, the American people are ready to take the mature approach. They recognize that every single item in the federal budget needs to be on the table for discussion.

Beyond that, exempting military spending is especially impractical. As has already been noted, national security spending is one of the three major components of government spending. Spending on the military and veterans' affairs makes up about one-fourth of the entire federal budget. It's an even bigger share if you include the cost of Homeland Security and other defense-related spending. Still, national security is a difficult topic to discuss in budgetary terms because we cannot put the nation's safety at risk just to make the accounting ledgers balance. As

---

1. Rasmussen Reports, "67% Favor Finding Spending Cuts in All Government Programs," Aug. 2011.

Ronald Reagan once put it, "Defense is not a budget issue. You spend what you need."

Reagan's attitude is obviously correct in the most basic sense. If we can't defend our nation, nothing else matters, but it's also important to remember that Reagan was speaking in a particular place and time. Recognizing that the Soviet economy could not keep up with the more vibrant US economy, he was seeking to put financial pressure on the communist empire and hurry its collapse. That Reagan succeeded is one of the key reasons we can consider different approaches in the twenty-first century.

The question before Americans today is exactly the same as it was in Reagan's time: how much do we *need* to spend on defense? While the question is the same, the threat environment is fundamentally different. In Reagan's era, we faced a rival superpower with massive military capabilities and a desire to defeat the forces of freedom. Today there is no such rival, but we do face a terrorist threat that has unnerved the nation for more than a decade. We also face cyber-war concerns that could not even have been imagined during the pre-Internet era when Reagan was in the White House.

Still, the question of what we *need* to spend is hard to even consider because most Americans hold a jumble of conflicting emotions and perceptions. These factors cloud the debate and shift the focus to everything but money.

Still, most of us recognize that the founding beliefs of our nation are worth fighting for and defending. Ninety percent agree with the key assertion in the Declaration of Independence that truly set our nation apart from every other nation in the history of the world: "We are all endowed by our Creator with certain inalienable rights, among them life, liberty, and the pursuit of happiness." Just 4 percent disagree.[2] While recognizing the nation is not perfect, 79 percent would rather live in the United States than anywhere else in the world.[3]

---

2. Rasmussen Reports, "Americans Still Agree with Ideals Set Forth in the Declaration of Independence," June 2011.
3. Rasmussen Reports, "79% Happy to Call America Home," Oct. 2010.

Americans also have tremendous respect for those who have signed up to defend our country. In a time when people are cynical about government, big business, and many other large institutions, 81 percent have a favorable opinion of the US military.[4] You see this respect in many ways beyond the numbers. At airports, uniformed military personnel are often offered priority boarding for flights and no one complains. In parades, sports events, and other public forums, the response is typically enthusiastic when those who have served are introduced. In millions of more private moments, complete strangers take the time to thank those in uniform.

This respect and admiration for our troops exists alongside doubts about the jobs they've been asked to do. Most voters now believe it was a mistake for the United States to have gotten involved in Iraq,[5] most now want to see US troops brought home quickly from Afghanistan,[6] and there has never been much support for the military action in Libya.[7] On a grander scale, the United States has signed treaties requiring us to provide military assistance to fifty-four countries around the globe if those countries are attacked. We also have special and unique relationships with Israel and Mexico that informally commit us to a concern about their security issues. Taking a look at individual countries suggests that the American people are in a mood to dramatically reduce the scope of our military protection for other nations. Out of fifty-four countries covered by current obligations, plus two others with special relationships, a majority of Americans support providing such assistance to only twelve. The commitment to provide military assistance is supported by 60 percent of Americans for only four countries: Canada, the United Kingdom, Australia, and Israel.

Countries that don't reach the 50 percent mark include our oldest ally, France, along with Portugal, Spain, Greece, Japan, Denmark, Belgium, and Poland.

4.   Rasmussen Reports, "81% Share a Favorable Opinion of US Military," Nov. 2010.
5.   Rasmussen Reports, "51% Say US Shouldn't Have Become Involved in Iraq," Mar. 2011.
6.   Rasmussen Reports, "59% Want Troops Home from Afghanistan," Aug. 2011.
7.   Rasmussen Reports, "20% Now Support US Military Action in Libya," Aug. 2011.

Public Support for Providing Military Assistance to Selected Countries

Canada 80%	South Korea 59%	The Philippines 49%	Belgium 38%
United Kingdom 74%	Bahamas 58%	France 46%	Poland 37%
Australia 65%	Panama 58%	Spain 46%	Turkey 37%
Israel 61%	Netherlands 55%	Costa Rica 45%	Brazil 33%
	Germany 54%	Greece 44%	Argentina 30%
	Norway 53%	Iceland 44%	Thailand 30%
	Mexico 53%	Japan 43%	Chile 29%
	Italy 50%	Dominican Republic 42%	Czech Republic 29%
		Haiti 41%	Honduras 28%
		Hungary 41%	Portugal 28%
		New Zealand 41%	Venezuela 27%
		Denmark 40%	Ecuador 25%
			El Salvador 25%
			Paraguay 23%
			Peru 23%
			Trinidad and Tobago 23%
			Uruguay 23%
			Luxembourg 22%
			Guatemala 21%
			Latvia 21%
			Nicaragua 20%
			Croatia 19%
			Bulgaria 18%
			Lithuania 18%
			Romania 18%
			Slovakia 17%
			Slovenia 17%
			Albania 16%
			Bolivia 14%
			Colombia 14%
			Cuba 12%
			Estonia 12%

Source: Rasmussen Reports Polling Data[8]

---

8.   Rasmussen Reports, "Defending Countries."

Moving beyond individual countries, less than half (49%) believe the nation needs to remain in the NATO alliance.[9]

These findings highlight the central gap between the American people and the governing philosophy of the Political Class in the early days of the twenty-first century. Three out of four American believe that US troops should never be deployed for military action overseas unless vital national security interests are at stake,[10] but recent presidents have all adopted less restrictive approaches to sending troops abroad. Troops are often dispatched for humanitarian purposes or in a belief that the United States should police the world; only 11 percent of voters believe that the role of global policeman is appropriate.[11]

American voters reject isolationism and want the nation to play the leading role in world affairs. They see our nation as a force for good and reject those who tend to blame America first in any world conflict. At the same time, twenty-first-century voters reject the belief that we should send Americans first in the face of any global challenge. Instead, voters are seeking a strategy that might best be defined as Protect America First.

If the military protects the nation, our other national assets will win over hearts and minds around the globe. This suggests that it is quite possible to find a twenty-first-century strategy that will support our troops, protect our nation, be embraced by a solid majority of voters, and reduce military spending by hundreds of billions of dollars annually. I say this despite Rasmussen Reports polling showing just 32 percent of voters nationwide believe the United States spends too much on national defense. A nearly equal number (27%) say that we are spending too little on defense, and 37 percent say that the current spending levels are about right.[12]

Predictably, conservatives say we spend too little on defense and liberals say we spend too much, but even many conservatives are willing to

9. Rasmussen Reports, "Only 49% Think US Still Needs to Belong to NATO," June 2011.
10. Rasmussen Reports, "75% See Vital US Interests as Only Reason for Committing Military Forces to Overseas Action," July 2011.
11. Rasmussen Reports, "Just 11% Say US Should Be World's Policeman," June 2011.
12. Rasmussen Reports, "Voters Underestimate How Much US Spends on Defense," Jan. 2011.

support significant changes. To see how to make changes, we first need to take a look at what we currently spend on national defense.

Where We Are Today

In 2010, the federal government spent more than $875 billion on national defense and veterans' affairs. That's a big number, even in a total federal budget that spent $3.3 trillion. That defense spending includes about $160 billion for Overseas Contingency Operations, a category that is primarily supplemental funding for the wars in Iraq and Afghanistan. It also includes $155 billion for the direct costs of military personnel and $31 billion to care for "wounded, ill, and injured" members of the service and their families. It costs a lot to maintain a military with 1.4 million active-duty military personnel. Veterans' benefits and services total about $125 billion, including another $45 billion for health care.[13]

In addition to the military personnel and veterans, the national security budget includes nearly eight hundred thousand civilian personnel to support the military effort (again, this doesn't even include the people working for Department of Homeland Security and other defense-related areas). For most people, these numbers are simply too big to fathom, so we need to find some context to provide a sense of scale, and understanding.

One way to do this is to look at how fast national security spending has grown over the past decade. In 2001, the year of the horrific terrorist attacks on 9/11, the federal government spent approximately $350 billion on defense and veterans' affairs. If that spending had grown to keep pace with the population and inflation, it would total approximately $481 billion today. Current spending is 82 percent higher than that.[14]

---

13.   Historical Tables, *Budget of the United States Government, Fiscal Year 2012*.
14.   Ibid.

It's no surprise that defense spending went up following 9/11 and that the American people supported an increase, but it's legitimate to ask if an 82 percent increase was necessarily the right amount.

Taking a longer-term view, spending is higher today than it was when Ronald Reagan left office, even after adjusting for population growth and inflation. That's a staggering comparison since our Cold War adversary, the Soviet Union, still existed on Reagan's final day in the White House. We are spending more today than we did back then even though our primary enemy collapsed!

The same point can be found by going back a bit further to 1968. At that time we were fighting both the Cold War with the Soviet Union and a hot war in Vietnam. Even after adjusting for population growth and inflation, we are spending more on national defense today than we did when the United States had half a million soldiers on the ground fighting in Southeast Asia.

If we *need* to spend more today than we did during Vietnam and the Cold War to keep us safe, Americans will pay the cost. If an 82 percent increase in military spending since the 9/11 attacks is *needed* to keep us safe, Americans will pay that cost as well. Just because spending has gone up doesn't automatically mean we're spending too much. The real question is always what's *needed* to keep us safe; Americans would rather err on the side of spending a bit more than is needed rather than a bit less.

To address the real need, however, we should also look at the competitive environment. As the chart on page 64 shows, the United States today spends about as much money on national defense as the rest of the world combined. That will come as a surprise to many. Only 58 percent of voters are even aware that the United States spends more on defense than any other nation in the world. And an even smaller number, just 33 percent, recognize that our nation spends roughly as much as the rest of the world combined.[15]

Beyond highlighting how our nation spends as much as the rest of

---

15.   Rasmussen Reports, "Voters Recognize US Military Spending Tops Other Countries," Nov. 2010.

Global Military Spending, 2009

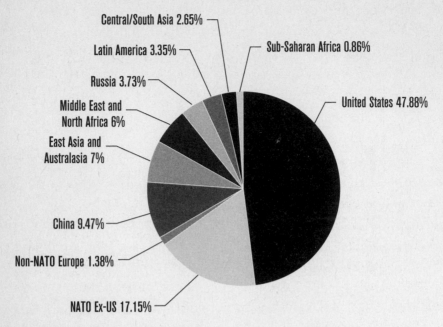

Central/South Asia 2.65%

Latin America 3.35%

Sub-Saharan Africa 0.86%

Russia 3.73%

United States 47.88%

Middle East and North Africa 6%

East Asia and Australasia 7%

China 9.47%

Non-NATO Europe 1.38%

NATO Ex-US 17.15%

Source: International Institute of Strategic Studies, the Military Balance, 2011

the world combined, a couple of other items in the chart are noteworthy. NATO, even without the United States, spends a bit more on the military than Russia and China combined. Overall, while the numbers are fairly close, US allies spend more than our enemies. We certainly don't want to leave our defense in the hands of Europeans, but it's reassuring to know that the bad guys aren't the only ones outside the United States with a military force.

Another way of looking at the data is to compare how much each nation pays per person on defense spending. The United States spends more than $2,500 per person on national defense; Russia and our NATO allies each spend about one-fifth of that amount. Nobody else in the world commits even one-tenth as much as the United States does to defense (see table on page 65).

It may be that these spending levels are the price we have to pay to be the world's dominant superpower. It's certainly better to be the country

Defense Expenditure per Capita, Constant 2008 US Dollars

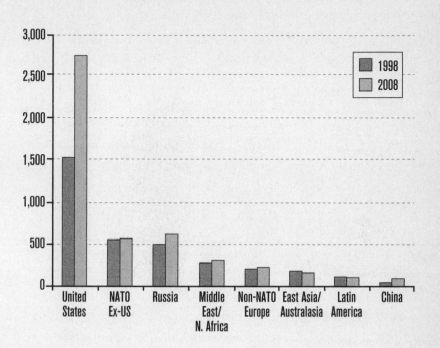

Sources: IISS, The Military Balance 1999–2000; IISS, The Military Balance 2010.

that has a bigger and more powerful military than anybody else, but that position comes with a cost that impacts US competitiveness and economic well-being. Think about how the average American is spending $2,000 a year more than the average European for defense. Is that a fair way to share the burden? Does it make sense at a time when only 46 percent of voters have an even somewhat favorable opinion of the NATO alliance?[16] What makes politicians think that voters would support such an unbalanced sharing of the burden?

It's not just the per capita numbers that highlight a spending gap. When examined in aggregate terms, the gap is equally staggering. While the United States is spending close to $900 billion on the military and

16. Rasmussen Reports, "Only 49% Think US Still Needs to Belong to NATO," June 2011.

veterans' affairs, China is spending less than $200 billion. North Korea, Iran, and Syria spend a combined total of under $30 billion. The Pentagon spends more on research and development alone than "Germany, the United Kingdom, France, Russia, or Japan each spend on their entire defense budgets."[17] If we are at risk militarily, it is certainly not for a lack of spending!

Budget figures tell only part of the story. It is also interesting to take a look at what that spending looks like in terms of military capacity. To take just one example, the United States has eleven aircraft carriers and hopes to have twelve in service in a few years. "No other nation has even one comparable ship,"[18] according to former defense secretary Robert Gates, who served under both President George W. Bush and Barack Obama. The US also has eight[19] WASP class helicopter carriers that are larger than just about every other *aircraft* carrier in the world.[20]

The US military has a physical presence in all fifty states plus a total of more than 250,000 soldiers deployed ashore in over a hundred countries worldwide.[21] Additionally, our navy has 280 ships and submarines to patrol the oceans.[22] Our air force controls most of the world's airspace as part of a military force that is the most dominant and expansive in world history.

But resource strains are showing on the US military today that suggest we may not be able to keep doing what we're doing for long. We have seen these strains in the need for soldiers to serve extended tours of duty in Iraq and Afghanistan. Additionally, National Guard forces have been called upon to supplement our war efforts in ways that have imposed tremendous difficulties and burdens on all involved. No amount of money can overcome the reality that we are following a game plan calling for more soldiers than we can find. One big strain is the challenge of recruit-

17.   Christopher A. Preble, *The Power Problem* (2009).
18.   Robert M. Gates, "Remarks on the Role of the Modern Navy," May 2010.
19.   United States Navy, *Fact File: Amphibious Assault Ships*, Jan. 2011.
20.   Christopher A. Preble, *The Power Problem* (2009).
21.   Ibid.
22.   United States Navy, *Status of the Navy*, Aug. 2011.

ing and retaining officers. This strain has even been acknowledged by a policy shift at West Point.

Back in the day, West Point cadets came to the academy and either sank or swam. A large number of the incoming plebes were not expected to be around when the class graduated four years later. Today, West Point helps cadets make it through rather than washing out those who can't make it on their own. Some of the alums aren't happy about the change, but more than anything else, this policy shift highlights how difficult it is for the army to recruit and retain the people they want as leaders.

In the narrow sense, the recruiting and retention strains lead to bigger budgets because it costs more and more to get the troops we need. In the larger sense, that we are having trouble recruiting enough officers and soldiers to support our current military strategy suggests a set of limits being imposed by the American people. Consent of the governed is not merely a concept for the voting booth; the government needs to earn it to support all its initiatives. If Americans aren't willing to serve in support of our military strategy, it does not have the consent of the governed.

In World War II, Americans showed their consent for a military effort needed to defeat Hitler's Germany and the emperor's Japan. Support for a military draft grew from 50 percent in May 1940 to 64 percent in June.[23] As war drew closer, 89 percent said the draft was a good idea.[24] Today, 67 percent oppose a military draft, and it is hard to imagine any scenario that would change that attitude.[25]

The military—and the nation at large—will have to consider the reality of more limited support.

From a budgeting perspective, it will have to be considered along with the assessment provided by Admiral Mike Mullen, chairman of the Joint Chiefs of Staff, who said, "The most significant threat to our

23.   Thomas J. Robinson, "Freedom Isn't Free: A Study of Compulsory Military Service in the US Army," 2006.

24.   Gallup Poll, "Timeline of Polling History: Events That Shaped the United States, and the World," 2011.

25.   Rasmussen Reports, "67% Oppose a Military Draft," Nov. 2009.

national security is our debt."[26] The American people have concerns on the economic front as well. In terms of threats to the United States, 82 percent of the nation's adults believe economic challenges are now a bigger concern than military challenges.[27]

From a political perspective, it's important to note that the budgetary and other strains on the military result from a gap between the American people and their political leaders. Voters want a strong but focused military with a mission to Protect America First. The nation's politicians, from both parties, have built a military designed to police the world. Ironically, the gap between public preferences and government policy has grown larger since the Cold War ended with the collapse of the Soviet Union just over two decades ago.

How Did We Get to This Point?

Following World War II, the United States and the Soviet Union each developed a string of global alliances that formed the framework of the Cold War. In his first inaugural address, President Dwight D. Eisenhower minced no words in defining the challenges of that era for the nation: "We sense with all our faculties that forces of good and evil are massed and armed and opposed as rarely before in history. . . . Freedom is pitted against slavery; lightness against the dark."

He raised a question that worried many Americans in the wake of the Depression and World War II: "Are we nearing the light—a day of freedom and of peace for all mankind? Or are the shadows of another night closing in upon us?" He acknowledged America's new role in the world: "Destiny has laid upon our country the responsibility of the free world's leadership."[28]

In assuming that leadership, Eisenhower believed that, given time,

---

26.   CNN Wire Staff, "Mullen: Debt Is Top National Security Threat," Aug. 2010.
27.   Rasmussen Reports, "When It Comes to Military Strategy, Voters Put American Interests ahead of World Peace," Jan. 2011.
28.   Dwight D. Eisenhower, "First Inaugural Address," Jan. 1953.

the superiority of freedom and democracy would win out over communism. His approach recognized the need for limits on nonessential military interventions and envisioned a path that could provide "security without paying the price of national bankruptcy."[29] He quickly ended what he saw as one costly diversion in Korea and kept the nation out of Vietnam. He "simply could not imagine the United States putting ground forces anywhere in Southeast Asia" and was "bitterly opposed . . . to such a course of action."[30]

Before leaving office, Eisenhower famously and accurately warned the nation to be wary of a military-industrial complex. But his basic blueprint for the Cold War—and the underlying economic superiority of a free economy over a communist economy—was solid enough to protect the nation until another president arrived who shared Eisenhower's confidence in America and the free world. President Ronald Reagan embarked on a major military buildup, largely because he believed that the Soviets couldn't keep up. "I think there's every indication and every reason to believe that the Soviet Union cannot increase its production of arms. . . . They've diverted so much to the military that they can't provide for consumer needs."

Reagan saw Soviet communism as "a form of insanity—a temporary aberration which will one day disappear from the earth because it is contrary to human nature." His goal was not an indefinite struggle. It was "We win and they lose."

In a 1981 speech at Notre Dame, Reagan declared, "The West won't contain communism, it will transcend communism. We will not bother to renounce it; we'll dismiss it as a bizarre chapter in human history whose last pages are even now being written."[31] Reagan later mocked communism by telling the British Parliament of a "great revolutionary crisis" within Soviet society, "a society where productive forces are ham-

29.   Quoted in Colin Dueck, *Hard Line: The Republican Party and US Foreign Policy Since World War II* (2010).

30.   Ibid.

31.   Ronald W. Reagan, "Commencement Address at Notre Dame," May 1981.

pered by political ones." He predicted a "march of freedom and democracy which will leave Marxism-Leninism on the ash heap of history."[32]

Reagan eventually went to Berlin and demanded, "Mr. Gorbachev, tear down that wall!" Shortly after Reagan left office, the Berlin Wall came down in 1989, and the era of international communism was brought to a close.

Following the collapse of the Soviet Union, the United States did cut defense spending by about 25 percent over a decade. Under the leadership of Colin Powell, who served as chairman of the Joint Chiefs of Staff, the military-industrial complex was put on the defensive and forced to trim its sails, but most overseas bases remained intact, along with the expanded alliances that had initially been created to contain the former Soviet Union. Some believe that "political pressures and bureaucratic inertia—precisely the military-industrial complex that Eisenhower had warned of three decades earlier—kept military spending much higher than dictated by necessity."[33]

Powell's efforts were challenged by many, including Bill Clinton's secretary of state, Madeleine Albright. She asked Powell, "What's the point of having this superb military that you're always talking about if we can't use it?"[34] Lacking a major foe that threatened the security of the United States, two Republican and two Democratic administrations began finding new things for the military to do. Some of the actions involved military action in such places as Iraq, Somalia, and Libya. Some merely involved the military as goodwill ambassadors following tragedies such as the earthquakes in Japan. As a result, more US military engagements occurred in the first decade following the end of the Cold War than in the entire forty-five-year history of that terrifying superpower showdown between the United States and the Soviet Union.

It is likely that voters would have brought the Political Class back into line with public attitudes early in the twenty-first century. Tragically,

---

32.   Ronald W. Reagan, "Address to British Parliament," June 1982.
33.   Christopher A. Preble, *The Power Problem* (2009).
34.   Ibid.

however, the 9/11 terrorist attacks forced the United States to aggressively deal with a new enemy that had launched an unprovoked attack upon our country. The hijackers killed thousands of innocent civilians and introduced America to a new terrorist threat. An aggressive response from the United States was expected, demanded, by millions of Americans who wanted their government to Protect America First.

It's been more than a decade since that horrible day that none of us will ever forget. Osama bin Laden has been killed, and the United States has survived. It is time to revisit the needed strategic reevaluation of our military strategy that was deferred by the horrors of 9/11. As we do so, it's important to recognize that the military-industrial complex of Eisenhower's time has been replaced by a terror-industrial complex today.

It's even more important to remember that the political elite has still not convinced the American people that we should police the world. Fifty-five percent of voters nationwide believe military strategy should be focused narrowly on defending America and its interests. Only 34 percent think the military's strategy should be the maintenance of worldwide stability and peace.[35]

The Disconnect between Public Opinion and National Defense Strategy

As in Eisenhower's time, a battle is ongoing where "freedom is pitted against slavery," and the United States is still the leading force for good in the world. But shadowy terrorists have replaced standing armies as the forces of evil; they represent a lurking threat to global peace and stability. Most also view economic concerns as a greater threat to our national security than military concerns.

As a result of this shifting environment, our nation needs a complete and thorough reassessment of its guiding foreign policy strategy today every bit as much as it did in the years following World War II.

---

35.   Rasmussen Reports, "When It Comes to Military Strategy, Voters Put American Interests ahead of World Peace," Jan. 2011.

Voters have a healthy understanding that this sometimes means our nation must carry more than its fair share of the burden. Despite doubts about the United Nations, 60 percent still believe the United States should remain involved in that international institution.[36]

At the same time, voters articulate a clear sense of balance and limits regarding what world leadership means in terms of military intervention. During the 2011 political turmoil in the Middle East, American voters clearly displayed this sense of balance. They overwhelmingly believed that it was good for the United States when dictators were toppled and replaced with leaders selected in free and fair elections. However, they wanted the United States to avoid direct involvement when dictators were challenged from Egypt to Libya.[37]

Voters wanted the United States to stay out of the Arab world turmoil even though they overwhelmingly believed it could lead to higher gas prices in the United States.[38] Most were also concerned that if the unrest expanded across more borders, it could become a threat to the security of the United States and drag our nation into a larger war.

Voters overwhelmingly and specifically wanted the United States to stay out of Libya. When President Obama launched military operations anyhow, he never received approval from a majority of Americans despite the general tendency of voters to rally around the flag at such times. After just a few months, only 26 percent favored continuing the military action in Libya.[39] Even when the objective of the intervention was met and longtime dictator Mu'ammar Gadhafi was killed, only 41 percent agreed with the president's decision to intervene in Libya.[40]

The reluctance for the United States to get involved stemmed partly from public doubts about the possibility for success. Fewer than half of

---

36.   Rasmussen Reports, "Only 27% See the UN as America's Ally," Apr. 2009.
37.   Rasmussen Reports, "63% Say US Should Stay out of Libya Crisis," Mar. 2011.
38.   Rasmussen Reports, "67% Say US Should Steer Clear of Political Unrest in Arab Nations," Feb. 2011.
39.   Rasmussen Reports, "63% Say US Should Stay out of Libya Crisis," Mar. 2011.
40.   Rasmussen Reports, "41% Now Agree with Obama's Decision to Take Military Action in Libya," Oct. 2011.

all Americans thought it likely that these Arab nations would make the transition to become free, democratic, and peaceful within the next few years.[41]

Just as important, Americans place national security over ideological purity when it comes to allies. By a three-to-one margin, Americans believe that our nation should be allies with any country that helps protect our own national security. Even by that more pragmatic measure, voters saw little upside from the Libyan venture: following the death of Gadhafi, only 18 percent expected the new Libyan government to become an ally of the United States.[42]

That pragmatic attitude, and the desire to stay out of fights that aren't essential to the larger strategic goals of the United States, is the same as the attitude displayed by President Eisenhower at the dawn of the Cold War.

While it's clearly inappropriate to use polling data as guidance for short-term military decisions, all longer-term military actions must be mindful of the potential public reaction. For example, in the fall of 2010, a flare-up occurred between North and South Korea. Rasmussen Reports polling found that 46 percent of voters thought the United States should provide military assistance to South Korea if it was attacked, but only 33 percent thought the United States should send additional soldiers.[43] The response to both questions showed that one out of four voters didn't even offer an opinion.

That tepid public reaction creates a tension for policymakers and strategists because the United States is bound by treaty to provide military assistance to allies such as South Korea. We currently have twenty-eight thousand troops in that county who might be forced into battle during any conflict on the Korea Peninsula. Yet, given the initial reluctance to provide any immediate support, how long could the military maintain support for any ongoing military activity in Korea?

---

41. Rasmussen Reports, "67% Say US Should Steer Clear of Political Unrest in Arab Nations," Feb. 2011.

42. Ibid.

43. Rasmussen Reports, "Many Voters Want to Help South Korea Militarily, but Not with More Troops," Nov. 2010.

Again, obviously, individual military actions should not be determined by public opinion polls. Eisenhower didn't conduct a poll to determine where and when to launch the D-day invasion. He sought counsel from military advisers and the president before taking the steps that eventually freed Western Europe and brought World War II to an end. That said, as the commander of US forces in Europe, Eisenhower did have broad public support for the overall military effort to remove Hitler from power. Later, as president of the United States, Eisenhower had similar public support for the effort to contain the Soviet threat. Today, however, a pretty serious disconnect exists between public opinion, our military strategy, and our ongoing treaty commitments.

As mentioned earlier, the United States is currently bound by mutual defense treaties to provide military assistance if any one of more than fifty nations is attacked. However, a majority of Americans think we should provide military assistance for only twelve.[44] This disconnect cannot be allowed to continue.

Eliminating that disconnect is the key to cutting defense spending. Seventy-nine percent of Americans believe we currently spend too much defending other countries around the world. Only 4 percent think we spend too little on others. Sixty-eight percent believe it is possible to significantly reduce the amount we spend defending other countries without putting the American people at risk.[45]

It would be a mistake to believe that the American people have a deeply thought-out national security strategy. Most voters are consumed by the day-to-day activities surrounding career, family, friends, faith, and more. But while it would be a mistake to think that the American people are sitting around discussing strategic national security options, it would be an even bigger mistake to dismiss the gut instincts of American voters. That's partly because voters are the sovereign power of the land, and partly because the commonsense instincts of voters almost al-

---

44. Rasmussen Reports, "Defending Countries."
45. Rasmussen Reports, "48% Think Major Cuts in Defense Spending Won't Put America at Risk," July 2011.

ways make more sense than the ideological preferences of the Political Class.

It's especially important to consider the gut instincts of voters on the big strategic questions before us. In terms of a federal budget discussion, that's where the money is. If our military strategy were geared to defend only twelve countries rather than fifty-four, the budgetary savings would be enormous.

Consider public opinion on some of the bigger choices before us. By a two-to-one margin, 55 to 28 percent, voters think we should withdraw our troops from Europe and let the Europeans defend their own land.[46] Support is found across partisan and ideological lines: Thoughts about the possibility of withdrawing troops from Japan tend to be similar to thoughts about withdrawing troops from Europe.[47]

It's remarkable that support for reducing our military commitments around the globe and removing troops from Europe and Japan is so strong. After all, no one in the Political Class has actively advocated such a policy. While the nation's current political leaders have refused to raise this issue, President Eisenhower was talking about it long ago: "We cannot be a modern Rome guarding the far frontiers with our legions."[48] Eisenhower grudgingly accepted the notion of troops in Europe as a temporary necessity following World War II, but never thought they would become a permanent feature of the strategic landscape.

As the US commitment to Europe has dragged on longer than anybody in the 1950s could have imagined, only 46 percent of voters nationwide have an even somewhat favorable opinion of NATO, the organization created at the end of World War II to bind the destinies of Europe and the United States.[49] Removing the troops we have in Europe and Japan alone would save somewhere in the range of $25 bil-

---

46.   Rasmussen Reports, "55% Want US Troops out of Europe," Oct. 2011.
47.   Rasmussen Reports, "Half Want Troops out of Europe, Japan, but South Korea's Another Story," Jan. 2011.
48.   Quoted in Colin Dueck, *Hard Line: The Republican Party and US Foreign Policy Since World War II* (2010).
49.   Rasmussen Reports, "Only 49% Think US Still Needs to Belong to NATO," June 2011.

lion annually and reduce future spending commitments by an even larger amount. That doesn't mean it's automatically the right thing to do, but this is where the debate should be focused. And it's worth noting that these poll results could shift dramatically if there was a substantive national debate on the issue.

If people understood that the average American is paying five times as much for defense as the average European, support would probably be much higher for this sort of reform. Support would also be likely to spike higher if Americans knew how much money could be saved by letting others shoulder a more equitable share of the defense burden. On the other hand, advocates of the current strategy would also make their case, which would resonate with some voters. However, it's likely that closing the gap between our current military strategy and voter preferences would lead to a reduced global military role for the United States.

Two Ghosts Haunting the Prospects of Reduced Military Spending

Before exploring the budgetary savings from military spending that could win public support, it is necessary to address two ghosts that haunt all such discussions: anti-Americanism and isolationism. The first might be called the ghost of George McGovern's convention. The 1972 convention that nominated the South Dakota senator to run against Richard Nixon was filled with antiwar fervor stemming from the Vietnam War. That was rather unremarkable given the times. However, it is stunning to realize that a plurality of convention delegates identified the United States as the greatest threat to world peace. This blame-America-first school of thought still attracts support from a vocal minority that is always advocating for the United States to retreat from its ideals and its commitments.[50]

That attitude will never be successful in the court of public opinion. In the eyes of most Americans, the United States represents the good

---

50.   Steven F. Hayward, *The Age of Reagan: The Fall of the Old Liberal Order* (2001).

guys in the earthly showdown between the forces of good and evil. Any military strategy that hopes for the support of the American people must incorporate this view and recognize the strategic value of having our nation as the leading advocate for freedom and liberty throughout the world.

The second ghost to address is the ghost of Robert Taft, a Republican senator and a leading spokesman for the isolationist movement on the eve of World War II. Most Americans would probably agree with Taft's assertion that "war should never be undertaken or seriously risked except to protect American liberty."[51] Most would probably also share his concern, expressed in 1939, that "no one has ever suggested before that a single nation should range over the world, like a knight-errant, protect democracy and ideals of good faith, and tilt, like Don Quixote, against the windmills of fascism."[52]

Taft's focus on avoiding entanglements blinded him to other concerns. In the same month that Hitler's troops and tanks overwhelmed France, Taft declared, "There is a good deal more danger of the infiltration of totalitarian ideas from the New Deal circle in Washington than there will ever be from any activities of the communists or the Nazi bund."[53] After Pearl Harbor, Taft did vote for US entry into World War II, and he eventually became a fairly strong advocate of containment during the early days of the Cold War, but his legacy as an isolationist lives on. It's a legacy the American people do not share.

Rather than longing for isolationism, 88 percent of voters say that our country's relationship with Europe is important, including 53 percent who say it's very important.[54] When disaster strikes in a place such as Haiti, Americans are quick to offer support and assistance. When a mining disaster occurred in Chile, an American company (not America's

---

51.   Robert A. Taft, *A Foreign Policy for Americans* (1951).
52.   Quoted in Colin Dueck, *Hard Line: The Republican Party and US Foreign Policy Since World War II* (2010).
53.   Ibid.
54.   Rasmussen Reports, "37% Agree That US Has Shown Arrogance and Been Dismissive of Europe," Apr. 2009.

government) provided the equipment for rescuing the miners. The list goes on and on. That's not something new for our nation; it's a deeply ingrained part of our national identity. In 1973, Canadian journalist Gordon Sinclair offered a stirring speech on behalf of the United States saying he could name five thousand times the Americans had helped others around the world, but not one time other nations had returned the favor. He said that the United States would have the right to thumb its nose at the rest of the world, but the United States never did.[55]

The notion that twenty-first-century America could drift into isolation is laughable, but that won't stop some in the Political Class from raising the alarm. That's one alarm it's safe to ignore. Bluntly, rather than retreat into isolation, the American people think our nation should lead the world. But their gut instincts on other issues suggest that voters also don't think leading requires having military forces in every nation around the globe.

As far as the American people are concerned, it is quite possible to have a healthy debate about bringing troops home from Europe and Japan without blaming America first or retreating to isolationism. As with just about every aspect of the federal budget crisis, the only real question is whether the Political Class will continue pursuing their own agenda or be forced to accept the commonsense wisdom of the American people.

Budgetary Implications

The *New York Times* and others in the Political Class may believe that the American people are opposed to cuts in specific programs, but that's not what the data reveals. Tremendous savings are possible by following the logic of the public's strategic preferences. Americans rightly reject a policy of blaming America first and have no desire to retreat from our nation's idealism and our role as a beacon of hope for those who believe

---

55.   Gordon Sinclair, "The Americans," 1973.

in liberty and freedom. They also reject the post–Cold War approach of the Political Class, which might be called Send Americans First.

Protect America First would mean returning to the more restrained military approach of Dwight Eisenhower and Ronald Reagan. Those presidents didn't hesitate to use military power when appropriate, but they had a limited definition of when that was appropriate. Like most Americans today, but unlike today's Political Class, they believed that US military forces should be used only when US national interests are at stake.

Reagan spelled out additional restrictions, adding that forces should never be sent without "the clear intent and support needed to win." He added, "There must be clearly defined and realistic objectives."[56] Reagan also believed in one other requirement before committing troops anywhere: there "must be reasonable assurance that the cause we are fighting for and the actions we take will have the support of the American people and Congress." Americans today believe those remain valid guidelines.[57] And even when all those parameters are met, Reagan emphasized that "our troops should be committed to combat abroad only as a last resort."

Aligning US military strategy with public opinion would save trillions of dollars over the coming decade and dramatically reduce the debt burden we are passing on to future generations. By reducing the federal debt, this important alignment would also help America to defend against the serious economic challenges facing the nation today. Most of all, however, aligning our military strategy and spending with public opinion would strengthen the most important values of the nation by reaffirming that "governments derive their only just authority from the consent of the governed." The people are sovereign and the politicians are to serve them. We want to display this attitude for the entire world.

Alignment, however, is difficult to achieve. Leadership expert Jim Collins cites this concept as a key difference between good and great

---

56.   Ronald Reagan, *An American Life* (1990).
57.   Rasmussen Reports, "75% See Vital US Interests as Only Reason for Committing Military Forces to Overseas Action," July 2011.

companies. He says, "The essence of a visionary company comes in the translation of its core ideology and its own unique drive for progress into the very fabric of the organization—into goals, strategies, tactics, policies, processes, cultural practices, management behaviors, building layouts, pay systems, accounting systems—into everything that the company does."[58] The core ideology of Americans is a belief in freedom and self-governance. The military's role, as most Americans view it today, is to Protect America First. That means protecting our people, our territory, and our ideals.

In practical terms, there must be alignment at several levels. This includes alignment between public attitudes and military strategy, between military strategy and alliance commitments, and between these commitments and the resources provided. As Collins suggests, the alignment must be found in everything the military does. To pursue this course in a disciplined manner is challenging in a political environment, but the benefits are well worth the effort. The impact that this will have can be seen by looking at supplemental budget requests, the baseline military budget, and the costs of caring for veterans.

Supplemental Budget Requests. The supplemental budget for operations in Afghanistan and Iraq cost the United States $163 billion in 2010 and $181 billion in 2011.[59] The Obama administration has initially projected reducing spending to approximately $118 billion in 2012.

Most Americans have decided it is time to bring these troops home within a year.[60] Clearly, in this area aligning the budget to the interests of voters will save a lot of money and lives. The withdrawal of troops must be responsive to battlefield concerns. However, regardless of precisely when and how we withdraw our final troops from Afghanistan, Iraq, and Libya, the public wants those missions completed sooner rather than later. The challenge from a budgetary perspective will be to make sure that the money stops when the mission does.

---

58. James C. Collins and Jerry I. Porras, *Built to Last: Successful Habits of Visionary Companies* (1997).

59. *Budget of the United States Government, Fiscal Year 2012.*

60. Rasmussen Reports, "59% Want Troops Home from Afghanistan," Aug. 2011.

Baseline Military Budget. General military spending, or the baseline budget, totals about $530 billion for 2011. The only way to substantially reduce that number is through strategic decisions concerning troop levels and deployments. Obviously, a complete review of military strategy is well beyond the scope of this book. Any strategic changes made must be done thoughtfully following an extended and healthy public debate. Military leaders would have to guide the process, allies must be consulted, and the reforms must be implemented over time. Many of the savings would not fully materialize for five to ten years. While many areas of the budget would be cut, some would increase as the nation focused on the differences between the military threats of the 1950s and the terrorist threats of the twenty-first century.

Additionally, an emerging strategy would take into account more than just military issues. Building the nation's economic strength clearly helps our long-term defense strategy. Showing that our government actually responds to voters is another strategic bonus that helps the United States retain its ideological advantage compared to totalitarian alternatives. Some might consider development of US oil reserves as part of a national defense strategy.

From a budgetary perspective, however, the biggest savings can be found in the gap between the more than fifty nations we are pledged to defend and the twelve countries that most Americans are willing to defend. If the mission is reduced, the cost will be, too. Simply put, fewer troops are needed to just defend the United States than are needed to police the world.

To give a sense of how much a Protect America First strategy could save, consider that even Defense Secretary Robert Gates said we should consider "the massive overmatch the US already enjoys. Consider, too, the growing anti-ship capabilities of adversaries. Do we really need eleven carrier strike groups for another thirty years when no other country has more than one? Any future plans must address these realities."[61]

A former naval officer and current Cato Institute scholar describes

---

61.   Robert M. Gates, "Remarks on the Role of the Modern Navy," May 2010.

the situation by saying our navy is "focused more on the defense of others than on the defense of the United States."[62] If our navy was committed only to the defense of vital US interests, it might be possible to concentrate the fleets in the Western Hemisphere rather than ranging across the seven seas. This could reduce the number of aircraft carriers, submarines, support staff, and sailors.

Apply the same thought process to the air force. Why is the US air force controlling the airspace in most of Europe and parts of Eastern Asia? A Protect America First strategy would be focused on protecting the skies over our nation and all air approaches that could threaten our nation. Military leaders would have to debate and define the right number of fighters and other aircraft that would be needed to fulfill this more basic mission. Two things, however, are certain. First, it would be a much smaller number of aircraft than are currently contemplated. Second, it would still be the largest and most powerful air force in the world.

In addition, bringing home troops currently deployed in Western Europe and Japan will result in direct savings of approximately $25 billion every year. All of these changes would reduce procurement budgets because we won't need as many new weapons, ships, and aircraft each year. When you think of a budget with over eighty major weapons systems that each cost billions of dollars, reducing procurement budgets can add up to real savings quickly. Training and recruiting costs would go down. So would administrative costs and the number of civilian support personnel. When the civilian workforce approaches eight hundred thousand people, these savings can add up pretty quickly.

By reducing the number of strategic commitments in places such as Europe and Japan, it is certainly reasonable to envision military spending returning to 2001 levels (with increases to adjust for population growth plus inflation). Some might balk at setting such targets for national defense and then expecting the military to fit within those parameters, but that's the approach Dwight Eisenhower used in the 1950s. He recognized the need to balance military power with domestic resources.

---

62.   Christopher A. Preble, *The Power Problem* (2009).

It would be irrational to demand that the military continue to police the world with a reduced budget, but it is quite rational to expect the military to accomplish the narrower mission of Protect America First with a budget appropriate for that role.

That would still provide for around $420 billion in annual military spending, nearly three times as much as what China or anybody else in the world spends. Our military would remain the most powerful in world history. And that spending level would be more in line with voter preferences. If anything, it might be a bit on the high side. Just 25 percent of voters believe that the United States should always spend at least three times as much as any other nation. Forty percent disagree and think such a target is too high.[63]

Once the initial cutbacks and savings have been fully implemented over five to ten years, it would be essential to set in place some long-term budgetary discipline in line with a reasonable goal for all federal spending. So long as the strategic environment remains the same, annual military spending increases should be held to just enough to keep up with population growth and inflation. Obviously, if a new military rival emerged, it would be time for a new assessment of the strategic situation, but it is difficult to envision a serious military rival emerging anytime soon that could threaten the territory of the United States.

It should be noted that there is no magic to the 2001 budget year as the starting point, but it does have the advantage of clarifying the strategic choices. If we would spend as much today as we did in 2001, but reduced our legacy commitments from the World War II era, we could cut overall spending levels while devoting additional resources to fighting the challenges of the post-9/11 world.

The specifics of how to deploy those resources should be the focus of intense debate and experimentation. To be aligned with voter attitudes, the focus would be more on defending the United States than on a broader global role. Obviously, substantial resources would be deployed

---

63.   Rasmussen Reports, "Voters Underestimate How Much US Spends on Defense," Feb. 2011.

to address the terrorist threat, and it's quite likely that some of the money would be used to help secure the southern border of the United States.[64]

It is important to remember that these changes are likely to offend both Republicans and Democrats among the Political Class. Many in power like having a military they can use to promote global and humanitarian goals, even if those goals do not affect the vital national security interests of the United States. The American people have rejected that approach.

Veterans' Affairs. Simply put, if we cut back on the number of soldiers today, we cut back on the number of veterans we need to serve in the future. Additionally, if we have fewer casualties now, we will have fewer disability payments, lower medical costs, and fewer survivors' benefits to pay in the future.

It sounds pretty basic, and it is. But the impact is huge. By reducing the number of soldiers today, we will reduce the total spending burden we are passing on to future generations by trillions of dollars. Consider this: "Of the 700,000 men and women who served in the Gulf War, 45 percent filed for disability benefits, and 88 percent of these requests were approved. On average, disabled Gulf War veterans receive $6,506 every year; this amounts to $4.3 billion paid out annually by the U.S. government."[65] That's the cost paid every year for veterans of just one military engagement.

These savings won't show up right away in the official budget calculations (the official budget shows the price we're paying today to support yesterday's veterans), but as with other unfunded liabilities, that accounting issue says more about the faulty way we measure federal budgets and deficits than it does about the magnitude of the savings.

While looking to the long term for savings in the veterans' affairs budget, there must never be a reduction in the benefits we have already promised to our veterans. We made promises to those who have served and they must be honored.

---

64.   Rasmussen Reports, "67% Say Military Should Be Used on Border to Stop Illegal Immigration," May 2010.

65.   Christopher A. Preble, *The Power Problem* (2009).

Conclusion

It would be a mistake to sacrifice the nation's defense just to balance the federal budget, but by aligning the military mission with popular opinion it is possible to save trillions of dollars over the coming decade. Alignment with popular opinion means rejecting isolationism and embracing America's role as world leader. It means letting our ideals and our economy take the lead internationally in many settings. The military should be freed from both the Blame America First school of thought and the Send Americans First attitude. Instead, the focus must remain where the American people think it should be with a strategy to Protect America First.

A strategy to Protect America First means deploying US military personnel overseas only when vital US interests are at stake. It means sending troops into battle only when victory is expected and the mission is clearly defined. The support of the American people is essential. These were the guidelines laid out by President Ronald Reagan in the 1980s, and they are still embraced by voters today.

In budgetary terms, this means ending military interventions in Afghanistan, Iraq, and Libya. It means bringing military spending closer to pre-9/11 levels. There would be no cuts in programs defending the United States, but significant cuts in programs that envision America as the world's policeman. There would also be serious cuts in alliances and troop deployments for alliances set up in the 1950s to counter the long-defunct Soviet Union. These might include bringing home troops from Western Europe and Japan, reducing the size and mission of the US navy, and having an air force that protects airspace in and around the United States. These steps would reduce personnel and procurement costs by hundreds of billions of dollars annually. Over the long haul, there would also be significant savings in veterans' affairs. The savings would come from having fewer veterans overall and, especially, fewer wartime casualties and veterans with disabilities.

I recognize that many on both sides of the partisan and ideological divides will be unhappy with this approach to military spending. That's especially true in the Political Class. For them, there is a simple solution: if you don't like the Protect America First strategy, go to the boss, the American people. This is the strategy they support today. It might be different if there was a vigorous national debate, but there's no telling whether the difference would be more or less to the liking of the Political Class. Still, if there are arguments to be made for a wider US engagement and for interventions in places such as Libya, make them. If there are reasons to leave US troops in Europe forever, state them. If we need to spend more, build support for the taxes needed to finance that spending. Don't sacrifice America's greatest asset—our commitment to self-governance—to pursue a more aggressive military strategy than the American people are willing to support.

4

---·---

How Voters Would Fix Social Security

While the details of addressing Social Security reform are different from those of national security, the underlying challenge is the same: getting the Political Class to follow the lead of the American people. Social Security remains the most lasting and popular policy legacy of the New Deal era. Even while approaching its eightieth birthday, the program is viewed favorably by 64 percent of voters nationwide.[1] In an era when distrust of government and government programs is the norm, that's an astonishing figure. Social Security has woven its way into the fabric of American society.

More than 50 million Americans receive Social Security benefits, a figure that includes nearly nine out of ten Americans sixty-five and older. For roughly two-thirds of senior citizens, Social Security provides a majority of their cash income, and about one in three derive at least 90 percent of their income from this program. FDR's dream legislation has been enormously successful at raising the standard of living for the nation's elders: even after adjusting for inflation, median income for those over sixty-five has more than doubled over the past half century.[2]

---

1. Rasmussen Reports, "One in Three Voters View Social Security, Medicare Unfavorably," June 2011.
2. US Social Security Administration, Social Security Online, Aug. 2011.

From the beginning, however, the program was designed to embrace Americans of all ages. When President Franklin D. Roosevelt signed the Social Security Act into law in 1935, he touched on this theme by noting, "Young people have come to wonder what will be their lot when they come to old age."[3]

Among those under sixty-five today, the most frequent interaction with the program is the payroll tax. Just about all workers directly pay 6.2 percent of their income in what are euphemistically called "contributions" in exchange for a promise of future benefits. The tax interaction is so significant that over 70 percent of families now pay more in Social Security taxes than they do in income taxes.[4] That personal tax payment is just half the total, since every individual tax payment is matched by employers, who are required to make an equal payment on the employee's behalf. When you add together both parts of the payroll tax, nearly one-eighth of a typical paycheck goes straight to the Social Security system.

Given this deep and substantive interaction, it's hardly surprising that voters of all ages want to make the system work and that efforts to tinker with Social Security are met with skepticism. Seniors are wary of any change that might threaten their primary source of income, a legitimate concern. Even critics who believe that today's seniors are getting back more than they paid in to the system recognize that the government made a promise to these retirees during their working lives. Now that those workers have retired, the promise they relied upon must be honored if the government is to retain any credibility.

While seniors are concerned about threats to their income, younger adults are wary of any tax hikes—a concern that is heightened by doubts about the ongoing solvency of the program. Only 26 percent of those under forty think it is even somewhat likely they will receive all their promised benefits. Only 5 percent think that happy outcome is very

---

3.   Franklin D. Roosevelt, "Presidential Statement Signing the Social Security Act," Aug. 1935.

4.   Tax Policy Center, "Historical Payroll Tax vs. Income Tax," Apr. 2009.

likely.[5] Regardless of the generation, the default position is to distrust politicians while looking for ways to keep Social Security working.

This deep attachment to Social Security is a tribute to the political genius of President Franklin D. Roosevelt. At the time he was promoting the program, many in his party complained about the inclusion of pay-roll taxes to cover the cost. They wanted the pensions to be paid directly out of the federal treasury. Many modern liberal activists still complain about the "regressive" nature of the Social Security tax. Roosevelt saw it differently.

Shortly after the first Social Security benefits were paid, Roosevelt explained his reasoning: "We put those payroll contributions there so as to give the contributors a legal, moral, and political right to collect their pensions and their unemployment benefits. With those taxes in there, no damn politician can ever scrap my social security program." He was right. Nobody to this day trusts politicians to make changes in Social Security. In fact, 64 percent believe that any proposed change to Social Security should be submitted to a vote of the American people before it could be implemented.[6]

FDR clearly understood the public mood of his day, and those under-lying attitudes remain with us in the twenty-first century. Americans did not want Social Security to be another form of welfare or government giveaway. Roosevelt sold the plan as an insurance program, and that's how people perceived it from the beginning.

Even more than a specific plan, Roosevelt sold an underlying logic that people embraced then and now. Recognizing the economic chal-lenges that come with aging, Americans instinctively and enthusiasti-cally grasp the idea of setting aside a little money out of each paycheck into an account that they can draw upon later in life. That attitude is clearly within the American tradition of assuming personal responsibility

5.   Rasmussen Reports, "Americans Under 40 Skeptical About Receiving Promised Social Security Benefits," July 2011.

6.   Rasmussen Reports, "51% Now Recognize Most Federal Spending Goes to Defense, Medicare, and Social Security," June 2011.

to avoid being a burden on society. Applying the logic to an entire nation was a way to get rid of the fear that people would outlive their income and other resources.

The concept was simple, but implementation was a bit more challenging. Initially, the program had to overcome a deficit brought on by funding the first generation of beneficiaries. The first person to receive a monthly Social Security check was Ida May Fuller from Ludlow, Vermont. During her working life she paid a total of $24.75 into the system. Her first monthly check returned just about that entire amount, $22.54. Over the next thirty-five years, she received a total of $22,888.92 in benefits.[7] While Fuller's return of nearly $1,000 for every dollar paid in taxes was exceptional, just about all of the first generation of Social Security recipients received far more than they paid into the system. Economic growth in the postwar era helped to bridge the gap, and so did an ongoing series of tax increases. When the program began, workers paid only 2 percent of their income into the system. That figure has risen to 12.4 percent today, a total paid half by the employee and half by the employer. To pay all currently promised benefits, the taxes will have to go even higher.

During the 1960s, when economic growth was strong and the retirement program was young, the politicians missed an opportunity to address the shortfall caused by the first generation of Social Security recipients. Rather than doing so, they added to the fiscal challenge by promising even more benefits and pushing the problem off to another generation: ours. As mentioned earlier, deceptive accounting practices implemented by President Lyndon Johnson made it easier for those who wanted to provide short-term benefit hikes while ignoring long-term costs. Ironically, while Johnson was a Democrat, his accounting trick helped Republican president Richard Nixon just as much. Nixon, on the eve of his reelection bid in 1972, announced he had "signed [legislation which] . . . constitutes a major breakthrough for older Americans,

---

7.   Larry DeWitt, "Research Note #3: Details of Ida May Fuller's Payroll Tax Contributions," July 1996.

for it says at last that inflation-proof Social Security benefits are theirs as a matter of right."[8]

Once again, the president of the United States had indicated that Social Security benefits were earned as a right by paying payroll taxes. That's the way the contract between the government and the American people is understood. Unfortunately, the payroll taxes being collected today are not enough to cover the benefits promised in the future. Sixty-five percent of Americans recognize this to be true, while only 19 percent think the current level of taxes is sufficient.[9] According to official government documents, the Social Security trust fund has a long-term deficit of $17.9 trillion. They claim the trust fund has enough reserves to keep paying benefits in full until 2036, although many critics point out that the trust fund as currently run is nothing more than a promise from the government to pay future benefits.[10]

In addition to the economic challenge posed by this reality, the long-term funding shortfall creates a political challenge because 89 percent of voters think it's important for the trust fund to collect enough in taxes so that all promised benefits can be paid.[11] Additionally, 73 percent of voters believe the best way to provide security for retirees is to protect the trust fund and make sure it has adequate revenue. Just 10 percent believe the trust fund should be scrapped so that the federal government could just pay promised benefits out of the general operating budget.[12] Once again, these results confirm that Americans bought into the concept sold so convincingly by Franklin Roosevelt in the 1930s.

That is what leads to the political dilemma facing the nation today. Many politicians are quite content to ignore the issue and push it further down the road. Senate majority leader Harry Reid took this approach

8. Richard M. Nixon, "Statement on Signing the Social Security Amendments of 1972," Oct. 1972.

9. Rasmussen Reports, "65% Say Current Taxes Not Enough to Fund Medicare, Social Security Promises," June 2011.

10. *The 2011 Annual Report of the Board of Trustees of the Federal Old-Age and Survivors Insurance and Federal Disability Insurance Trust Funds.*

11. Rasmussen Reports, "65% Say Current Taxes Not Enough to Fund Medicare, Social Security Promises," June 2011.

12. Rasmussen Reports, "30% Favor Tax Hikes to Keep Social Security, Medicare Solvent," June 2011.

by declaring, "Two decades from now, I'm willing to take a look at it, but I'm not willing to take a look at it right now."[13] While anything's possible, it's highly unlikely Reid will be in office when that day arrives. After all, he'd be ninety-one at that time. That's the type of fiscal policy leadership displayed by Lyndon Johnson and Richard Nixon, and it's a big part of what got us into the problems we face today.

Other politicians take the government's promises to seniors a bit more seriously and are interested in solving the funding gap. But, as you might expect, they tend to line up along partisan lines. Most Democrats say all that's needed is one more Social Security tax hike and the problem can be solved. The Social Security trustees estimate that would require raising the combined employee and employer tax from 12.4 percent of payroll today to just over 14.6 percent.[14] Most Republicans say that the promised benefits need to be cut either by raising the retirement age or reducing the growth of future benefits.

A few on each side would like to go further. Some on the left would like to see taxes raised even more than is needed to make the system solvent. They want benefits for retirees to go up even higher. On the right, many advocate privatization of the program so that individuals can opt out of Social Security. Neither of these approaches enjoys widespread popular support, and it's hard to envision that changing in the next generation or so. Voters are divided on the more modest approaches as well. Given a choice of how to deal with the problem, 34 percent say the retirement age should be raised for future generations, 30 percent say taxes should be raised, and 15 percent want benefits to be cut.[15] Just about everyone agrees that something needs to be done, but there's little agreement on what should be done.

When you ask about specific changes, the results break down along expected lines. Seniors are okay with tax hikes to ensure the solvency of the system. Of course, they're not paying those taxes now. Younger voters

---

13. *America's Newsroom with Bill Hemmer & Martha MacCallum*, Mar. 2011.

14. *The 2011 Annual Report of the Board of Trustees of the Federal Old-Age and Survivors Insurance and Federal Disability Insurance Trust Funds.*

15. Rasmussen Reports, "30% Favor Tax Hikes to Keep Social Security, Medicare Solvent," June 2011.

reject that approach because they know they'll end up paying the higher taxes, but aren't sure they'll see the benefits.

Stats like these are used by politicians to blame the voters. Democrats and Republicans in the Political Class tend to think of themselves as leaders advocating the responsible approach. They are frustrated that every politician who talks about changing the system in any way runs into a wall of opposition. No matter how they talk about Social Security, the polls show that voters don't like what Washington proposes. It's become known as the "third rail of politics."

That's because, as with so many issues that have come before, the political dynamic surrounding Social Security finds politicians lagging behind the public. Most Americans live in a dynamic world and have constantly been adjusting their views and attitudes based upon encounters with reality. Voters overwhelmingly embrace the concept of Social Security, but recognize that the trade-offs between taxes and benefits might require different approaches for a new generation. The Political Class lives in a static, bureaucratic world and has assumed its traditional role as the primary defender of the status quo.

In the case of Social Security, this has left politicians hiding their heads in the sand, acting as if the only issue at all is an accounting question about how to balance the long-term income and expense streams of the trust fund. In the real world, while voters desperately want the Social Security system to be fiscally sound, bigger challenges stand in the way of desired reform.

The first is one that politicians refuse to acknowledge: people just don't trust individual politicians, Congress, or the larger political system. By a three-to-one margin the American people believe that no matter how bad something is, Congress can always make it worse.[16] With that mind-set, protecting an unsustainable status quo is less risky for voters than trusting congressional reform. Even if Congress crafted the perfect reform plan (if there is such a thing), and even if voters loved what they

---

16. Rasmussen Reports, "Voters Continue to Believe Congress Can Always Make Things Worse," Jan. 2011.

heard about the plan, popular support would be withheld because voters don't trust Congress.

The second issue is that many young adults no longer believe Social Security is a good deal for them.[17] They like the concept and they'd like to buy what FDR sold an earlier generation, but the returns for twenty-somethings today will never be close to the returns of Ida May Fuller. As a result, young workers today are looking at the trade-offs between taxes and benefits differently than their grandparents did. It is important to craft a system that meets the needs of today's workers without passing the burden on to another generation.

The third, and vitally important, issue is to close the gap between political rhetoric, public expectations, and the reality of the Social Security trust fund. The starting point is to address the trust issue. The only way to do that is to take decision-making authority out of the hands of politicians. Two out of three American voters think voters should have the right to approve or reject any proposed solutions recommended by Congress.[18] Conceptually, such a requirement makes sense. For more than seventy-five years, Social Security has been presented to voters as a contract between the government and individual American workers. To change a contract lawfully requires approval from both parties. If the government wants to change the contract, it should be required to get approval from those on the other side of the bargain.

There's another reason for requiring the politicians to submit their work for voter approval: it could help provide needed legitimacy for fundamental changes to an important federal program. This is especially important at a time when just 17 percent believe our government has the consent of the governed.[19]

It is hard to overstate the importance of seeking voter approval for any

---

17. Rasmussen Reports, "Americans Under 40 Skeptical About Receiving Promised Social Security Benefits," July 2011.
18. Rasmussen Reports, "51% Now Recognize Most Federal Spending Goes to Defense, Medicare, and Social Security," June 2011.
19. Rasmussen Reports, "New Low: 17% Say US Government Has Consent of the Governed," Aug. 2011.

changes to Social Security. Such a step or steps represent an essential ratification of a new contract between the federal government and the American people. Our generation has been called upon to do double duty on Social Security. We need to cover the deficit passed on by politicians in the 1960s, and on top of that, we need to adequately fund our own retirement years so that we don't become a burden to future generations. For people to shoulder such a burden, they must have a final say on whether the proposal makes sense.

While it makes sense, the idea of voters ratifying congressional action is something that has never been done before in the American experience. Some may doubt whether it's even allowed within the Constitution, but the mechanism for accomplishing this task is quite simple. Congress has the authority to enact legislation that becomes law when signed by the president. Over the years, Congress has sometimes included requirements that must be met before a certain provision can be enacted. Voter approval would be a requirement that must be met before fundamental changes in Social Security can be implemented. This is simply adding another check to the system of checks and balances envisioned by the drafters of our governing charter.

In practical terms, the referendum should be held when congressional elections are held. Politicians, especially at the state and local level, always like to stick ballot measures that might restrict their power on ballots for low-turnout elections. They know that the Political Class is more likely to turn out when it's time for a primary election or other choice that most voters don't care about, but for a fundamental reform in a program such as Social Security, the election should be held at a time of maximum potential turnout. That means a general election. Additionally, the rules should be much simpler than the rules for the electoral college. If most voters favor the reform proposed by Congress, it becomes law. If not, it doesn't.

Requiring voter approval will also make it much easier to pass needed reforms because voters are far more willing than their politicians to make hard choices and move on. The key is to move decision-making power as far away from politicians and bureaucrats as possible. The more that individuals can make decisions at their kitchen table or in conversations with friends, family, and others, the better the decisions will be and the better off the nation will be. If the long-term Social Security trade-off is a choice between a higher retirement age and higher taxes, why should politicians have the power to force a single answer on every single American? What gives them the right to dictate the appropriate balance for individual retirement planning? Some workers might be interested in paying more now and retiring sooner. Others would prefer to pay less in taxes now but begin collecting their benefits later.

Sixty-five percent of voters believe individuals should have the right to select their own retirement age in this manner. Only 23 percent disagree. Significantly, while support for the concept is higher among those under sixty-five, a majority of senior citizens (53%) agree as well.[20] That support is consistent for both the way Social Security has been sold to the American people over the decades and for traditional American notions of self-reliance and self-governance. It is an acknowledgment that one-size-fits-all solutions don't make sense in a society as big and diverse as that of the United States.

Any reasonable proposal would also acknowledge that people might change their mind along the way. It would seem logical to let people make an initial decision about taxes and retirement age when they first enter the workforce, but to also address that the world might look different at fifty-five than it does at eighteen. It would make sense to offer people a chance to revise their choice at, say, ages thirty-five, forty-five, and fifty-five. Whatever the choice and the age, the underlying concept would remain the same—people would make trade-offs that affect their own retirement planning without impacting the long-term balance of the trust fund.

It should also be noted that this concept is consistent with Franklin D. Roosevelt's initial concept of Social Security. He envisioned a

---

20. Rasmussen Reports, "65% Believe Americans Should Have Right to Pick Own Social Security Retirement Age," June 2011.

program that would grow to include a combination of "compulsory contributions," supplemented by voluntary contributions made in exchange for increased benefits. The mandatory contributions would set a minimum level of coverage, but people would be free to contribute more in exchange for more benefits.[21]

The concept of letting people choose their own retirement age within the existing Social Security program is so unremarkable that it may be difficult to initially grasp the impact this would have on the nation's finances. If one person traded off a higher retirement age for lower taxes, the impact would be minimal, but when a generation moves in that direction and tens of millions of people make that choice, the impact is huge. While no one wants to be forced to wait those few extra years before collecting benefits, many will find the trade-off appealing if it is their own choice and they can pay a little bit less along the way. Over the long term, people's choosing later retirement ages could cut the cost of Social Security nearly in half.

Another way to consider the impact is to think of a twenty-eight-year-old worker today. When that worker turns sixty-seven, there will be approximately 35.1 million people in America over the age of sixty-seven, or old enough to collect Social Security under the current system. But, by letting people choose their own retirement age, that number could drop as low as 20.4 million, a reduction of 42 percent.[22] That translates directly into a smaller burden for future generations by simply letting individuals make their own choice.

If Congress considered a plan like this, voters would be skeptical and wonder what the hidden provisions might be. People would worry about expensive and inappropriate last-minute provisions inserted to buy votes or to protect friends of the Political Class. However, since the final product would be submitted to a vote of the American people, the process would be protected from Political Class gamesmanship.

---

21. Franklin D. Roosevelt, "Message to Congress on Social Security," 1935.
22. Calculations derived from US Census Bureau, "US Population Projections," 2008.

By presenting the issue to voters, this approach would demonstrate conclusively that the American people are willing to cut spending far more than their politicians. Consider that 36 percent of workers under forty would defer their retirement age to seventy-five in exchange for a lower payroll tax. No one in the political realm is suggesting pushing the retirement age back to anything close to age seventy-five. The same point comes through loud and clear when we look at the response of those already in their fifties. While politicians tiptoe around the issue and promise such workers that no changes are needed, 44 percent of those aged fifty to sixty-four would trade lower taxes for a higher retirement age.[23]

The simple fact is that most Americans support FDR's concept of setting aside some money during your working years to earn benefits during your retirement years. But many aren't happy with the current mix of taxes and benefits. They are looking for ways to make Social Security work better for today's workers. By freeing people to make their own choices, the long-term cost of Social Security benefits will be reduced far more than anybody in Congress would dare propose. On top of that, it would be accomplished with the consent of the governed and in a manner that improves everybody's confidence in Social Security.

It is hard to overstate the value of eliminating the $17.9 trillion deficit in the Social Security trust fund. Removing that debt will strengthen the economy just as much as the overall reform strengthens and improves individual retirement planning. It would do so by dramatically reducing the level of "compulsory contributions" to Social Security and make tens of millions of workers feel more secure about their retirement. For younger workers willing to wait until they're about seventy-five to collect their first Social Security check, it could mean completely eliminating their employee portion of the Social Security tax!

---

23.   Rasmussen Reports, "65% Believe Americans Should Have Right to Pick Own Retirement Age," June 2011.

How Does It Eliminate the Deficit?

Because an approach like this has never seriously been discussed in the halls of power or in the tumult of a campaign, it would be foolish to claim an ability to predict precisely the final form of legislation that voters might eventually approve. Moving from concept to reality always takes twists and turns, even when the concept is broadly supported and consistent with our nation's heritage and our understanding of Social Security. It is, however, quite possible to lay out a rational starting point that is broadly consistent with public opinion and to highlight some of the key decisions in the debate. The first decision is how to address the long-term actuarial deficit in the Social Security trust fund. Simply letting people trade off lower taxes for a higher age of collecting retirement benefits doesn't necessarily fix the long-term problem. If the long-term value of the tax and benefit trade-offs are equal, there would be no deficit reduction.

One approach to bridging the gap would be to protect those who are happy with the status quo and to place the entire cost upon those who want to change their current Social Security retirement age. The system could be set up so that those who want to change would receive tax savings that are not as big as the deferred benefits. If a person deferred their retirement age enough to give up $1,000 in promised benefits, they might receive only $700 in offsetting tax reductions. Essentially, every person who opted for a higher retirement age would also be kicking back a bit of money to help the system remain solvent. Those who wanted no change in either their retirement age or the tax rate would be fully protected. To eliminate the trust fund's long-term deficit, this approach would require up to half of all workers to select a higher retirement age.

A different approach would be to spread the burden across all working Americans in two steps. The first step would be to formally increase the standard Social Security taxes from the current total of 12.4 to 14.6 percent. That's the amount Social Security trustees say is needed to bring the system into long-term balance.

I recognize that talk of raising taxes will instantly make some stomachs turn, but it's important to remember that nobody would be required to pay the new level of taxes. Companies would be required to pay their share of the payroll tax for all workers. But the employee's share of the tax would be entirely optional. The only people who would pay it are those who would voluntarily send more money to the trust fund in exchange for a lower retirement age. With this approach, the mandatory Social Security tax paid by both employer and employee would decline from 12.4 percent today to 7.3 percent.

Some might prefer a different way of raising taxes to eliminate the trust fund deficit. Many Democrats have advocated eliminating the salary cap on Social Security payroll taxes (currently set at just over $100,000). Polls show public support for such a tax hike, but also show that those who pay more should receive more in benefits.[24] This would certainly be an option to consider, but its impact would be limited. That's because the higher the taxes go for individuals, the more likely they are to defer their retirement age in exchange for lower taxes. As a result, eliminating the salary cap for Social Security payroll taxes would simply encourage more upper-income earners to defer their retirement age a few years.

Regardless of which tax scenario is pursued, the trust fund would be in balance over the long term, and the second step would be to let individual workers choose the right mix of taxes and retirement age for themselves. In this scenario, the trade-offs would be equal. If people defer their retirement age enough to give up $1,000 in promised benefits, they would receive $1,000 in offsetting tax reductions. Using this approach, the trust fund would be balanced for the long term regardless of whether anybody selected a different retirement age.

The second approach is likely to be more appealing from a political perspective. Raising the tax rate for everyone would probably seem fairer to most because it requires everybody to share equally in the burden of

---

24.   Rasmussen Reports, "62% Support Social Security Taxes on All or Most of Income," Aug. 2008.

saving Social Security. So, while acknowledging that there are other approaches, I will focus on this for the rest of the chapter.

To put it in real-world terms, young workers willing to defer receiving Social Security benefits until roughly age seventy-five would probably be able to stop paying their share of Social Security taxes immediately (their company would still pay the employer's share). That would be an instant and significant increase in take-home pay that could be used for current expenses, a home down payment, private retirement accounts, or other purposes. This trade-off is possible without hurting the trust fund because the young worker, upon retirement, would be getting benefits for only half as long as he or she would under current law.

For young workers who want to collect benefits earlier than age seventy-five, but later than the current retirement age of sixty-seven, interim options would be available and the tax savings would be less dramatic. If any young workers wanted to begin collecting full Social Security benefits younger than age sixty-seven, they would have the opportunity to pay even more in Social Security taxes.

While the biggest impact would be on young workers, many people into their forties and fifties would also consider a similar trade-off. The personal impact would be less dramatic, but a fifty-five-year-old would have the option to stop paying personal Social Security taxes by deferring retirement benefits for just a few years. Many might find that appealing. With this approach, the trust fund deficit would be eliminated regardless of how many people decide to switch and how many don't. That's because the initial tax increase would bring the trust fund into long-term balance, and individual changes would not impact that balance. While the individual decisions wouldn't affect the trust fund balance, they would impact millions of lives in positive ways. That's why it's important to allow individuals to make the best decisions for themselves.

It's important to note that those who would trade paying less in taxes for a later Social Security retirement age are not automatically planning on retiring later. They are simply opting to receive Social Security benefits later. Sixty-three percent of those who would make such a choice say they would set the tax savings aside in a private retirement account.[25] Some might invest the money with the idea of bridging the gap from an earlier retirement age until their Social Security benefits kick in. Others might wait and invest the savings for a higher income during retirement. Many might simply feel more secure having real money in the bank rather than a government IOU. It's also true that some might use the money for things other than retirement. For some, the tax savings might allow for a down payment on a first home or be set aside for a child's education. Some might simply plan on working past their mandated Social Security retirement age, whether for the satisfaction of accomplishing something or because they need the money. These are all the sorts of decisions that should be made by individual citizens and not politicians.

Some may wonder why my example suggests that the employer portion of the tax remains unchanged while the trade-off involves only the personal Social Security taxes. There are several reasons. By making the change only on the personal tax, the actual trade-offs are more transparent. Also, it avoids a conflict of interest in which employers might be tempted to pressure workers into cutting the employer's taxes and taking a later retirement age. Ultimately, all the taxes come out of the compensation paid to workers, but keeping personal choices on the personal tax side of the ledger seems prudent.

With a larger share of the revenue coming from employers rather than being shared equally, there are legitimate concerns about abuse by politicians seeking more hidden revenues. Given these concerns, it is important to build protections into the process, and those will be discussed with other tax issues in chapter 6.

Regardless of the details, the basic concept is simple. Giving all Americans the chance to select their own Social Security retirement age is a potentially popular and effective way to eliminate the $17.9 trillion trust fund deficit. It is also an effective way to give people more con-

---

25. Rasmussen Reports, "65% Believe Americans Should Have Right to Pick Own Social Security Retirement Age," June 2011.

trol over their own retirement plan and give everyone more confidence about financing their retirement years. Just as important, it would pay off the debts that have been passed on to us since the 1960s and pay for our own retirement years without passing a burden on to our children and grandchildren.

Trust Funds

In addition to eliminating the long-term deficit in the Social Security system, promised benefits need to be paid on time each month. Nearly $3 trillion is currently held in the Social Security trust fund, more than enough to cover the benefit payments during a transition as people make individual choices to select their own retirement age.[26]

However, this assumes that there really is a trust fund with $3 trillion in assets dedicated solely to paying Social Security benefits. As discussed in chapter 2, the government disputes that notion and claims, "The Federal Government owns and manages the assets and earnings of most federal trust funds." Remember, the government claims the right to "unilaterally change the law to raise or lower future trust fund collections and payments or change the purpose for which collections are used." According to official documents, the trust fund surplus is nothing but a scam.[27]

This reality—and the need for reform—was highlighted by the Obama administration in 2011. Early in the year, the president's director of the Office of Management and Budget recited the traditional line by saying, "Social Security benefits are entirely self-financing. They are paid for with payroll taxes collected from workers and their employers throughout their careers. These taxes are placed in a trust fund dedicated to paying benefits owed to current and future beneficiaries."[28]

---

26. *The 2011 Annual Report of the Board of Trustees of the Federal Old-Age and Survivors Insurance and Federal Disability Insurance Trust Funds.*

27. *Budget of the United States Government, Fiscal Year 2012.*

28. Jacob Lew, "Opposing View: Social Security Isn't the Problem," Feb. 2011.

A few months later, during the political struggle to raise the debt ceiling, President Obama said he couldn't guarantee that Social Security checks would go out on time.[29] His assertion flatly contradicted the claims of his OMB director that there was a "trust fund dedicated to paying benefits owed to current and future beneficiaries."[30] At the time Obama spoke, nearly $3 trillion was allegedly sitting in the Social Security trust fund. If that was true, the upcoming payments should not have been at risk. But the president, perhaps inadvertently, spoke the truth as it is understood in Washington: the trust funds are just another piggy bank for the politicians to use when it suits their purposes.

This is not what FDR sold to the American people, and it's not what voters believe today. It is absolutely essential to align government policy with voter expectations. That will require setting up a real trust fund with real assets rather than just government promises. It may also require a new set of trustees who represent the American people rather than the federal government.

This is harder to accomplish than it might at first seem. For example, private pensions invest some of their money directly in corporate stocks and bonds. That's not a viable option for the Social Security trust fund. The last thing the American people want is for a federal program to get even more involved in ownership of private companies.[31] It's sickening to think of how poorly politically directed investments might destroy both the trust funds and the larger economy. Direct real estate investments are also not a viable option, especially given the Fannie Mae and Freddie Mac debacle.

One possible approach might follow the adage of not putting all your eggs in one basket. The United States has something approaching $25 trillion in bank deposits, mutual fund investments, and municipal

29.   Corbett Daly, "Obama Says He Cannot Guarantee Social Security Checks Will Go Out on Aug. 3," July 2011.

30.   Jacob Lew, "Opposing View: Social Security Isn't the Problem," Feb. 2011.

31.   Rasmussen Reports, "Most Americans Say Government Has Too Much Power over Economy," Oct. 2010.

bonds. Maybe the trust fund should be distributed among these and other fairly safe investments in a manner that ensures no single group or investment is dominant.

Two guidelines would have to be in place for this to work. First, the trust fund could never account for more than a minor share of any deposit or investment vehicle. Second, no single investment or bank deposit could account for more than a sliver of the total trust fund assets.

Even with these broad guidelines, the practical realities are challenging. The first challenge is the sheer amount of money involved. You couldn't just put all the money in banks because the trust fund deposits would make up more than a quarter of all bank deposits in the country. Still, putting the money into small bank deposits across the country might be a good start. With eight thousand banks in the nation, and diversification as the goal, it's easy to envision rules to insure prohibiting any one bank from receiving more than one-half of 1 percent of the total trust fund dollars deposited in bank accounts. There would also be strict limits so that the trust fund deposits never exceeded a modest share of the total deposits for any one bank and no money could be placed in foreign banks. Some might also prefer restrictions against putting money into banks that were bailed out. After that, some money could be invested in high-quality mutual funds or municipal bonds, but with limits so that the Social Security trust fund never owned more than a minor portion of any particular mutual fund or bond distribution.

There would even be provision for the trust fund to purchase some Treasury bills on the open market, but that would have to be restricted to a minority share of the trust fund assets. The key point is to create a real trust fund with real marketable assets and a diverse fund that is not overly dependent upon one class of assets. Some assets will do better than others, but future retirees will be much more secure with real assets rather than just promises from the government.

To bring this about it is probably necessary to change the trustees responsible for overseeing the trust fund. Under current law, the trustees include the secretary of the Treasury, two other cabinet members, the commissioner of Social Security, and two other members appointed by the president. These trustees all face a conflict of interest as they have obligations to the federal government, which is currently borrowing money from the trust funds. The conflict is highlighted by the current claim that money in the Social Security trust fund belongs to the federal government rather than potential beneficiaries of the trust fund. Nobody is looking out for the American people in this arrangement.

A new approach might eliminate the conflict of interest by preventing federal officials from serving as Social Security trustees. The new trustees could be selected by governors and county officials throughout the nation. These trustees would be entrusted solely with protecting the Social Security trust fund and representing the beneficiaries of the trust fund. They would not have the dual role of serving both the federal government and the trust fund.

Fortunately, there is time to work this all out. Over the next several years, the trust fund will be getting smaller and smaller no matter what reforms are enacted. That will provide the time needed to debate and solidify the reforms needed to make the trust funds real and build in adequate protections. It should be noted that letting workers select their own retirement age will also help with the problem by reducing the size of the trust fund. The more that people defer their own retirement age, the less money needs to be stored in a trust fund for future use.

Taking time to do it right is also important because making the trust fund real must be done in a manner approved directly by voters. This should probably be done after voters have already approved the concept of letting people select their own retirement age. The issues are sufficiently different that it would be wise to have them considered at different times.

While the details may vary, two important concepts must survive any reform of the Social Security trust fund. First, the fund must be filled with real assets rather than simply promises from the federal government. Second, the trustees must be pledged to serve only the beneficiaries of the trust fund rather than having a dual loyalty to both the fund and the federal government. If these changes can be implemented, Americans will be able to sleep better at night rather than worrying what will be their lot when they come to old age.

Conclusion

Social Security has become the most popular policy legacy of the New Deal era for a reason: its fundamental values are consistent with American heritage and culture. FDR didn't convince people to support a government handout; he convinced them to accept a new tool to enhance our national belief in personal responsibility. It made sense that people should set aside a bit of money during their working lives to provide for their retirement years. It still does.

Other New Deal programs, such as the National Industrial Recovery Act, never connected with voters and failed to survive because they fundamentally rejected the American traditions of free markets and individual responsibility. Americans today want Social Security to work, and allowing workers the right to select their own retirement age is a reform the public may be willing to embrace. It intuitively makes sense in the same way that the original Social Security program made sense. It is hard for many to imagine a reason why people should be denied the right to select their own retirement age. Shifting decision making away from politicians and back to individual citizens is clearly a step in the right direction.

Ultimately, the challenge in reforming Social Security is not finding a program voters can support, it's finding a political forum that voters trust to make the reforms. Congress and official Washington have no credibility on the subject. That's why it is important for the government to intentionally seek approval for fundamental changes in important programs. It's the only way to build legitimacy for the government and insure that these reforms have the consent of the governed. No matter what the proposal, a requirement for voters to approve any change in

Social Security will help keep the Political Class from doing too much damage. Any politician who is afraid to submit his or her reform to a vote of the people should not be taken seriously.

Politicians who are willing to follow the lead of the American people hold the key to making Social Security work for twenty-first-century Americans. Even more, those who recognize that the American people are once again far ahead of their politicians hold the key to solving America's fiscal crisis.

5

---·---

How Voters Would Fix Medicare and Health Care

President Barack Obama and Congressman Paul Ryan both deserve credit for drawing attention to the issues surrounding the cost of medical care and doing so at great political cost to themselves and their own political party. During the 2006 and 2008 elections, when Democrats gained control of Congress and President Obama won the White House, Democrats were consistently trusted more than Republicans on the health care issue by wide margins. In November 2008, the soon-to-be president declared, "The question isn't how we can afford to focus on health care. The question is how we can afford not to."[1]

Believing they had a mandate from the people, congressional Democrats and President Obama began pushing a major health care plan. Within just a few months, well before any legislation was passed, the Democrats were on the defensive. Republicans gained the upper hand as the party most trusted on health care, and it helped them win big in the midterm elections of 2010.

By January of 2011, as the new GOP majority in the House took office, Republicans enjoyed a 14-point advantage over Democrats on

---

1.   Foon Rhee, "Push for Healthcare Reform Quotes Obama," Nov. 2008.

the health care issue. Then Paul Ryan proposed his budget plan featuring fundamental changes in Medicare, and it cost the Republicans dearly. The GOP's 14-point advantage disappeared, and the parties were essentially even, with voters not feeling particularly good about any of what they were hearing from either team in Washington.[2]

The unpopularity of both Obama's and Ryan's plans was confirmed by other polling as well. From the moment it became law, a majority of voters favored repeal of the president's plan and perceived it as a drag on the economy.[3] Ryan's plan is not nearly as well-known, but among those with an opinion, opponents outnumbered supporters by nearly a two-to-one margin.[4] The plans also hurt their sponsors. The president's job approval rating declined and negative perceptions of Ryan soared.

Obama and Ryan struggled politically partly because they took on an enormously complex industry encrusted with layer after layer of rules and regulations. Additionally, there was no popular support for a major crusade. While there is a medical-care cost crisis for the government and the business community, most Americans are satisfied with the medical care they receive and with their own insurance coverage. Two-thirds of all Americans rate their own coverage as good or excellent.[5] That means most Americans entered the debate over health care reform thinking they had more to lose than to gain. These people, the vast majority, needed to be assured that any change would make things better rather than worse. As in all discussion of medical ethics, a good starting point is "First, do no harm."

The importance of protecting people against change was highlighted in polling conducted a few years ago that showed that half of all Americans supported providing free health care to all Americans. They did so even though most thought it would increase the overall cost of care while hurting the quality of care. Additionally, when the taxes to pay for

---

2.   Rasmussen Reports, "Trust on Issues," July 2011.

3.   Rasmussen Reports, "Health Care Law," Aug. 2011.

4.   Rasmussen Reports, "Opposition to Ryan Budget Plan Grows," Apr. 2011.

5.   Rasmussen Reports, "70% of Insured Rate Health Insurance Coverage as Good or Excellent," May 2009.

it were included, 52 percent expected to pay more with such a system in place. Only 28 percent expected to save money with a system of "free" health care. Apparently, people were willing to pay such a price so that everyone could have coverage.[6]

However, while paying a bit more was acceptable, giving up their own insurance coverage was not. Only 31 percent supported "free" health care for all if it meant giving up their own coverage and joining a government program. Both Obama and Ryan think that times are desperate enough that voters ought to be willing to make such a change, but voters don't see things that way. Even if they did, politicians are the last people they'd trust to fix the problem.

To protect themselves from political shenanigans, 64 percent want any changes in Medicare approved by voters before implementation.[7] Neither the Obama plan nor the Ryan plan could possibly win such a referendum because they were ideological in nature rather than practical. Obama's plan drew support primarily from those who favored a single-payer health care system and saw it as a step along the way to a complete government takeover of medical care in the United States. Ryan talked about how his plan would work from a government budgeting perspective, but not from a personal perspective.

Any plan that can win popular support must shore up the current Medicare system, at least in the interim, until alternatives can be presented that merit the support of the American people. This is consistent with a "do no harm" approach to health care reform. In the best of all worlds, senior citizens will have a choice between the existing system and a series of alternatives. Over time, as better options prove themselves, all of us will benefit. But, until then, it is inappropriate to experiment with the health and well-being of senior citizens just to score ideological or political points.

While it is necessary to shore up the current system in the short term,

---

6. Rasmussen Reports, "Free Health Care? Not If It Means Switching Insurance Coverage!" Oct. 2007.

7. Rasmussen Reports, "51% Now Recognize Most Federal Spending Goes to Defense, Medicare, and Social Security," June 2011.

long-term and fundamental changes in Medicare cannot be avoided. Richard W. Fisher, president of the Dallas Federal Reserve Bank, noted in a formal address, "The good news is that the Social Security shortfall might be manageable. . . . The bad news is that Social Security is the lesser of our entitlement worries. It is but the tip of the unfunded liability iceberg."[8]

As noted in the previous chapter, a solution to the Social Security challenge that can win voter support can be found. However, Fisher warns that to cover the unfunded liabilities of the Medicare program "you would be stuck with an $85.6 trillion bill. That is more than six times as large as the bill for Social Security. It is more than six times the annual output of the entire U.S. economy."

The Cato Institute's Mike Tanner put it to me this way: "I much prefer talking Social Security reform rather than Medicare reform. With Social Security, whatever the problems, there are solutions that leave people better off. But, with Medicare, at the end of the day, people are simply going to get less than we have promised them." *Washington Post* business columnist Robert Samuelson looked at the situation and concluded, "It is only a slight exaggeration to say that unless we end Medicare 'as we know it,' America 'as we know it' will end."[9]

The prospect of reforming Medicare is understandably terrifying to the many who rely upon it to pay their medical bills. After all, who wants politicians making decisions about their health care? That's why reform is needed. The present system is unsustainable. Figuring out ways to handle the cost of medical care may be the biggest fiscal issue facing the nation today. While national security and Social Security represent a similar share of the federal budget, paying for medical care is much more than a federal budget issue. It affects every state, county, and local government in the nation. It affects every business and individual. If the cost of financing medical care can be reduced, it will provide a huge boost to the US economy by reducing costs all along the supply

8.   Richard W. Fisher, "Remarks Before the Commonwealth Club of California," May 2008.
9.   Robert J. Samuelson, "Why We Must End Medicare 'As We Know It,'" June 2011.

chain. More specifically, getting the cost of medical care under control will increase private sector hiring by reducing the cost of adding new employees.

The numbers are staggering. The United States spent about $2.5 trillion on medical care in 2009, nearly as much as the entire federal budget. That's more than $8,000 per resident or $33,000 for a family of four. The cost of medical care consumed 17.4 percent of our nation's gross domestic product (GDP). In 1960, the cost of medical care was just a few hundred dollars per person and the total equaled just 5.1 percent of the total economic output.[10]

The Medicare program, which didn't even exist until 1965, has grown to cost more than $500 billion annually, and the expense is projected to grow much faster than the population and inflation for many years to come.[11] Those figures don't even include the cost of providing medical insurance for nearly 2 million federal government employees. These budget-busting figures caught the attention of politicians such as Barack Obama and Paul Ryan. To liberals, the escalating costs of paying for medical care crowds out other federal spending and makes it difficult to fund other government initiatives. To conservatives, the costs are part of an unacceptable growth in government spending and a burden on the economy.

Figures provided by the Obama administration show that if health care costs are not brought under control, all federal spending would consume fully 81 percent of the nation's GDP by the end of this century.[12] With state and local government spending added to the mix, nothing would be left for the private sector. Obviously that's impossible. The economy would collapse long before federal spending reached the 81 percent mark. But the projection illustrates just how dire the long-term situation has become.

Another way of looking at the costs is to consider what it might take

10. Numbers derived from the 2008 and 2010 Economic Reports of the President, as well as data from the Organization for Economic Co-operation and Development.
11. *Budget of the United States Government, Fiscal Year 2012.*
12. *Budget of the United States Government, Fiscal Year 2011.*

to bring the entire Medicare program into long-term actuarial balance. Without fixing the cost side of the equation, the basic payroll tax would have to jump from 2.9 percent today to roughly 15 percent. One-seventh of every paycheck would go to Medicare. That would come on top of Social Security taxes and income taxes. Such a tax hike would jolt the economy in ways that no one wants to imagine.

Because the Medicare numbers are so much worse than those for Social Security, it's not possible to come up with a clean and simple solution. As with Social Security, it's important to make the Medicare trust funds real, rather than simply a set of empty promises from the government. Giving people the right to select their own retirement age can help as part of the Medicare reform effort. As part of that plan, a more modest tax hike might make sense, but it won't make any difference unless the long-term costs of providing health care are brought into line. These steps alone cannot solve the entire problem because they do not, by themselves, bring down the out-of-control cost of medical care.

The real question is not how to pay for Medicare, but how to bring down the cost of medical care in the United States. American voters, not surprisingly, believe that free market principles can help. By a 69 to 23 percent margin, voters believe that greater free market competition between insurance companies would do more to reduce health care costs than more government regulation.[13] Unfortunately, insurance companies today are largely prohibited from any meaningful competition. They receive special protection from the government in the form of antitrust exemptions. Sixty-eight percent of voters want those exemptions repealed. Seventy-six percent see another avenue of increased competition in allowing employers and individuals to buy insurance plans across state lines.[14] That, too, is currently prohibited by law.

Another barrier to competition is a federal mandate that every insurance plan cover exactly the same procedures with exactly the same

13. Rasmussen Reports. "69% Think Competition Between Health Insurers Better for Consumers Than More Government Regulation," July 2011.

14. Ibid.

deductibles. That's the twenty-first-century equivalent of Henry Ford saying that consumers could have any color car they wanted as long as it was black. Voters have other ideas. Seventy-eight percent say individuals should have the right to choose between different types of health insurance plans, including some that cost more but cover just about all procedures, and some that cost less while covering only major medical procedures. Only 7 percent side with federal policymakers and think this choice should be prohibited.[15]

In addition to favoring a choice of the medical procedures covered, 77 percent think individuals should have the right to choose between plans with a mix of higher deductibles and lower premiums, and plans with a mix of lower deductibles and higher premiums. Just 6 percent don't think consumers should have this choice. In theory, a lot of people might be better off if they got lower-cost insurance to cover major and unexpected medical events, while paying for routine visits to the doctor with savings from reduced premiums. One of the choices offered for all individuals should be the right to buy the same health insurance plan offered to members of Congress. Seventy-eight percent of Americans support that notion.[16] The same logic should probably apply to state legislators and other government workers. If individuals want to buy a health insurance plan available to government employees, they should be allowed to do so.

If Americans are given the right to choose their own type of health insurance, barriers in the tax code must be overcome as well. Under current law, health insurance premiums paid by companies are tax exempt but those purchased by individuals are not. Also, the tax code offers a significant preference for insurance plans that provide high premiums and low deductibles rather than lower premiums and higher deductibles. For Americans to have a real choice, the tax code should treat all medical-care expenditures equally.

---

15. Rasmussen Reports, "39% Say Health Insurance Companies Should Be Required to Cover Contraceptives," Aug. 2011.

16. Rasmussen Reports, "78% Say All Americans Should Be Able to Buy the Health Insurance That Congress Has," Sep. 2009.

These government barriers to free market competition are part of the unhealthy alliance between Big Government and Big Business. Those corporate welfare arrangements are unseemly, but can be challenged when they are visible and there is a public desire to do so. However, while acknowledging the potential value of free markets in the fight against medical-care costs, voters also want to place some limits of their own on market forces. For example, if someone without health insurance has been in a terrible accident, 91 percent of Americans believe that person should receive emergency room treatment.[17] In fact, this belief is so strong that 76 percent believe illegal immigrants should receive emergency room care following an accident.[18] That's virtually the only government service that most voters are willing to provide for illegal immigrants. Voters are opposed to providing any government funding to help illegal immigrants receive insurance, to providing them with driver's licenses, and any other type of government assistance. But emergency room treatment is recognized as a special case.

American voters also think the normal free market rules shouldn't apply in some other circumstances. In those cases, voters believe other values are more important. They want health care made available to the poor, the elderly, and people with chronic conditions, such as diabetes.[19] Most favor providing a free medical school education for doctors who agree to serve five years helping those living in poverty without health insurance.[20]

Sixty-three percent agree with President Obama that "we must make it a priority to give every single American quality affordable health care."[21] Before voters are willing to consider any new approaches, they want to make sure that these values are honored. If free market forces

---

17. Rasmussen Reports, "91% Think Emergency Rooms Should Treat Those Without Health Insurance," Aug. 2011.

18. Ibid.

19. Rasmussen Reports, "Only 18% Say Those with Chronic Conditions Should Pay More in Health Insurance," July 2009.

20. Rasmussen Reports, "58% Favor Free Schooling for Doctors Who Will Serve the Poor," Sep. 2009.

21. Rasmussen Reports, "63% Support Affordable Health Care for 'Every Single American,'" Mar. 2009.

were working in other aspects of the health care world, it would be fairly easy to think of ways to address these concerns.

However, in addition to eliminating legal barriers, another huge hurdle must be overcome before competition could help drive prices down. Medical-care consumers want more and more decision-making authority, but they currently pay only a small portion of the overall cost. While the ever-rising costs have huge implications for government budgets and private businesses, the cost growth has been largely invisible to consumers. In 1960, Americans spent 3.6 percent of their disposable income for the out-of-pocket costs associated with medical care. Nearly half a century later, in 2009, Americans were spending an even smaller portion of their income on out-of-pocket expenditures, just 2.7 percent. That's because just over half of all medical costs were paid out of pocket in 1960 and just 14 percent are paid that way in today's world.[22] Certainly the increased provision of medical insurance, especially for the elderly, has been a major step forward for the nation over the past half century, but while medical-care spending has exploded overall, the out-of-pocket costs for consumers have declined. For most Americans, the only visible impact of the cost problems has been the increased hassle of dealing with insurance company rules and scheduling issues. Those hassles are the result of insurance companies dealing with the costs that individuals don't worry about.

This is especially a problem because consumers want to make their own decisions. Americans are fairly evenly divided as to whether they fear insurance companies or the government more in the health care debate, but are fundamentally agreed that both should have less to say about individual medical decisions.[23] This means shifting decision making about health care back to individuals, their families, and their doctors. The only way to do that is to aggressively take power away from politicians, employers, and health care bureaucrats in both the government and in-

22.   Numbers derived from the 2008 and 2010 Economic Reports of the President, as well as data from the Organization for Economic Co-operation and Development.

23.   Rasmussen Reports, "On Health Care, 51% Fear Government More Than Insurance Companies," Aug. 2009.

surance companies. After all, your doctor knows what you need better than some senator you've never met. Ultimately, solutions will be found by focusing more on how health care is delivered and how choices are made rather than fighting about how to pay for the status quo.

In the fight to reduce the cost of medical care, it is hard to overstate the significance of consumers' paying less out of pocket today than they did a half century ago. That is a key reason that insurance companies and governments are reducing consumer medical-care choices and becoming ever more annoying. Costs can only be controlled when the people footing the bill are making the choices. If more decision making is transferred to people who pay only a fraction of the total cost out of pocket, prices will continue to rise and the situation will get even worse. On the other hand, forcing individuals to pay more out of pocket for health care is a nonstarter. That's the opposite of what everyone is trying to achieve. Voters want health care reform to reduce costs rather than increase them. This means that a key challenge in the health care debate is finding mechanisms that give people more control over their health-care dollar without increasing the out-of-pocket costs they pay.

One way to do this would be to give consumers more control over the money their employers pay for medical insurance. More than 150 million Americans receive insurance coverage from employers, so the impact could be enormous. If a worker wants a different health insurance plan than the one provided by his employer, and that plan didn't cost the employer any extra money, 82 percent believe the worker should be allowed to pick his or her own insurance plan.[24] Since the average annual employer-provided premium costs more than $5,000 and the average family plan is roughly $14,000, this simple reform could give consumers control of nearly a trillion dollars annually.[25] Adding even more control, 52 percent think that the worker should be able to keep any savings resulting from his or her health insurance choices. If a family plan for a

---

24.   Rasmussen Reports, "82% Say Workers Should Be Allowed to Choose Their Own Insurance," July 2011.

25.   Kaiser Family Foundation and Health Research & Educational Trust, "Employer Health Benefits: 2010 Summary of Findings," 2010.

worker costs $1,000 a month and the worker finds a plan that he or she likes for $800, the worker gets to take home an extra $200 a month.

As with other efforts to give Americans more control of their own medical-care decisions, barriers to choice will have to be removed from the tax code in this area as well. If people choose a different health insurance plan from the one picked by their employer, they should not be slapped with an extra tax burden for making that choice.

Giving workers this kind of control would give them many opportunities to improve their overall level of health care while reducing its cost. For example, the nation spends twice as much on medical care as it does on food.[26] Yet for many families, especially low-income families, better meals would do more to improve their health than more doctor visits. The choices are never simple and clear-cut, but that's why they should be made by individuals rather than employers, insurance companies, or government bureaucrats.

This thought process is entirely consistent with public attitudes about health care choices as well. Sixty-two percent of voters nationwide believe that exercise, diet, and lifestyle choices have a bigger impact on someone's health than health insurance and medical care.[27] This view is also shared by many experts. An article in the *New England Journal of Medicine* stated, "The single greatest opportunity to improve health and reduce premature deaths lies in personal behavior."[28] These findings aren't limited to academic articles. I recently met a respected heart surgeon who told me that most of his surgeries were unnecessary and could have been prevented by better diet and exercise.

Giving workers control over the money their employers spend for health insurance will only help if a variety of insurance products are available. Unfortunately, government regulators have done just about everything within their power to limit the options available to consum-

26.   Carlos Angrisano et al., *Accounting for the Cost of Health Care in the United States* (2007).
27.   Rasmussen Reports, "62% Say Personal Responsibility for Health More Important Than Health Insurance," Oct. 2011.
28.   Steven A. Schroeder, "We Can Do Better—Improving the Health of the American People," Sep. 2007.

ers. For example, some people might prefer to pay a lower premium and higher deductibles. With such a policy, they would be covered for any hospital stays or serious issues but would pay for more routine costs out of pocket. Some people might think that's a great deal while others think it's a lousy deal, but Congress decided that nobody should be allowed to make such a choice on their own.[29] In the pursuit of promising lower deductibles for all, the politicians in Washington eliminated an opportunity for many to pay lower premiums. Just 12 percent of voters agree with that new government policy. Seventy-six percent disagree and think Americans should be allowed to buy health insurance coverage for such issues as unexpected surgeries or cancer, but pay for routine doctor visits on their own without insurance.[30]

It's not just Washington that limits consumer choices in health insurance. Many state legislators also add mandatory coverage rules that eliminate any meaningful difference between insurance products offered within their state. Again, it's not a question of whether a decision is right or wrong; it's a question of who gets to make it. What is the right trade-off between lower out-of-pocket costs for preventative care and lower co-pay for hospitalization? That should be an individual decision, not a government or insurance company or employer decision.

Giving consumers more choice in the selection of insurance products is one step toward aligning with the 69 percent of voters who believe increased competition between insurance companies would help reduce costs, but it doesn't get to the core issue of saving money by changing the way that health care is delivered.[31] To understand the potential savings that could result from real competition, walk into your local drugstore. You can buy off-the-shelf and inexpensive equipment to check your blood pressure, your blood sugar, your cholesterol, and more. You can buy a test to see if your children have illegal drugs in their

29. *Compilation of Patient Protection and Affordable Health Care Act*, 2010.

30. Rasmussen Reports, "70% Favor Individual Choice over Government Standards for Health Insurance," Oct. 2011.

31. Rasmussen Reports, "69% Think Competition Between Health Insurers Better for Consumers Than More Government Regulations," July 2011.

system, or if your wife is pregnant. Other self-monitoring tests are clearly possible, and it's far cheaper to buy the equipment and perform the tests at home than to go the doctor's office for a blood test. It's also a lot more convenient to do the test at home.

Moving routine health-care testing out to individuals gives them the ability to improve their own health at a lower cost. This is not a theory; it's already proven itself in the fight against diabetes. Not so long ago, diabetics had their blood sugar levels checked once every three months in the doctor's office. The doctor would evaluate the results and give the patient a diet and insulin routine for the next three months. Now those with diabetes can check their own blood sugar many times a day—and they can do it wherever they are. The benefits are not only fewer health complications and lower costs, but a dramatically improved quality of life for millions of Americans with diabetes.

While it's easy to understand how embracing competition could dramatically reduce the cost and improve the quality of health care for most Americans, it is more difficult to think of how to establish a competitive environment. That's especially true when you think of the other values Americans bring to the medical-care debate. Those who are happy with their current medical care and insurance must not be harmed in any way. Quality, affordable care must be available to all—including those in poverty, those near the end of their life, and those with chronic conditions.

Figuring out the best way to reliably deliver more and more low-cost monitoring to individuals is never going to happen until workers have more control over their insurance options. Finding new ways to serve consumers is the work of entrepreneurs, not bureaucrats. A study by McKinsey and Company noted that "misaligned incentives" currently favor expensive new technology and other factors that lead to higher costs. "Innovative technologies that actually reduce costs to the patient are less common." That's what happens when the government is paying the bills. The reason for this is fairly clear. "Supplier behavior—from physicians, to hospitals, to insurance companies—is highly rational in response to the set of economic incentives each faces." In other words, if the government offers someone more money to deliver a more expensive product, suppliers are happy to oblige. That's the opposite of what happens in consumer-driven industries where "technological innovation drives prices down."[32]

This gravy train for some of the largest medical-care companies will generate strong resistance to the concept of allowing competition to reduce the cost of medical care. When you add in their allies in government bureaucracies, the difficulty of doing so is almost impossible to overstate. Just imagine, as one small piece of the puzzle, the resistance that will be raised against the idea of eliminating antitrust exemptions for health insurance companies! Eight-six percent of the funding for the status quo is provided by either government sources or heavily regulated insurance companies.[33] More than half of all medical-care costs are paid directly by the government or a government-run program. The introduction of competition offers a huge potential windfall for consumers but an even bigger threat to those who profit from the system. It remains to be seen whether the current financial crisis surrounding medical care can generate enough interest and influence to bring about the needed change.

The needed change can't possibly be determined through the corrupt legislative and regulatory process in Washington. Consider an issue that rises up from time to time in the political realm; medical malpractice lawsuits and the need for reform. Malpractice lawsuits, plus the practice of defensive medicine to avoid more suits, cost up to $200 billion a year.[34] That's approaching 10 percent of the nation's total health care tab, or nearly $3,000 for a family of four. Most voters would like to see that number trimmed dramatically and support some kind of reform to limit potential liabilities,[35] but no easy and obvious solution is available. Obviously, frivolous lawsuits and excessive awards drive up the cost of

---

32. Carlos Angrisano et al., *Accounting for the Cost of Health Care in the United States* (2007).

33. Numbers derived from the 2008 and 2010 Economic Reports of the President, as well as data from the Organization for Economic Co-operation and Development.

34. Carlos Angrisano et al., *Accounting for the Cost of Health Care in the United States* (2007).

35. Rasmussen Reports, "Voters Favor Tort Reform by a Two-to-One Margin," Dec. 2009.

care for everyone. Just as obviously, occasionally doctors commit serious errors and deserve to be punished. What's not obvious is the best way to balance these competing interests.

Some in Washington might say that this is a task for a wise and impartial regulator or group of regulators with the wisdom of Solomon. But, as mentioned in chapter 1, while those in Washington may see themselves in such a light, hardly anybody else does. Instead, most Americans are skeptical of a revolving-door arrangement that bears the strong appearance of legalized corruption. Fifty-nine percent believe some companies routinely hire regulators to get favorable treatment from the government, and nearly as many (53%) think companies that regularly hire former regulators get special treatment.[36] Regulatory corruption is one of the key reasons that seven out of ten Americans believe Big Government and Big Business work together against the rest of us.[37] It's also one of the reasons our health care system is in such trouble today.

The only way to find the right balance on the issue of medical malpractice or many other financial issues in the medical-care debate is competition between the states. Let states fulfill their role as "laboratories of democracy" and try a variety of approaches. Some would be too favorable to the doctors and some too favorable to those filing lawsuits. Some might lead to higher costs while others lower the tab. Some might cause doctors to leave the state, some might draw them in. Some states might attract patients seeking care, while others might cause patients to flee. Jobs and investment would move to the states with the best ideas and the right balance. Those states would see their system copied while other methods will be rejected. That approach is also consistent with the basic attitudes held by most Americans. Fifty-six percent believe that letting states compete to determine the most effective standards and guidelines would do more to lower costs than establishing a single set

---

36. Rasmussen Reports, "51% Think It's Bribery When a Company Offers a Government Regulator a Job," 2011.

37. Rasmussen Reports, "68% Believe Government and Big Business Work Together Against the Rest of Us," Feb. 2011.

of federal regulations. Just 33 percent think having a single set of rules would be better.[38]

Letting states compete and experiment can help us find the right balance on a number of issues in the medical-care debate. Voters overwhelmingly believe that nurse-practitioners should be allowed to provide more of the services currently performed by doctors.[39] This could save money and let doctors focus their energies on more serious cases, but where do you draw the lines? What kind of care requires a doctor and what does not? Should nurses and nurse-practitioners be allowed to write some more common prescriptions without going to a doctor? Some states would give more authority to nurses and some would give less. The answers might lead some states to have more conveniently located walk-in clinics for routine care and minor emergencies. Malpractice reform and letting nurse-practitioners handle more services are just two of the many issues that could be resolved more effectively by letting states compete. Another is the potential conflict of interest surrounding the role of doctors.

Doctors are thrust into an awkward situation in today's world, being told to straddle the role of trusted adviser to patients, while also being asked to contain costs or promote certain products. No federal bureaucrat, no matter how smart, can figure out a magic formula to eliminate these conflicts. That's why competition between the states is so important. Different states would have different approaches, and the results could be studied to see what works best. Some approaches will work better in different states; Texas is not New York, after all. Shifting more control to the hands of consumers is a reasonable approach to reducing the cost of care, but having several states try different approaches also provides an important safety net. If one state's approach doesn't work out, the state would have plenty of other approaches to consider.

---

38. Rasmussen Reports, "56% Think Competing State Standards More Likely to Lower Health Care Costs," July 2011.

39. Rasmussen Reports, "67% Favor Expanding Use of Nurse-Practitioner for Routine Care," Apr. 2011.

How Would State Competition Work?

Most voters believe that individual states should have the right to opt out of the health care law passed by President Obama and congressional Democrats in 2010,[40] but few have given any thought to what that might really mean. To allow some form of meaningful competition consistent with voter beliefs, each state should probably be allowed to choose from one of three options. The first would be to stay within the existing guidelines and rules of the federal government, the second would be to implement a single-payer system within the state, and the third would allow for more competition utilizing a free market approach.

Some on the right might object to the first two options. After all, they represent exactly the opposite of giving consumers more control, but true competition must allow for a wide range of outcomes, not just the outcomes preferred by one segment of the population. Nationally, 34 percent of voters favor a single-payer plan, and such voters may constitute a majority in some states.[41] Vermont has already signed such a system into law, pending federal approval.[42] Those who believe it's the best approach should have a chance to try it. Those who believe that competition will produce better results should not be afraid of a little competition. Bluntly, the American people would benefit from seeing a wide variety of options so that they could make informed decisions over time. For those who believe that a single-payer health plan won't work, the best way to prove it is to let the American people see it in action.

Some states may not want to go in the single-payer direction, but still prefer to have the federal government set national standards. Any state that wants to do so should be able to stick with the status quo. Again, those who believe there are better options should not be afraid of a little competition. And, of course, those states that restrict the options avail-

---

40. Rasmussen Reports, "54% Say States Should Have Right to Opt out of Health Care Law," Feb. 2011.

41. Rasmussen Reports, "34% Favor Single-Payer Health Care System," Dec. 2009.

42. Zach Howard, "Vermont Single-Payer Health Care Law Signed by Governor," May 2011.

able to their residents should be prepared to explain why it makes sense to do so.

Those states that choose to embrace competition should be encouraged to push as much decision-making power and financial control as possible to health care consumers. One requirement for choosing this path could be to allow citizens to buy insurance policies from any other state that has chosen to go the competitive route. Each state would come up with its own approach to issues such as tort reform, nurse-practitioners, and conflict-of-interest issues. Even more, they could explore ways of giving consumers more choices in both insurance coverage and the delivery of care while preserving other core values in the health care debate.

Medicare recipients in these states could remain part of the federal program and be fully protected, but the states might also come up with other options to offer seniors. Many proposals have been suggested that would give seniors a viable set of choices between the existing Medicare plan and other options. The proposals typically involve some form of mechanism for the Medicare program to help defray the insurance costs for individual patients while also reducing the net cost to the Medicare system. Each state would have to come up with its own plan and negotiate with the federal Medicare system before putting it into effect. One simple approach would be to let seniors purchase the same insurance plan that's provided to federal and state employees. And consistent with the philosophy of first doing no harm, the choice would be up to individuals, not politicians. Regardless of the specific plans developed, it's likely that such a competitive environment would lead to options providing better care for seniors, a reduced cost for the Medicare system, and a lower cost of health care for all.

It is, of course, impossible to predict what might emerge when entrepreneurs are unleashed to serve the needs of medical-care consumers. A system that responds to consumers of medical care rather than bureaucrats would be less centralized and less expensive. It would make it easier and more convenient to obtain routine care and less dependent upon waiting for insurance company authorization. And if a majority of

Americans are correct, a system that relies upon competition and consumer choice will produce better far better health results at a lower cost than a system directed by the government.

One of the most obvious immediate changes would come in the increased variety of insurance plans available to consumers. Some workers could consider a low-cost major medical plan and pay for most routine care out of pocket. Because such a plan would cost so much less than most employer-based plans, the worker could receive hundreds of dollars extra each month in his or her paycheck. Others might consider trade-offs between different levels of coverage, co-pays, and maximum risk. Some might want a wider choice in doctors, while others might prefer to pay a bit less, but have fewer choices. New ideas would be introduced as well. It's possible that some insurance companies would add features such as giving customers the right to increase their coverage as they age regardless of their health at the time. Again, as with all other such examples, it's not that there is a right or a wrong choice; it's that different choices are right for different people. With a system aimed at pleasing consumers rather than bureaucrats, the result would be a dramatically different and more user-friendly medical-care system.

The variety of insurance options would begin to change the medical-care landscape and changing delivery options would follow. It's likely that more and more home monitoring would become the norm. In many cases, the results of daily or weekly tests would be forwarded electronically to a doctor or other care provider. That's the type of delivery change that could both improve health outcomes and lower costs.

The President's Health Care Plan

While much passion has been devoted to the topic of repealing (or protecting) the health care law passed by President Obama and congressional Democrats in 2010, this topic has not been a key part of the discussion in this chapter. That's because the real question is not whether that law is repealed, but what comes next. Seventy-five percent of voters nationwide believe major changes are needed in that health care legislation.[43] Some believe it should be repealed and replaced, while others are okay with leaving it in place but fixing the biggest problems.

The president appears to believe that federal government regulation is the best way to control the cost of medical care, but 75 percent of voters believe his program will cost more than projected.[44] Most also believe it will raise the cost of care, hurt the quality of care, and increase the federal deficit.[45]

The president's plan also prompted a large number of "waivers" for companies, unions, and others who were having a hard time complying. Most voters are opposed to the approach of giving waivers and believe that any exemptions should apply to all.[46] The law, passed in 2010, was unpopular nationally both before and after it became law. Letting states opt out of that plan is consistent with what voters want and avoids any unnecessary wrangling about what is repealed and what is left. Those states that want to remain in the current system could do so and presumably would lobby for changes they consider appropriate.

Conclusion

Addressing the cost of Medicare is perhaps the most pressing fiscal problem facing the federal government today. Ultimately, the only way to address the problem is to reduce the cost of delivering medical care for all Americans. To accomplish that, most voters embrace the idea of competition: competition among states and competition among insurance companies. They also bring other values to the debate, including the

---

43.   Rasmussen Reports, "75% Want Health Care Law Changed," Jan. 2011.
44.   Rasmussen Reports, "75% Think Health Care Law May Cost More Than Estimated," Jan. 2011.
45.   Rasmussen Reports, "55% Favor Health Care Repeal, Just 17% Say New Law Will Improve Quality of Care," June 2011.
46.   Rasmussen Reports, "Majority of Voters Still Question Health Care Waivers, Think They Should Be Given to All," Jan. 2011.

belief that vulnerable citizens should not be hurt during a transition period. Among other things, that means bolstering Medicare's short-term financial picture.

The Medicare program has four separate parts, none of which are adequately funded. In 1965, Lyndon Johnson created a Hospital Insurance trust fund (HI) and a Supplemental Medical Insurance trust fund (SMI). The first, designed to cover the cost of hospitalization for the elderly, was set up something like Social Security with dedicated revenues from a payroll tax. As costs have mushroomed, the dedicated tax has proven inadequate, leaving a large unfunded liability. Sadly, this is the best-financed part of Medicare.

The Supplemental Medicare Insurance trust fund was set up to handle nonhospital care such as routine doctor visits. This program has no dedicated payroll taxes, although seniors are required to pay a modest premium, which is deducted from their Social Security benefits. With no dedicated tax revenue, this fund is also burdened with a huge unfunded liability. In one of the true outrages of federal reporting, the government claims that this program is fully funded. How can they make this absurd claim? Because with no dedicated revenue, the government simply contributes whatever is needed each year. In other words, the part of Medicare that has dedicated revenue to offset a significant part of the cost is considered a problem, but the part with no revenue for the trust fund is fine. It's hard to find a clearer example of the Political Class view that the trust funds mean nothing more than trust the government.

For what it's worth, the prescription-drug benefit passed during the Bush administration uses the same faulty logic. There is a modest insurance payment, but no tax revenue to offset the costs. Since there is no significant revenue, the government promises to make up the difference and has deemed the program adequately funded. The promise to pay Medicare benefits without any offsetting Medicare tax revenue costs the federal government hundreds of billions of dollars every year. That money comes straight out of the general operating budget.

That's not at all the way people think the Medicare system is supposed to work. Like Social Security, Medicare is envisioned as a program where people set aside money during their working lives to be drawn on as benefits during retirement.

The first step to strengthening Medicare would be for the government to provide a sound base of financing for the promised long-term benefits. All parts of Medicare should be financed with a Medicare payroll tax, with no separate funding from the federal government's general operating budget. That's what voters believe should happen, and they're the boss. As with Social Security, there would also be a need to make the trust funds real, rather than simply a set of promises from government.

Once the trust funds are established, the next step would be to provide adequate funding for the current program. As mentioned earlier, with the current cost projections this would require increasing the payroll tax from 2.9 to 15 percent (paid equally by employer and employee). That would destroy the economy and eliminate millions of jobs, so a better approach would be to select a more modest increase. Perhaps the tax could go from 2.9 to 7.9 percent over a period of years (it would probably make sense to hold off the first increase until the recession has ended). Additionally, as with Social Security, workers could select their own retirement age by trading off a later retirement age for lower taxes.

Given public opposition to tax hikes, it is important to note that this increase in Medicare could never be considered on a stand-alone basis. It would be possible only in conjunction with the Social Security tax changes mentioned in the previous chapter. By combining both the Social Security and Medicare tax proposals, the overall mandatory tax for each worker would be lower than it is today.

It's also important to note that this increase in dedicated tax revenue for Medicare would reduce the federal government's contribution from the general operating budget to Medicare by hundreds of billions of dollars annually. That will help eliminate the need for other tax hikes to close the budget deficit. Even more important, it moves Medicare closer to being what people think it should be by bringing the costs and the benefits of the program more closely into alignment.

In terms of long-term debt reduction, these changes would do more than any other proposal in this book or any proposed by anyone in the political arena. The extra dedicated tax revenue would immediately eliminate nearly 40 percent of the $85.6 trillion unfunded liability for a debt reduction in the range of $30 trillion. As some employees defer their Medicare benefits in exchange for lower taxes, additional savings would materialize, probably in the range of $10 trillion $15 trillion in long-term savings. Workers who deferred their benefits might stay on an employer's health care plan a bit longer or use some of their savings to find other interim insurance. But it would be their choice and would contribute to improving the financial condition of the Medicare system.

The rest of the unfunded liability would have to be eliminated by taking steps to reduce the cost of providing medical care. As noted earlier in the chapter, the savings would be generated by carving out safe areas for the use of free market competition to drive costs down. Those with chronic conditions, those living in poverty, those who are near the end of their life, and other vulnerable Americans would be protected. They, like all Americans, would also benefit from the general reduction in medical-care prices. Over time, the cost savings could well prove significant enough to trim the Medicare payroll tax as well.

Instituting competition requires far more than just having government regulators step out of the way. That's the kind of approach that leads to debacles such as the financial industry meltdown. Instituting real competition requires breaking the damaging alliance between Big Government and Big Business. It means giving individual consumers more power over their own medical-care choices. In practical terms, this means shifting the decision making in medical care away from employers, insurance companies, and government bureaucrats.

The steps outlined in this chapter that address Medicare directly include:

- Requiring voter approval for any changes in Medicare.
- Making the Medicare trust fund real rather than merely a promise from the federal government.
- Allowing those over sixty-five the chance to opt out of Medicare.

- Giving workers the right to trade off lower taxes for a higher retirement age.
- Insuring the short-term solvency of the Medicare program by raising the payroll tax over several years. The mandatory portion of the tax for a worker would go from 1.45 percent of payroll today to 3.95 percent in a few years. This tax increase would be offset by a larger tax cut in the Social Security program, leaving workers with a net cut in their mandatory payroll taxes.
- Funding all Medicare expenses out of trust fund revenues. This would eliminate the hundreds of billions of dollars annually that the federal government contributes to Medicare from the operating budget.

The Medicare changes would be supplemented by other efforts to reduce the overall cost of medical care:

- Removing antitrust protection for health insurance companies.
- Allowing businesses and individuals to buy health insurance coverage across state lines.
- Enabling all consumers to have more control of their health care expenditures by letting them select their own insurance coverage with their employer's health care program. If workers choose a less expensive program, they could keep the change.
- Eliminating barriers to choice in the federal tax code by treating all health care expenditures the same.
- Allowing consumers to buy the health insurance plans offered to Congress, state legislators, and other government workers.
- Allowing individuals to choose among a variety of insurance coverage options including policies that cover different medical procedures and those with various mixes of premiums and deductibles.
- Encourage competition among the states to address issues such as tort reform, authority of nurse-practitioners, conflicts of interest, and more.

- Each state could select either a statewide single-payer system, maintenance of the status quo with federal regulations, or a consumer-driven model that (among other things) lets every citizen buy insurance policies across state lines.

States that pursue additional competition would likely take the lead in developing new, low-cost, and high-quality methods of delivering medical-care services. Whether it's finding the right balance in tort reform, determining how much authority is appropriate for various caregivers, or encouraging the natural trend toward more home health monitoring, the "laboratories of democracy" will determine in the real world what works and what doesn't.

This approach has the added benefit of acknowledging that the so-called health care debate in Washington is not really about health care. It's about how to finance the status quo for one segment of the health care industry. That segment is huge—the delivery of specialized medical care—and hugely important, but there's still more to health care than questions about how to pay for the current system. Just about all Americans recognize that regular exercise improves their health, but memberships to exercise clubs are not covered by insurance or included in the health care debate. As mentioned earlier, some Americans would benefit more from an improved diet rather than more medical care. These are the type of trade-offs that are ignored in the current debate and can be made only by individuals.

Besides, the posturing in Washington about funding the status quo system of delivering care misses the most important point in the entire debate. The status quo is the problem. As with national security and Social Security, the solutions to Medicare funding require finding broad policies that align with voter expectations and make sense standing alone. Voters can embrace a Protect America First military strategy because it makes sense to them, not just because it reduces spending and helps the economy. The same can be said about letting voters select their own retirement age as a way to address the Social Security challenges.

There is no value in cutting the budget just to keep the accountants and the bondholders happy.

The challenges in funding Medicare are far greater. They require strengthening both the short-term financing of the program and the long-term dedicated-funding commitments so that promises made by the government can be honored. It requires making the Medicare trust funds real and protecting them from the federal government. It also requires aggressive steps to break the stranglehold of the large insurance companies and other health care providers allied with the federal government. Whenever Big Government and Big Business work together, it's bad for the rest of us. Ultimately, while the details of the Medicare fix are different, the solution is to shift power away from politicians and bureaucrats so that individuals can have more control over their own lives.

6

———•———

How Voters Would
Fix the Tax System

Many years ago I saw a cartoon sketch of a teenaged boy with his electric guitar standing in front of a full wall of amplifiers and other equipment searching for just the right sound. His father, listening from just a few feet away in a comfortable chair, looked puzzled as his son proudly proclaimed, "Dad, I finally got it to sound just like an acoustic!" Obviously, it would have been much easier to just buy an acoustic guitar rather than buying all kinds of digital bells and whistles to try to approximate the sound of one.

It was worth a laugh in a guitar magazine, but it's not so funny when our nation's political leaders take a similar course on tax policy. On taxes, politicians seek to make the simple complex and hope that in many cases it's just plain impossible to understand. They do this because they know that, if they were honest, voters wouldn't let them get away with their schemes.

For voters, the issue is simple: sixty-four percent believe that the United States is overtaxed.[1] That's the reason every winning presidential candidate for the past forty years has been the candidate most credible on

———

1. Rasmussen Reports, "64% Say Americans Are Overtaxed, Political Class Disagrees," Apr. 2011.

the issue of cutting taxes. It's the reason President Obama campaigned in 2008 on a promise to cut taxes for 95 percent of Americans, and why he later agreed to extend the Bush administration's tax cuts.

Three out of four voters believe average Americans should pay 20 percent or less of their income in taxes.[2] To reach that goal would require quite a tax cut since we're currently paying about 28 percent of our income in taxes.[3] Most Americans consistently believe that tax cuts are good for the economy, and only about one in four hold the opposite view.[4] Any effort to align government policy with voter preferences must address this core fact and lead to lower taxes over time. In a government that claims to derive its just authority from the consent of the governed, there is no other choice.

No matter how the topic is presented, the resistance to higher taxes is a key defining feature of America's political landscape:

- Sixty-eight percent prefer a government with fewer services and lower taxes. Just 22 percent want more services and higher taxes.[5]
- Seventy-one percent are unwilling to pay higher taxes to help reduce the federal budget deficit.[6]
- When the *New York Times* reported that "economists across the political spectrum say a consumption tax may be inevitable,"[7] just 22 percent of voters supported the idea. Sixty-five percent were opposed.[8]
- When the Federal Trade Commission (FTC) recommended taxes to help the struggling newspaper industry, 84 percent opposed a tax on monthly cell phone bills; 76 percent opposed a tax on the

2.   Rasmussen Reports, "74% Say They Should Pay No More Than 20% of Their Income in Taxes," Apr. 2011.

3.   Kail M. Padgitt, "Tax Freedom Day Arrives on April 12," 2011.

4.   Rasmussen Reports, "Most Voters Still Think Tax Cuts, Spending Decreases Benefit Economy," June 2011.

5.   Rasmussen Reports, "68% Prefer a Government with Fewer Services, Lower Taxes," Jan. 2011.

6.   Rasmussen Reports, "20% Would Pay Higher Taxes to Reduce Deficit," Mar. 2011.

7.   Catherine Rampell, "Many See the VAT Option as a Cure for Deficits," Dec. 2009.

8.   Rasmussen Reports, "National Sales Tax Still Unpopular," Mar. 2010.

purchase of consumer electronic items such as computers, iPads, and Kindles; and 74 percent opposed a tax on websites such as the Drudge Report.[9]

- When Transportation Secretary Ray LaHood proposed a mileage tax, 73 percent of Americans were opposed.[10]

The list could go on and on. No matter what new tax is suggested and no matter what the purpose, the American people say no. That's problematic for a Political Class that views government as the center of the nation, if not the universe. As the tax issue became dominant in the 2011 debt-ceiling debate, a senior editor at the *New Republic* articulated the frustration felt by many in the Political Class: "The [sad] irony here is that nobody in Washington is talking about seriously expanding government right now." Jonathan Cohn lamented that even if all the Bush tax cuts are allowed to expire and a massive middle-class tax hike is imposed on an unwilling nation, "We'd still have a lower tax burden than our European counterparts."[11] Think about that. Even if taxes were raised to the highest level in American history, Cohn is concerned that our taxes would still be too low!

Washington Post blogger Ezra Klein expressed the smug assumption of the Political Class in a post claiming the only way to "have a serious conversation about taxes" is to talk about hiking them: "We cannot fund anything close to the government's commitments if we don't raise taxes."[12] He then quoted other longtime DC insiders about the impossibility of cutting spending. Inadvertently, Klein's column highlights the similarity in the way today's Political Class views the American people and the way the British government viewed the American colonies in the prerevolutionary era.

In 1765, the British imposed the massively unpopular Stamp Act

9.   Rasmussen Reports, "74% Oppose Taxing Internet News Sites to Help Newspapers," June 2010.

10. Rasmussen Reports, "Americans Strongly Reject Mileage Tax, Gas Tax Hike," Mar. 2011.

11. Jonathan Cohn, "John Boehner Is Wrong: Bigger Government Goes with Bigger People. Just Ask the Dutch," July 2011.

12. Ezra Klein, "One Shot on Taxes: Don't Blow it, Democrats," Aug. 2011.

while George Grenville was prime minister. After the protests erupted, Grenville expressed his frustration:

> *Protection and obedience are reciprocal. Great Britain protects America; America is bound to yield obedience. . . . When they want the protection of this kingdom, they are always very ready to ask it. That protection has always been afforded them in the most full and ample manner . . . Now, when they are called upon to contribute a small share toward the public expense—an expense arising from themselves—they renounce your authority, insult your officers, and break out, I might almost say, into open rebellion.*[13]

Just like the Political Class today, the man who imposed the Stamp Act on the colonies thought he was just being rational. In his arrogance, he assumed the colonies could never defend themselves without the British. Therefore, in his view, they should pay for it. The colonial view was different and led to riots filled with cries of "No taxation without representation!" Grenville was not amused: "Ungrateful people of America! Bounties have been extended to them."

Perhaps it was a blessing that Grenville did not live long enough to see the Declaration of Independence. What he saw as protections and bounties was described by Jefferson as sending "swarms of Officers to harass our people and eat out their substance." The document complained that the British "kept among us, in times of peace, Standing Armies without the Consent of our legislatures" and also mentioned a problem with "quartering large bodies of armed troops among us." Just like the Political Class today, Grenville couldn't grasp that the benefits he offered cost more than the price Americans were willing to pay. In fact, some of what Grenville considered benefits were seen as burdens by those on the receiving end. That same dynamic continues today, and it was captured best in Ronald Reagan's line about the most frightening

---

13.   William Jennings Bryan, ed., *The World's Famous Orations* (1906).

words in the English language: "I'm from the government and I'm here to help."

It's also worth noting another perspective from England in the prerevolutionary era. William Pitt debated Grenville and acknowledged, "The Americans have not acted in all things with prudence and temper."[14] That was true then and it certainly applies to today's unrest with politics and politicians as well, but Pitt put it in context by saying the colonists "have been wronged: they have been driven to madness by injustice." Who in Washington today is willing to admit that it is the very actions of the Political Class that have provoked the American people?

The deeply held voter belief that the United States is overtaxed clashes with the Political Class's lust for more government revenue and illuminates a central tension between the American people and their political leaders. Trying to honor voter demands for lower taxes should be a foundational objective of all participants in the budget debate. Instead, politicians routinely seek ways to ignore the voters and pursue their own agenda.

Advocates of higher taxes are correct in stating that the US collects a smaller share of its income in taxes than other developed nations around the world, but that's hardly a reason for raising taxes to European levels. It's like the argument little kids use when their parents say no: "But, Mom, everyone else is doing it." The answer from grown-ups to children always points out the absurdity of making bad choices just because somebody else is doing it, too.

Sometimes, like Grenville long ago, the Political Class claims that voters want more government than they are willing to pay for. It's a good line, but it's not true. As shown in the preceding three chapters, and throughout the rest of this book, the American people are quite willing to trim the size of government starting with reasonable and thoughtful changes in national security, Social Security, and Medicare. A more accurate description of the dynamic is to note that the Political Class wants

---

14.   Ibid.

more government than Mainstream Americans are willing to pay for. That's why 79 percent of Mainstream voters think Americans are over-taxed, and 87 percent of those who support the Political Class disagree.[15]

Stats like those are the reason politicians try to muddy the waters with talk of revenue-enhancing reforms, closing loopholes, marginal rates, regressive structures, LIFO accounting rules, and more. They'd rather talk about anything besides their desire for higher taxes. Voters opposing tax hikes are viewed as a problem to work around rather than as the boss sending a message. It's frightening that so many politicians and activists place a higher priority on getting more money for the government than on honoring the clearly expressed desires of the American people. It's just another case of the Political Class wanting to take us back to 1775 while the American people are looking to the future.

Despite the strong voter belief that the nation is overtaxed, American voters would probably be willing to pay a small tax hike to clean up the mess made by their politicians. It's not that they like the idea; it's just that they don't want to pass on a burden to their children and grandchildren. Still, even that support for modest tax hikes is possible only if voters are convinced that the extra revenue would be used for deficit reduction rather than new spending, that government spending had really been cut as much as possible, and that a temporary tax hike is absolutely needed to bring the nation's books in balance. Those are difficult conditions to meet when most Americans believe that if taxes are raised to reduce the federal deficit, the new tax money will not be used for deficit reduction. Sixty-two percent believe the new revenue would be spent instead on new government programs.[16]

That's why polls sometimes show the appearance of early support for deficit reduction plans that include tax hikes and why that support fades as the details become clear. People like the idea of a compromise to move everyone forward, but they don't believe the politicians will de-

---

15.   Rasmussen Reports, "64% Say Americans Are Overtaxed, Political Class Disagrees," Apr. 2011.

16.   Rasmussen Reports, "If Taxes Hiked to Reduce Deficit, 62% Think It Will Be Spent on New Pro-grams," Sep. 2011.

liver on their promises. It is just about impossible to overstate the level of skepticism voters bring to this debate.

When President Obama's deficit commission issued its report, many voters indicated that a mix of spending cuts and tax hikes could be part of the solution. Forty-three percent thought only spending cuts should be considered, while 44 percent said a mix of spending cuts and tax increases should be on the table.[17] But they clearly wanted the over-whelming majority of the deficit reduction to come from spending cuts. However, when all was said and done, the particular mix didn't really matter. Only 30 percent thought Congress was likely to actually make any spending cuts proposed by the deficit commission. At the same time, 78 percent thought it likely that Congress would implement the tax hikes proposed by the commission.[18]

The same dynamic was found in the 2011 debacle surrounding the debt ceiling. The president promoted a "balanced" mix of tax hikes and spending cuts and said only corporations and the wealthy would pay the higher taxes. Congressional Republicans claimed to want all deficit re-duction to come from spending cuts. Yet, voters feared that taxes would go up too much and spending would not be cut enough. Three-fourths of all voters said it was likely that the result would be higher taxes for the middle class.[19]

The skepticism is part of every political discussion. Voters have learned over the years that when politicians get together, taxes are likely to go up. That's why the old line warns, "Congress is in session, better hang on to your wallet." Politicians do promise spending cuts all the time, but voters have learned that they deserve all the credibility of a six-year-old boy caught with his hand in the cookie jar and promising to be good for the rest of his life.

Weak as their credibility is on the spending side, voters have even less

---

17. Rasmussen Reports, "Americans Say Congress More Likely to Raise Taxes Than Cut Spending If Deficit Commission Recommends It," Apr. 2010.
18. Rasmussen Reports, "Voters Skeptical About Spending Cuts in Debt Ceiling Debate," July 2011.
19. Rasmussen Reports, "75% See Middle Class Tax Hikes as Likely in Debt Ceiling Debate," July 2011.

trust in politicians when it comes to taxes. Many Americans still remember the first president Bush, who campaigned on a clear message: "Read my lips, no new taxes." But once in office he forgot the promise, raised taxes, and was then voted out of office. One of the constants throughout history is the tendency of governments and taxes to grow and to never be satisfied with their share of the pie. Whether kings rule or elected politicians, wars and crises have always been an excuse for more taxes. Somehow, when the crisis ends, the taxes always remain higher than they were when the problem began.

A *Hagar the Horrible* cartoon captured the attitude beautifully. It showed big, strong tax collectors approaching Hagar and the other Vikings. They acknowledged how difficult it was for people to pay their taxes after paying for food, shelter, and clothing. So, to address the problem, the king had decided that people should pay their taxes first.

Adding to the problem, temporary taxes have a habit of becoming permanent. An Alabama tax first installed to pay pension benefits for Civil War soldiers is still being collected in the twenty-first century, decades after the last Confederate soldier in the state died.[20] After the Johnstown Flood in 1936, a temporary one-year tax was passed charging 10 percent on the sale of all alcohol. It was extended temporarily for fifteen years before being made permanent. That permanent tax is now at 18 percent.[21]

An *Investor's Business Daily* column claims, "The granddaddy of the temporary tax zombies is the telephone excise tax. It was enacted in 1898 to finance the Spanish-American War, and supposedly died in 2007, but the government is scheduled to collect $2.3 billion over the next five years. During its inglorious history as a revenue generator, taxpayers have paid $360 billion (inflation-adjusted) in telephone taxes." The article, by Sam Batkins and Douglas Holtz-Eakin of the American Action Forum, noted, "There are five excise taxes that were instituted generations ago that have failed to expire. Together, the gas, telephone,

20.   "Ala. still collecting tax for Confederate vets," July 2010.
21.   Ann Gonzalez Ribeiro, "'Temporary' Taxes That Stuck," Feb. 2010.

tire, sports, and firearms tax have collected more than $1.4 trillion (adjusted for inflation) from taxpayers."[22]

That track record makes it hard for politicians to win support for temporary tax hikes in the twenty-first century, so politicians have looked for other ways to divert attention from the voter belief that the nation is overtaxed. An old standby in the effort to distract attention from talk of lower taxes is class warfare. What is often unrecognized, however, is that both Republicans and Democrats in the Political Class resort to this technique. One of the most troublesome story lines to pop up in recent years has been based upon the fact that roughly half of all Americans don't pay any federal income tax.[23] On talk radio and other forums, this has morphed into a general class-warfare argument that only half the nation pays taxes. I can't begin to tell you how many times I've heard or read responses to Rasmussen Reports polling data that says something like "Well, the half who favor government programs are the half that don't pay any taxes."

The problem with this idea is that it's just plain wrong. While only about half the nation pays federal income taxes, the overwhelming majority pay a whole variety of taxes including state and local taxes, payroll taxes, sales taxes, property taxes, sin taxes, and more. Those who aren't paying federal income taxes don't consider themselves free from taxation; they still see too much money taken out of their paycheck and too much added on to everything they buy.

In addition to being wrong, attacking those who don't pay federal income taxes as if they don't pay any taxes at all is a particularly stupid political tactic. Opposition to tax hikes is stronger among lower- and middle-income Americans than it is among the upper-middle-class and wealthier Americans. Those with higher income are less resistant partly because they can always hire a good accountant to keep the tax burden down a bit, and partly because they can absorb the hit much easier than

---

22.   Sam Batkins and Douglas Holtz-Eakin, "Toll in 'Temporary' Taxes: $1.4 Trillion," July 2010.

23.   Rachel Johnson et al., *Why Some Tax Units Pay No Income Tax* (2011).

those who earn less. So, by attacking those who don't pay federal income taxes, advocates of lower taxes are attacking a big part of their constituency.

For conservatives who fashion themselves as followers of Ronald Reagan, it's also worth remembering that Reagan's 1986 tax reform removed 6 million lower-income Americans from the need to pay federal income taxes.[24] Reagan considered that feature an important part of the overall objective that ended up reducing the marginal tax rates for all Americans.

Of course, others play the class-warfare card at the opposite end of the spectrum and suggest that the answer to any revenue problem is to raise taxes on the rich. Such an approach taps into and reinforces an underlying belief that middle-class taxpayers pay a larger share of their income in taxes than those who are wealthy.[25] Besides, it's hard to feel sorry for those who make millions of dollars while millions are pinching pennies. This class warfare has some value for its practitioners, but its effectiveness has practical and political limits. Practically, there aren't enough rich people around to raise the kind of money needed to have a serious impact on the government's finances. So while the rhetoric is about those who own corporate jets, the legislation ends up targeting the middle class, too. Voters know this, so when politicians talk about raising taxes on the rich, most voters suspect that their own taxes will be heading up, too.[26]

Another part of the political challenge is that, while voters want the wealthy to pay their fair share of the tax burden, few want to "soak the rich." Sixty-four percent of adults think the middle class pays a larger share of its income in taxes than wealthy Americans do.[27] No wonder they want the rich to pay more. That belief explains why the so-called

24. Ronald W. Reagan, "Radio Address to the Nation on Tax Reform," June 1987.
25. Rasmussen Reports, "64% Say Middle Class Americans Pay the Largest Share of Their Income in Taxes," Mar. 2011.
26. Rasmussen Reports, "75% See Middle Class Tax Hikes as Likely in Debt Ceiling Deal," July 2011.
27. Rasmussen Reports, "64% Say Middle Class Americans Pay the Largest Share of Their Income in Taxes," Mar. 2011.

Buffett rule resonated with so many people. It would be outrageous to design a tax code where a billionaire such as Buffett paid a lower tax rate than his secretary.

But that doesn't mean most voters want to impose punitive rates on those who earn more than they do. In fact, 69 percent of likely voters believe that if someone earns twice as much, they should pay twice as much in taxes. Only 13 percent believe that they should pay more than twice as much. This once again highlights the foundational belief of voters in treating everyone equally. They don't want special breaks for the wealthy, but they also aren't keen on special penalties. Further weakening the effectiveness of the class-warfare argument, many voters believe that raising taxes on the wealthy is bad for the economy.[28]

Put it all together and the argument about raising taxes on the rich splits the nation. Most would prefer an approach that cuts middle-class taxes. Still, when given a choice between one candidate who opposes all tax hikes and another who promises to raise taxes only on the rich, voters are fairly evenly divided.[29] During the 2010 election, the public was also evenly divided between extending the Bush tax cuts for all Americans and extending them for all but the wealthy.[30] At other times, a modest plurality prefers the candidate who would raise taxes only on the wealthy.[31]

Any discussion that splits the electorate on taxes is a tactical victory for the Political Class. Whether it's a discussion about taxing the rich or complaining about those who don't pay federal income taxes, the Political Class would rather talk about class warfare instead of addressing the 64 percent who believe the nation is overtaxed.

The Political Class is determined to talk about side issues because

---

28. Rasmussen Reports, "61% Favor Simpler Tax Code, but Have Doubts About Flat Tax Plans," Oct. 2011.

29. Rasmussen Reports, "45% Favor Candidate Who Promises to Only Raise Taxes on Wealthy, Highest Level in Over Two Years," Feb. 2011.

30. Rasmussen Reports, "Voters Still Give the Edge to Extending Bush Tax Cuts for All Taxpayers," Nov. 2010.

31. Rasmussen Reports, "47% Favor Candidate Who Raises Taxes on Wealthy over One Who Opposes All Tax Increases," Oct. 2011.

it recognizes that voters have firmly entrenched attitudes on taxes. As a result, those who favor lower taxes should have the edge in this debate. They do, but elected politicians claiming to advocate lower taxes often fumble away the advantage. Some elected politicians calling for lower taxes talk a good game about cutting spending in general, but fail to present any specific cuts that they can present to the voters. That undermines the credibility of their position on taxes. Simply put, any advocate for lower taxes should be willing to explain how they will bring government spending down to a level that the American people are willing to pay for. For those who say it's not possible, the proposals mentioned in the preceding three chapters accomplish that goal. The savings generated by a Protect America First strategy go a long way toward balancing the budget without any new or increased taxes. The proposals to let people select their own retirement age for Social Security and Medicare directly lead to lower taxes. The mandatory payroll tax would be cut from 15.3 percent today to 11.25 percent, while insuring the long-term solvency of both programs. Other measures will be mentioned later in the chapters that follow. In a nation where 68 percent prefer a government with fewer services and lower taxes, there is no excuse for anyone to advocate tax restraint without articulating spending cuts as well.[32]

But the Political Class has no interest in advocating either tax restraint or spending cuts. With this reality, and with the public's strong belief that the nation is overtaxed, it's necessary to think about protections that will prevent the politicians from keeping more dollars in taxes than they should. The most basic protection of all is a requirement that all tax hikes must be approved by the American people before they can be implemented. Fifty-seven percent of voters nationwide support this approach, and a referendum could be held in the same manner as described earlier for changes in Social Security and Medicare.[33] Politically,

32.   Rasmussen Reports, "68% Prefer a Government with Fewer Services, Lower Taxes," Jan. 2011.

33.   Rasmussen Reports, "53% Say Voter Approval Needed for Changes to Medicare and Social Security," Apr. 2010.

this should be equally easy to adopt. It requires only one person to implement so long as that person is the president of the United States. A candidate for president could simply make it clear that he or she would never sign a tax hike unless it was first approved by voters. Later, it might be a good idea to have that provision enshrined as a constitutional amendment, but it can be made effective without waiting.

A national referendum could solve the problem that some politicians face after signing a no-tax-hike pledge. These candidates are always under pressure to break their pledge in exchange for some deal that promises to bring down government spending. If a credible deal was really presented, these candidates would be able to let the people decide directly. Of course, it would be up to other politicians to figure out how to convince those voters that the promised spending cuts would actually happen. More likely, the requirement of a voter referendum would call the bluff of those who claim the American people are ready to pay higher taxes.

The notion of requiring voter approval for any tax hikes is consistent with our great national heritage of self-governance. When the Constitution was drafted, the House of Representatives was the only branch of government given the authority to initiate tax hikes. The thinking was that the House would be the branch closest to the people and, therefore, most resistant to taxes. That was true in the eighteenth and nineteenth centuries when congressional turnover averaged roughly 50 percent every election cycle. Today, however, it's safe to say that most members of Congress are more comfortable with the Political Class than Mainstream Americans. That's what happens when elected officials have more job security than a tenured college professor.

Voters overwhelmingly believe their so-called representatives listen more to party leaders and lobbyists than to voters in the district. Hardly any voters get to participate in a competitive election for a new representative, and only one in four believe their own representative is the best person for the job. The distrust leads 59 percent to conclude that most members of Congress routinely get reelected because election rules are rigged to benefit those already in power. Only 17 percent think incumbents get reelected because they do a good job representing their constituents.[34]

In this environment, politicians cannot be trusted to represent the views of the public on taxation. As recognized in the Constitution, controlling the power of the purse is essential to limiting the power of the government. All tax increases, at any level of government, should be approved by voters before they can be collected. That's common sense, popular with voters, and a logical extension of the rallying cry that founded the nation—"No taxation without representation." With today's technology and communications capabilities, there is absolutely no rational reason to keep voters out of the loop on the fundamental issue of how much they want to pay for government services.

Sometimes, the power of these procedural issues to protect voters is hard to envision. To get a sense of scale, all we have to do is go back to the 1960s and '70s when American politicians found a great way to have their cake and eat it, too. The tax code at the time was not indexed for inflation, so when people got raises to cover the cost of inflation, they were pushed into a higher tax bracket. This phenomenon, known as bracket creep, was extremely aggravating to most Americans, but a boon to politicians. Bracket creep enabled tax revenue to grow far faster than the economy year in and year out. Congress had so much extra money to spend that it could even afford to vote for "tax cuts" before just about every election. Of course, the tax cuts were never enough to fully offset the impact of bracket creep, so Congress had more money to spend while also being able to brag to voters about passing a tax cut.

Ronald Reagan put an end to all this political fun in 1981. As part of his tax reform package, he changed the rules so that income brackets in the tax code get adjusted every year for inflation. With this in place, government tax revenue continued to grow just about every year, but it no longer grew faster than the economy. For most Americans, this was a blessing. Never again would their taxes go up just because of inflation. For DC politicians, Reagan's reform meant the fun was over. It was one

---

34.   Rasmussen Reports, "Fewer Voters Than Ever Believe US Elections Are Fair," Aug. 2011.

of the first substantive challenges to the spendthrift culture of the 1960s and '70s and has had a substantial impact on reducing the growth of taxes over the past thirty years.

What's especially interesting about this brief trip down memory lane is that the indexing of the tax brackets is rarely discussed in the battle over Reagan's legacy. A lot of attention is paid to his initial plan that became the Kemp-Roth tax cuts, which cut income taxes 10 percent in the first year, 10 percent in the second, and 5 percent in the third. These cuts played a key role in reviving the economy and spurring economic growth that lasted for two decades, but in terms of lasting impact, it's hard to think of anything that changed the course of the nation's fiscal history as much as the lesser-known decision to index the income tax brackets.

In addition to requiring voter approval for tax hikes, more disclosure and transparency would also help protect taxpayers. A starting point could be to require employers to disclose all the payroll taxes they pay on behalf of their workers. Let the workers see the cost of local, state, and federal government on each and every paycheck. This becomes even more important in a system where the employer is paying a larger share of the Social Security and Medicare cost than their workers. Naturally, the smallest employers could be exempted, and provisions could be made for workers to see other costs as well including the cost of medical-care benefits.

A Taxpayer Disclosure Act could also give people an annual summary of each taxpayer's total tax bill from all levels of government. This would include federal income taxes, payroll taxes, state income taxes, property taxes, sales taxes, gasoline taxes, taxes paid by the employer, and whatever else we pay taxes on. Obviously, some of the figures would be estimates, and there could probably be a website where people could follow up and get a more precise handle on their own tax bill. This seems like a basic concept of good governance. Governments properly require private businesses to disclose all costs to customers, including hidden costs. The government should be required to do the same.

Finally, on a grander process issue, the topic of tax reform is a double-edged sword for voters. They like the concept but distrust those who would be called upon to implement it. Sixty-four percent think it's better to have lower tax rates and few deductions than to have higher rates and lots of deductions. Only 16 percent prefer higher tax rates and more deductions. That makes sense since higher rates and lower deductions gives the government more control over spending decisions. With fewer deductions, people can decide how to spend their own money without worrying about the tax implications.[35]

Americans are also fed up with special loopholes for companies and industries favored by the Political Class. This is consistent with voter desires to eliminate corporate welfare in all forms, as discussed in chapter 8. Two-thirds say it's more beneficial for the economy if the government treats all companies and industries on an equal basis. Only 21 percent disagree.

Just about everybody agrees that lower tax rates, fewer deductions, and the elimination of corporate loopholes would be good for the economy. Anything that gets the government out of deciding how people and corporations should spend their money is a step in the right direction. Plus, requiring everyone to pay the same rate addresses the broad middle-class concern that the rich are able to use loopholes to pay less than their fair share.

Still, while voters like the concept of tax reform, they are rightly skeptical when politicians from all across the political spectrum talk of tax reform as a way to get more money for the government. Like all other proposals that increase some taxes, any tax reform plan should be submitted to the voters before it can be implemented. It's too important an issue to leave to the politicians.

While a serious reform of the tax code is likely to help the economy, which would also help reduce the budget deficit, it should not be treated as a magic elixir that eliminates the need to cut government spending. Unfortunately, that's just what many politicians do. They say they'll balance the budget, never talk about serious spending cuts, and say that

---

35.   Rasmussen Reports, "64% Favor Lower Tax Rates with Fewer Deductions," Aug. 2011.

tax reform will let the genie of economic growth solve all the problems without raising anyone's tax rate.

A better approach, consistent with voter preferences for less government spending, is to implement reductions in spending like those described throughout this book. That will help spur economic growth by eliminating the debt burden, restoring confidence, and shifting more resources to the private sector. Tax reform can be added to the mix, but it is not a substitute for the serious work of aligning federal spending with popular opinion.

Then, as the economy grows, the American people are clear that any extra revenue that comes in from economic growth should be used for debt reduction. Once there's a surplus, 80 percent say that the surplus should first be used to pay down whatever remains of the $100 trillion debt accumulated by the government during earlier times. No new spending programs and no tax cuts. Pay down the debt.

In terms of the budget debate, the tax issue is simple. Sixty-four percent of voters believe that the nation is overtaxed. Any plan that respects the will of the people must put the nation on a long-term path to lower taxes. The proposals for allowing individual workers to select their own Social Security and Medicare retirement age accomplish that goal.

Additionally, it's important to remember that voters are concerned with out-of-control government spending and see tax restraint as a tool to enforce spending restraint. That context needs to be explained again and again and again. Without it, there is no rationale for simply opposing tax hikes.

This is part of a larger problem that plagues advocates of limited government. They put all their focus on a side issue—the size of government—and fail to recognize that people don't really care about limited government or big government or anything about government. The government is merely one institution among many that makes a self-governing society work. It's a means to an end. What voters care about is the society and the world they live in. If limited government is part of a vibrant and free society that is generally fair and decent, people will love it. If a larger government threatens those benefits, people will hate it, but the focus should always be on addressing the larger goals first and explaining how limited government or lower taxes will help achieve those goals.

The key policy reform on taxes is simple. Before any tax hike can be implemented, it should be approved by voters. That should be supported by a more complete disclosure of how much individual Americans are paying in taxes. The Political Class won't like either approach because they are annoyed by ongoing public resistance to tax hikes, but the country is not here to serve the Political Class, the Political Class should be here to serve the nation.

7

---•---

How Voters Want to Be Generous

While voters are quite generous when it comes to helping those in need, just 20 percent believe that the array of welfare programs reduce the nation's level of poverty. Highlighting just how big the gap is between policymakers and the nation, 49 percent of American adults believe that the government programs increase the level of poverty.[1] As on so many other issues, the Political Class and Mainstream voters disagree. Most who support the Political Class think welfare programs reduce poverty, while most in the Mainstream do not.

One reason voters are skeptical is that official government figures for measuring poverty show virtually no change in poverty over the past forty-five years.[2] Even more dubious, the official figures show that the economically disastrous year of 1973 had the lowest level of poverty recorded since Lyndon Johnson's War on Poverty began in 1964. If those figures reflected reality, and if there were truly no improvement after decades of spending trillions of dollars, voters would rightly demand to shut down all the government's antipoverty efforts. After all, even after adjusting for inflation, the nation spends five times as much for each

---

1. Rasmussen Reports, "Only 20% Think Government Anti-Poverty Programs Really Work," Aug. 2011.
2. Nicholas Eberstadt, "Poverty Rate," 2008.

person in or near poverty today as we did in the 1960s.[3] Shouldn't we expect to see something for all that money?

The reality is that many programs have had an impact, but we don't have good ways to define or measure the effectiveness and celebrate the successes. The official government definition of poverty was established in 1965 based on a rule of thumb about the ratio of food costs as a share of income. This approach has several problems, including that the ratio selected was inappropriate for low-income Americans. Additionally, data show that low-income Americans typically spend far more income than the Census Bureau says they have. Part of this comes because the Census Bureau does not count food stamps and the Earned Income Tax Credit when measuring income. Other factors are involved as well.

Such a poor measure was established at a time when many of those involved in launching the War on Poverty wanted to come up with a number that showed massive numbers of Americans living in poverty. To do so, they created a measure that defines many Americans as poor even though their lifestyle does not match what Americans think of as living in poverty.

Currently, about 40 million Americans are officially defined as living below the poverty line. Yet most of those have adequate levels of food, shelter, clothing, and medical care. Sixty-three percent of American adults believe such a family is not living in poverty. The average American living in what is officially defined as poverty enjoys more living space than the average European family.[4] Only 16 percent believe that a family is living in poverty if it has two color televisions, cable or satellite TV, a DVD player, and a VCR. However, the average family living in poverty—as defined by the US government—has those items.[5]

None of this is to suggest that lower-income families are living a life

3.   Ron Haskins, "Fighting Poverty the American Way," June 2011.
4.   Robert Rector and Rachel Sheffield, "Understanding Poverty in the United States: Surprising Facts About America's Poor," Sep. 2011.
5.   Rasmussen Reports, "Many See Those in 'Poverty' as Not So Poor," Aug. 2011.

Amenities in Poor Households

Percent of Poor Households Which Have Each Item

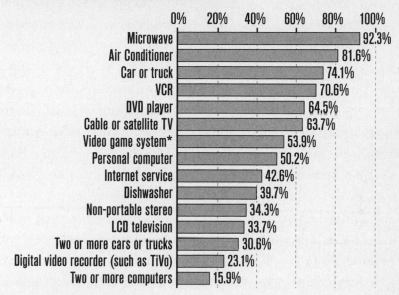

Microwave	92.3%
Air Conditioner	81.6%
Car or truck	74.1%
VCR	70.6%
DVD player	64.5%
Cable or satellite TV	63.7%
Video game system*	53.9%
Personal computer	50.2%
Internet service	42.6%
Dishwasher	39.7%
Non-portable stereo	34.3%
LCD television	33.7%
Two or more cars or trucks	30.6%
Digital video recorder (such as TiVo)	23.1%
Two or more computers	15.9%

*Among families with children in 2005

Sources: US Department of Energy. Residential Energy Consumption Survey, 2009, at http://www.eia.doe.gov/emeu/recs/ (June 22, 2011), and US Department of Housing and Urban Development and US Census Bureau, *American Housing Survey for the United States: 2009*, at http://www.census.gov/prod/2011pubs/ h150-09.pdf (September 8, 2011).

of ease, but it does show that what the government defines as poverty is vastly different from what most Americans envision. If the measuring tool doesn't make sense, it's hard to measure effectiveness or success.

Besides the fact that the official government measure of poverty is essentially worthless, another factor should be considered in determining why voters don't think government antipoverty programs reduce poverty. That's because most of those programs are not intended to reduce poverty. They are designed to help those who somehow slip through the cracks of the economy and need temporary or special assistance. Certainly, someone who has been helped with a good meal is in better shape to find a job and get that first step back on the ladder of success, but the meal is to combat hunger, not to reduce the level of poverty itself.

This is an important distinction. It is one thing to combat poverty, and another to battle with its symptoms. A doctor does not target merely the fever, but the disease itself. Still, it is often important to keep the fever down while dealing with the underlying issues. And no matter how much is done to reduce poverty in America, some will always slip through the cracks and need help. Sadly, poverty seems to be a part of the human condition.

Some of the confusion is intentional. Many of the initial activists in the War on Poverty had grandiose ambitions to do more than address poverty; they wanted a fundamental redistribution of income in America. Even today, of course, some reject the American way of hard work and self-sufficiency. For example, a surprisingly large body of research exists about granting people the right *not* to work.[6]

I thought ideas like that had faded away with the 1960s and '70s. However, some university professors and others today advocate providing every member of a society with a basic income grant sufficient to live a modest life. Nobody would have to work for that grant, but those who want to work could do so without the pressure of needing to provide for themselves or a family. Perhaps the objective might be to find work that is more satisfying, if less financially rewarding. Just about all Americans think people have the right *not* to work. But hardly anybody thinks that those who choose not to work have the right to demand financial support from others. Only 11 percent support the notion of providing every citizen with a basic income grant, whether or not they choose to work.[7]

Out of this confusing discussion arose a bewildering array of government and charitable programs to try to help those truly in need, even if we can't figure out how many people are in that situation. Robert Rector of the Heritage Foundation has found, "The means-tested welfare

6. Philip Harvey, "The Right to Work and Basic Income Guarantees: Competing or Complementary Goals?"
7. Rasmussen Reports, "11% Think Government Should Provide Basic Income Grant for All," Sep. 2011.

system consists of 69 federal programs providing cash, food, housing, medical care, social services, training, and targeted aid to the poor and low income Americans."[8] Spending on these programs will be about $940 billion in 2011, a figure that rivals the total for defense spending and veterans' affairs. More is spent on these means-tested programs than the total amount spent by local, state, and federal governments on education for 50 million K–12 students. It also tops the amount spent on Social Security or Medicare.

The total includes $695 billion paid directly by the federal government with the remaining quarter of a trillion dollars coming from state government spending. Rector notes, "In recent years, 52% of total means tested spending went to medical care for poor and lower-income Americans, and 37% was spent on cash, food, and housing aid. The remaining 11% was spent on social services, training, child development, targeted federal education aid, and community development for lower-income persons and communities." A list of the sixty-nine programs is provided on the next page.

All told, these programs work out to a cost of $3,000 for every man, woman, and child in America or $12,000 for a family of four.

That funding is supplemented by large amounts of charitable giving. According to a report by the Giving USA Foundation, Americans gave $291 billion to charity in 2011. Seventy-three percent of that total, $212 billion, came from individuals.[9] Additionally, according to the Independent Sector, more than 60 million people contributed $169 billion in volunteer time during 2009. Put it all together and private sector giving reached two-thirds of all federal welfare spending.[10]

Of all the giving, 35 percent went to religious organizations, 14 percent to education, 9 percent directly to human services, 8 percent for health organizations, and another 8 percent for public-society benefits

8. Robert Rector, "Uncovering the Hidden Welfare State: 69 Means-Tested Programs and $940 Billion in Annual Spending," Aug. 2011.

9. Giving USA Foundation, *Giving USA 2011: The Annual Report on Philanthropy for the Year 2010.*

10. Corporation for National and Community Service, "Research Brief: Volunteering in America Research Highlights," 2010, http://independentsector.org/volunteer_time.

Spending on Means-Tested Programs
Fiscal Year 2008

In Millions of Dollars

Program	Federal Spending	State Spending	Total Spending
SSI/Old Age Assistance	43,872	5,146	49,018
Earned Income Tax Credit (Refundable Portion)	40,600		40,600
Child Credit (Refundable Portion)	34,019		34,019
AFDC/TANF	7,889	7,582	15,471
Foster Care Title IV-E	4,525	4,040	8,565
Adoption Assistance, Title IV-E	2,038	1,316	3,354
General Assistance Cash		2,625	2,625
General Assistance to Indians	118		118
Assets for Independence	24		24
Medicaid	201,426	150,667	352,093
SCHIP—State Supplemental Health Insurance Program	6,900	2,021	8,921
Medical General Assistance		4,900	4,900
Indian Health Services	2,925		2,925
Consolidated Health Centers/ Community Health Centers	2,021		2,021
Maternal and Child Health	666	500	1,166
Healthy Start	100		100
Food Stamps	39,319	3,482	42,801
School Lunch	7,863		7,863
WIC—Women, Infant, and Children Food Program	6,170		6,170
School Breakfast	2,307		2,307
Child Care Food Program	2,029		2,029
Nutrition Program for the Elderly, Nutrition Service Incentives	756	106	862
Summer Program	312		312
Commodity Supplemental Food Program	141		141
TFAP—The Emergency Food Assistance Program	190		190
Needy Families	54		54
Farmers' Market Nutrition Program	20		20
Special Milk Program	15		15
Section 8 Housing (HUD)	24,467		24,467
Public Housing (HUD)	7,526		7,526

Program	Federal Spending	State Spending	Total Spending
State Housing Expenditures		2,085	2,085
Home Investment Partnership Program (HUD)	1,969		1,969
Homeless Assistance Grants	1,440		1,440
Rural Housing Insurance Fund (Agriculture)	1,312		1,312
Rural Housing Service (Agriculture)	926		926
Housing for the Elderly (HUD)	1,008		1,008
Native American Housing Block Grants (HUD)	572		572
Other Assisted Housing Programs	584		584
Housing for Persons with Disabilities (HUD)	320		320
LIHEAP—Low Income Home Energy Assistance	2,663		2,663
Universal Service Fund—Subsidized Phone Service for Low-Income Persons	819		819
Weatherization	291	159	450
Pell Grants	18,000		18,000
Title One Grants to Local Education Authorities	14,872		14,872
Special Programs for Disadvantaged (TRIO)	885		885
Supplemental Education Opportunity Grants	759		759
Migrant Education	425		425
Gear Up	303		303
Education for Homeless Children and Youth	64		64
LEAP, formerly State Student Incentive Grant Program (SSIG)	64	64	128
Even Start	66		66
TANF Work Activities and Training	1,964	540	2,504
Job Corps	763		763
WIA Youth Opportunity Grants (formerly Summer Youth Employment)	984		984
WIA Adult Employment and Training (formerly JTPA IIA Training for Disadvantaged Adults & Youth)	827		827
Senior Community Service Employment	483	53	536
Food Stamp Employment and Training Program	351	166	517
Migrant Training	83		83
YouthBuild	60		60
Native American Training	53		53
TANF Block Grant Services	5,704	1,383	7,087
Title XX Social Services Block Grant	1,843		1,843

(*continued on next page*)

Program	Federal Spending	State Spending	Total Spending
Community Service Block Grant	654		654
Social Services for Refugees, Asylees, and Humanitarian Cases	592		592
Title III Aging Americans Act	351		351
Legal Services Block Grant	346		346
Family Planning	300		300
Emergency Food and Shelter Program	154		154
Healthy Marriage and Responsible Fatherhood Grants	150		150
Americorps/Volunteers in Service to America	93		93
Headstart	6,877	1,719	8,596
Childcare and Child Development Block Grant	4,164	2,176	6,340
TANF Block Grant Child Care	1,736	1,045	2,781
Community Development Block Grant	7,849		7,849
Economic Development Administration (Commerce)	238		238
Appalachian Regional Development	74		74
Empowerment Zones, Enterprise Communities, Renewal Communities	17		17
UDAG—Urban Development Block Grant	3		3

Source: The Heritage Foundation, from current and previous presidential budget and OMB documents, and other historical data from official government agency websites and resources.

such as United Way. Eleven percent went to foundations for later distribution, 5 percent for international concerns such as the crisis in Haiti, and 2 percent went directly to individuals. The balance went to arts, culture, and humanities programs (5%) and environmental or animal-related concerns (2%). This funding provides employment for 13 million people in the nonprofit sector.

It's not just the amount of money and time that is significant. Seventy-five percent have confidence that their contributions will be used effectively.[11] That's quite different from the 20 percent who believe government antipoverty programs have actually reduced poverty. That may be one reason that, to be a good citizen, 66 percent say it's more im-

---

11.   Rasmussen Reports, "More Americans Plan on Giving to Charity This Year," Dec. 2010.

portant to do volunteer work for church and community organizations than it is to get involved in politics and political campaigns.[12]

With all that activity, 45 percent of voters say the federal government is now spending too much on welfare and other programs to help those in financial need. Just 25 percent say too little is being spent, and those figures come at a time when the economy has been at its weakest point in generations.[13]

They also come at an interesting time in relation to the federal budget. It is common sense to recognize that when the economy gets worse, more people will need financial assistance either from the government, from charitable organizations, or from family and friends. The reverse of that is also easy to grasp: when the economy gets better, fewer people should need such help. But under current budget plans produced by the Obama administration, spending on means-tested programs is slated to continue growing dramatically even after the recession comes to an end. Part of that comes from provisions affecting Medicaid in the president's health care law and partly from a desire to revise the official definition of poverty so that more people are eligible.

It's important to note that, even before the recession, spending on means-tested government programs had grown rapidly. Rector found, "For the past two decades, means tested welfare or aid to the poor has been the fastest growing component of government spending, outstripping the combined growth of Medicare and Social Security spending, as well as the growth in education and defense spending."[14]

So, government spending on means-tested programs grew rapidly before the recession, grew even more during the recession, and is projected to keep growing after the recession. As in so many other aspects of the federal budget, the plans of the government are heading in the opposite direction from the preferences of the American people. An overwhelm-

12.   Rasmussen Reports, "57% Would Rather Be Called Good Citizen Than a Patriot," June 2011.
13.   Rasmussen Reports, "62% Prefer Minimum Wage States Jobs as an Alternative to Welfare," Sep. 2011.
14.   Robert Rector, "Uncovering the Hidden Welfare State: 69 Means-Tested Programs and $940 Billion in Annual Spending," Aug. 2011.

ing 71 percent believe that too many people are receiving welfare who should not be eligible. Only 18 percent have the opposite concern.[15] That suggests a desire to reduce spending on such programs and offers an idea for how to get there: tighten the official measures of poverty to reduce the number of eligible recipients.

To drive this process, Rector has a reasonable proposal to treat all sixty-nine means-tested programs as a single budget category and then put limits to how much the spending can grow for all sixty-nine. Such an approach would highlight six broad categories of federal spending: national defense, Social Security, Medicare, means-tested welfare programs, interest, and everything else. That has the added benefit of bringing clarity to the overall budget and helping people understand where the money goes.

To stay within the limits on spending growth for all means-tested programs will require a lot of effort to ensure that those most in need don't get hurt. It may require using money more effectively to get better results. For example, the United States currently spends around $31 billion on preschool programs. Ron Haskins of the Brookings Institution notes that some of this money has funded programs producing a lasting impact on school performance. He adds, "Unfortunately, a substantial portion of that money is being spent on preschool programs without an educational focus or on Head Start (about $7 billion in 2010), which has been shown to have almost no impacts by the end of first grade."[16] In the current budget process, all programs fight for their own funding. If all means-tested programs are treated as a single budget item, choices would have to be made and less effective programs would be reduced or eliminated. This would free up funding for better programs while also providing a means to reduce the overall growth in spending. In some cases, the federal government will also have to seek help from the states, such as considering approaches recommended by governors on joint federal-state programs such as Medicaid.

---

15.   Rasmussen Reports, "71% Say Too Many People Get Welfare Who Shouldn't," Aug. 2011.
16.   Ron Haskins, "Fighting Poverty the American Way," June 2011.

But, ultimately, a big part of the solution will come from defining who is eligible to receive payments from the vast array of means-tested programs. Currently, 71 percent believe too many people are receiving benefits who should not be eligible. Government policy will be aligned with voter attitudes on this point when the number believing too many people are receiving benefits is essentially the same as the number who believe too many are being denied benefits who should be eligible.

In the short term, that would probably come from adjusting eligibility standards using the current official measures of poverty. Longer term, it will require better measures of poverty and near poverty.

Before looking at some of the realities of what new measures of poverty might look like, it's important to note that many Americans are eligible for means-tested programs who earn more than the official poverty threshold. This is by design and serves a valuable purpose. The concept is to ensure that people have incentives to work and eliminate the need for benefits. So, imagine the case of a person who is offered a job that pays just enough to get them above the poverty threshold. If they lost all their benefits by taking the job, they might be worse off by working. So the reasonable policy approach would be to gradually reduce their benefits as income grows. In practical terms, this means that people earning two or three times as much as the official poverty level still receive some benefits from means-tested programs. If official measures of poverty change, adjustments will have to be made across a whole array of government programs. However, as the nation focuses more attention on those most in need, great consideration will still need to be given to the near-poor and to providing appropriate paths to self-sufficiency.

In developing a new measure of official poverty, a sense of the challenge can be gained by looking at data on food security. At some point during a typical year, approximately 5 percent of US households experience what is called "very low food security." Bureaucratically, that means the "food intake of some household members was reduced, and their normal eating patterns were disrupted." That means they missed meals and went hungry because they couldn't afford to buy food. Among households with children, about 1 percent experienced a time when this happened to the children. While these numbers are smaller than the 40 million officially living in poverty, it is still horrifying to realize that more than half a million households had children who went hungry at some point during the year.[17]

The story doesn't end there. Most of those people facing challenges don't face them every day. On an average day, about 1 percent of households have someone who is forced to miss a meal. And, on any given day, children are hungry in about a quarter of a percent of homes with children. It is not my intent to minimize the problem, but to identify it. In many ways these numbers are more horrible than the official poverty numbers. That 1 percent of households in which someone can't find adequate food on any given day is more than 1 million people missing a meal. To know that, in America, more than 1 million people are forced to cut back on a meal every single day is far more troubling than to envision 40 million people with lower incomes than most, but with adequate food and housing.

To solve that troubling issue of hunger in America, we need to focus on the reality of such circumstances rather than being diverted by a bloated estimate of families living in poverty. To drive home the distinction, consider the following data from the US Department of Agriculture collected in the recession year of 2009:[18]

- 96 percent of poor parents stated that their children were never hungry at any time during the year because they could not afford food.
- 83 percent of poor families reported having enough food to eat.
- 82 percent of poor adults reported never being hungry at any time in the prior year due to lack of money for food.

17. United States Department of Agriculture Economic Research Service, "Food Security in the US," Aug. 2011.

18. Robert Rector and Rachel Sheffield, "Understanding Poverty in the United States: Surprising Facts About America's Poor," Sep. 2011.

Defining a more sophisticated and useful measure of poverty is necessary, but cannot be addressed in a single chapter. An appropriate measure would help direct resources where they are needed the most and also show how various programs alleviate the burden of poverty. Policymakers should know if the 1 percent who are hungry on any given day would have been two or three times as many without intervention from the government and nonprofit sources. To help guide future policy choices, measures should distinguish between those who had a bad month and those who have struggled for years. These measures would help the nation understand the depths of true poverty, but also identify people with below-standard incomes who need a different type of assistance. Perhaps most important of all, it would provide a way to identify how many people escaped poverty over time and moved on to self-sufficiency. It would be especially helpful if we could better understand how they did so. What is needed is not a political gimmick such as the original poverty threshold, but a serious tool that can help improve the way we treat those whom our society is in danger of leaving behind.

Discussion of poverty in America can never end with a discussion of means-tested programs for helping those currently in need. The more pressing issue is how to reduce poverty in America. If we have a better tool for measuring it, that's fine. But it will only be great news when a reliable measure shows that poverty in America is truly in decline.

In general, policies and programs that significantly reduce poverty will be found outside the means-tested welfare budget. As just one example, the most effective government antipoverty program of all time has been Social Security, which dramatically reduced poverty among the elderly over the past half century.

Ron Haskins of the Brookings Institution points out "four major causes of poverty in America." The first is lack of jobs. Obviously when the economy offers more and better jobs it reduces poverty. During tough economic times the reverse is true. A plurality of Americans (43%) agrees that "free market capitalism is the best antipoverty program in the world,"[19] but even those who won't go that far recognize that a vibrant private sector economy is a necessary foundation for all efforts to reduce poverty.[20]

The second primary cause of poverty identified by Haskins is lack of education. This also makes intuitive sense. Somebody who has received an education has certain skills that enable them to more effectively earn a living. Over the long term, improving education reduces poverty.

"Family composition" is the third item on Haskins's list, and it concerns the decline in marriage rates and rise of single-parent households. While many view this issue in moral or religious terms, the objective and measurable impact on poverty rates is easy to see. Single-parent households are four times as likely to live in poverty as those households with both parents in place, and the share of single-parent households has increased dramatically in recent generations.

The final item on Haskins's list is immigration, a major factor in poverty discussions because one out of every five adult immigrants has less than a ninth-grade education. The average immigrant male now earns about 20 percent less than non-immigrant males. In earlier times, immigrants earned a bit more than others in the country.

In addressing these causes of poverty, Haskins also notes that solutions need to be developed in a manner consistent with the norms and expectations of American culture:

> *Engaging consistently in hard work has been a fundamental part of the nation's cultural ethic since the Pilgrims landed at Plymouth Rock. The tradition of hard work and self-sufficiency is so fundamental to the American ethic that it poses a constraint on US social policy. Americans think people should earn their own way and resent it when adults, including single parents, do not work and rely instead on welfare.*

19.   Rasmussen Reports, "43% Say Free Market Is Best Anti-Poverty Program," Sep. 2010.
20.   Ron Haskins, "Fighting Poverty the American Way," June 2011.

That attitude is clearly reflected in polling data. Most (53%) believe it is too easy to qualify for welfare, while only 22 percent believe it is too hard.[21] Fifty-five percent think that anyone who wants food stamps should be required to work for them.[22] Sixty-two percent think state governments should offer the long-term unemployed a minimum-wage job instead of welfare payments.[23]

Converting these cultural-norms into policy isn't likely to have a major impact on reducing poverty in the short term. If anything, making it a bit tougher to qualify for welfare might have a marginal impact by forcing a few people off the welfare rolls and into private sector jobs. These concerns still need to be addressed because it is important to assure taxpayers that their money is being used wisely and in a manner honoring bedrock principles of hard work and self-sufficiency. The measures may also have a longer-term impact by reinstilling time-tested expectations of self-sufficiency.

When 70 percent of voters nationwide believe that any welfare recipients using drugs should lose their benefits, that view should be respected by the Political Class. Most voters (53%) believe that every potential welfare recipient should be tested for illegal drugs before receiving benefits.[24] This may reflect a concern that welfare funds will be used to buy drugs, or perhaps voters think that anyone who can afford to buy the drugs doesn't need the benefits. It might even be little more than a belief that welfare payments should be made to help those who are willing to help themselves. Certainly, this approach is not likely to save much money (in fact, with the cost of testing, the savings might be nonexistent or costs may even go up a bit). It is not going to reduce poverty in any significant manner, but it does send a signal that it is vitally important

---

21.   Rasmussen Reports, "53% Say It's Too Easy to Get on Welfare," July 2007.
22.   Rasmussen Reports, "55% Say Those Who Receive Food Stamps Should Be Required to Work," Apr. 2011.
23.   Rasmussen Reports, "62% Prefer Minimum Wage States Jobs as Alternative to Unemployment," Sep. 2011.
24.   Rasmussen Reports, "53% Support Automatic Drug Testing for Welfare Applicants," July 2011.

to respect the taxpayers in the debate over welfare while also trying to help those in need. Hardworking American taxpayers, including many who have formerly been in need themselves, are the solution to the challenges surrounding poverty rather than an obstacle to reform. The American people are generous and willing to help all who are trying to make a better life for themselves, but they don't want to be played for fools.

When considering the four major causes of poverty in the United States, following the instincts of the American people will do a lot more to reduce poverty than following the nation's Political Class. Considering the concepts mentioned in earlier chapters certainly will.

- Reforming national security, Social Security, and Medicare as described in chapters 3–5 will remove the enormous burden of more than $100 trillion in government debt that is dragging down the economy. By laying the foundation for a stronger economy, these reforms will also create jobs, the most important weapon in the fight against poverty.
- Allowing workers to select their own retirement age for Social Security and Medicare will give workers the chance to pay less in taxes. This extra take-home pay will be especially valuable for the working poor, those who are barely getting by.
- Demanding a better return on educational investments made by the taxpayers—as discussed in chapter 9—will set the stage for reducing poverty over the longer term.

Following the gut instincts of voters in other areas can help as well. The federal government can do little to reduce the number of single-parent homes. If change is possible at all, it will come from changes in the society at large, but the federal government can certainly help on the margin by eliminating any provisions in welfare programs or federal law that provide incentives for people to remain unmarried.

As for the impact of immigration on poverty, the voters have a lot to say about a subject that is among the most misunderstood by the nation's Political Class. Voters are fed up with illegal immigration. They are not angry at the immigrants, however. Eighty-three percent direct their anger at the federal government.[25] This makes sense, because just about everyone can understand why so many people would want to come to America and start a better life. A Gallup survey found that approximately 165 million people around the world would like to permanently move to the United States. No other nation comes close (Canada was second, at 45 million).[26] The United States accepts more new residents than any other nation in the world.

While people understand why others would like to come to the USA, they can't understand why the federal government won't even try to enforce its own laws. Most believe that government policies actually encourage illegal immigration; only 27 percent disagree. People are also unhappy with private sector enablers of illegal immigration.[27] Seventy-five percent want strict sanctions on companies that knowingly hire illegal immigrants. Fifty-nine percent want landlords who knowingly rent to illegal immigrants to be punished.[28] Sixty-one percent want repeat offenders shut down completely and put out of business. When authorities raid a place where illegal immigrants are seeking jobs, there is more support for punishing the employer than the immigrants.[29] "Americans are more comfortable going after those who profit from illegal immigration rather than individual illegal immigrants. That's roughly comparable to fighting the War on Drugs by going after big-time drug dealers and cartels rather than occasional users of illegal drugs.

It's easy to see there is a world of difference between opposing illegal immigration and opposing immigration. That's one of the things that the folks in DC have a hard time recognizing: most Americans welcome legal immigration. In regular polling, stretching back more than five

25.   Rasmussen Reports, "32% Angry About Immigration, but Not Mad at Immigrants," June 2008.

26.   Neli Esipova and Julie Ray, "700 Million World Wide Desire to Migrate Permanently," Nov. 2009.

27.   Rasmussen Reports, "60% Say Federal Government Encourages Illegal Immigration," May 2011.

28.   Rasmussen Reports, "75% Support Tough Penalties Against Employers Who Hire Illegal Immigrants," July 2011.

29.   Rasmussen Reports, "61% Favor a State Law That Would Shut Down Repeat Offenders Who Hire Illegal Immigrants," May 2011.

years, a solid majority of voters nationwide consistently supports welcoming anybody, except national security threats, criminals, and those who would come to live off our welfare system, into the country legally.[30] Republicans are actually a bit more welcoming than Democrats, but the bottom line is that America is a nation of immigrants and a nation of laws. Americans today are intent on honoring both parts of that tradition.

Still, 59 percent of voters believe that even those who enter the country legally should have to wait three years before they are eligible to collect welfare benefits.[31] That's a commonsense precaution to make sure those planning to come here are really seeking to secure the blessings of freedom and liberty for themselves and their families. It's so consistent with the American heritage of hard work and self-sufficiency that only 16 percent oppose any type of waiting period. It might also ultimately lead to requiring some qualifications based upon education, employment, and/or finances for immigration to the United States.

For lower-income and less educated foreigners, temporary work visas could be issued by select states—if they deem it appropriate. This would be consistent with polling showing that 49 percent believe immigrants take jobs that Americans won't take themselves.[32] Allowing people with a job and a willingness to work into the United States is consistent with basic American values.

It should be noted that none of these reforms for legal immigration are possible until the federal government convinces voters that it's serious about stopping illegal immigration. That would mean taking action against employers, landlords, and others who profit from the system. It would mean allowing law enforcement officials to check the status of those stopped for other law enforcement actions, and it would require cutting off federal aid for so-called sanctuary cities. All of those actions are supported by a majority of voters across the nation,[33] and they make

30.   Rasmussen Reports, "63% Still Believe Border Control is Top Immigration Priority," Apr. 2011.

31.   Rasmussen Reports, "71% Say Too Many People Get Welfare Who Shouldn't," Aug. 2011.

32.   Rasmussen Reports, "49% Say Illegal Immigrants Perform Jobs Most US Citizens Won't Do," Aug. 2011.

33.   Rasmussen Reports, "63% Favor Immigration Checks on All Routine Traffic Stops," Oct. 2011.

sense only when accompanied by a welcoming policy of legal immigration.

All of this suggests four steps to align the government's welfare policy with voter preferences:

1. Treat all means-tested programs as a single budget item and place overall limits on its spending growth.
2. Trim eligibility standards so that fewer people receive benefits but more attention is focused on those most in need.
3. Develop a new measure of official poverty that assesses program effectiveness and tracks success while also being consistent with voters' understanding of poverty and low-income status.
4. Recognize the importance of the nonprofit sector in doing things that government cannot or will not do to help those most in need.

That last step, recognizing the importance of the nonprofit sector, has dual value. The obvious initial benefit is that individuals acting in their local communities and churches can see special needs and circumstances that no government program could ever address. These efforts can never replace the government antipoverty programs, but they can fill in gaps that arise all of a sudden. They can find people in need who are invisible to bureaucratic approaches. When there's a fire or a flood or other unimaginable shock to someone's daily routine, it is heartwarming to see how communities respond.

Another equally important benefit of charitable giving and volunteer efforts is the impact on the people who get involved. It changes poverty from an abstraction to a person. My little town has a Missions 101 program that brings middle and high school students for a long weekend over the summer. The generally middle-class or affluent students have their world turned upside down as they work for people whose lives are nowhere near as comfortable as theirs. I have been blessed at times to hear the stories from these students and see the reports of eyes opened wide to a new reality. Making the invisible world of poverty visible to them is worth even more than the projects they do for those in need.

Keep in mind that these are merely the steps needed to help those who are in need of assistance. The challenge of actually reducing poverty in America can be addressed only by other programs that address the four major causes of poverty—job issues, lack of education, family composition challenges, and immigration.

PART THREE

—•—•—

How Voters Would Save the People's Money

8

————•————

Ending Corporate Welfare

Every year the federal government dispenses tens of billions of dollars in direct grants to large companies throughout the nation. Some of the biggest names in corporate America also receive other favors including loans, loan guarantees, and tax breaks.

To most Americans, corporate welfare is a disgusting abuse of the public trust. Why should taxpayers be providing grants and subsidies to companies such as Archer Daniels Midland, Boeing, Xerox, IBM, Motorola, Dow Chemical, and General Electric? Why should we bail out failing companies and give big bonuses to the executives who ran the companies into the ground?

While voters hate corporate welfare, politicians and Big Business leaders view it as the norm. Leading business executives such as Jeffrey Immelt, CEO of General Electric, see it as a way that "government can help business invest in our shared future."[1]

In the summer of 2008, before most Americans knew a financial industry meltdown was on the horizon, insurance giant AIG gave millions of dollars in campaign contributions to members of Congress and other political figures. The failed company later received hundreds of billions of dollars in bailout funding. Just to keep the numbers straight, the cam-

---

1.   Jeffrey R. Immelt, "A Blueprint for Keeping America Competitive," Jan. 2011.

paign contributions were in the *millions*, but the company received back hundreds of *billions*.

Along the way, those hundreds of billions in taxpayer bailouts allowed AIG to pay executive bonuses of $165 million.[2] Public outrage was so powerful that several of the highest-paid executives eventually gave back their bonuses, while others reportedly received death threats.[3] Some complained that they had taken a lower salary in exchange for promised bonuses and were offended by all the noise.

The entire issue would never have arisen if the politicians had listened to the American people and the company had been allowed to fail. Among all Americans, the AIG bailout was opposed by a 77 to 9 percent margin. Some opposed it only because the concept was offensive to traditional American values. But most (59%) also thought that letting the insurance giant fail would be better for the economy than bailing it out. While overall public opinion was clear, there was a notable exception — 70 percent of those with Political Class views thought it would be better to provide the subsidies needed to keep the company afloat.[4]

A similar tale took place at Citigroup, a company that had retained the services of the politically well-connected Robert Rubin nine years before when the bank needed a bailout. He developed those connections during a quarter century at Goldman Sachs and as Treasury secretary for President Bill Clinton. With that résumé, he was able to earn over $100 million over nine years providing advisory services at Citigroup. Early in his tenure, Rubin drew some criticism for his involvement in the Enron scandal.[5] Citigroup held a substantial amount of Enron debt and stood to take major losses if the credit-rating agencies downgraded

2. Edmund L. Andrews and Peter Baker, "AIG Planning Huge Bonuses After $170 Billion Bailout," Mar. 2009.

3. Brady Dennis and David Cho, "Rage at AIG Swells as Bonuses Go Out," Mar. 2009.

4. Rasmussen Reports, "Most Americans Say Let AIG Go out of Business, Political Class Disagrees," Mar. 2009.

5. Joseph Kahn and Alessandra Stanley, "Enron's Many Strands: Dual Roles; Rubin Relishes Role of Banker as Public Man," Feb. 2002.

Enron's credit. To address this concern, Rubin called senior Treasury Department official Peter Fisher and asked him to intervene. Fisher wisely refused and Enron later collapsed.

In November 2008, however, Rubin placed a call to Treasury Secretary Henry Paulson on behalf of his company. This time, Rubin's call started a process that gained Citigroup $45 billion in bailout funding, government guarantees of more than $300 billion to protect the bank from toxic assets, and other subsidies. The government investment totaled far more than the entire market value of the company. So the government could have taken over the entire company for less money.

Perhaps the most stunning aspect of the deal is that Citigroup didn't even have to make any management changes to get the money. The *Washington Post* reported that the government "could have enacted a highly punitive complete bailout, like that of American International Group, requiring terms that strongly punish existing shareholders and give the government control of the Citigroup board, as well as firing the chief executive. They rejected that approach."[6]

That they got to keep their jobs may have been the greatest value Rubin provided for his friends and colleagues. "The bailout of Citigroup, which put the government at risk of hundreds of billions of dollars of losses, was set in motion by three men whose professional lives have long been intertwined," according to *Washington Post* reporting on the subject. "Treasury Secretary Henry M. Paulson Jr.; Citigroup board member Robert E. Rubin; and Timothy F. Geithner, the president of the Federal Reserve Bank of New York, have for years followed one another in and out of jobs in government and industry. Their close relationships helped pave the way for one of the largest and most dramatic government interventions to date in the financial crisis."[7]

Think about how all of that played out. The government provided more funding to Citigroup than the entire corporation was worth after

---

6. David Cho and Neil Irwin, "Rubin, Paulson, Geithner, a Familiar Trio at Heart of Citigroup Bailout," Nov. 2008.

7. Ibid.

private investors wouldn't touch it. Seeing that the company was des-
tined to fail and that shareholders would lose their entire investment,
the government used hundreds of billions of taxpayer dollars to prop
up the company and let the shareholders keep the "profit." The "profit,"
it should be noted, came only because the government bailed out the
failing firm. And after all that, they didn't even fire the CEO, Vikram
Pandit. It's theoretically possible that the government carefully weighed
various alternatives and concluded he was the best person to guide the
firm forward. Of course, it's also probably no coincidence that Pandit
was an ally of Robert Rubin's.[8]

The Citigroup deal, like many others of the bailout era, was premised
on the notion that some financial institutions are simply too big to fail.
At the time, only 32 percent of Americans shared that view, but public
opinion didn't matter to Congress.[9] The interests of their friends in the
Political Class prevailed, as they often do on corporate welfare issues.
Today, there is even less support for the Political Class view. Just 24 percent believe the government should find a way to keep failing banks in
business. Most (56%) disagree and believe that if "some of the largest
banks in the country reach a point where they can no longer meet their
obligations," the government should let them go out of business.[10] Sixty-
four percent believe that letting banks fail is better for the economy.[11]

Voters saw the bailouts as a betrayal of basic American values. People
don't mind companies making a profit when sales are good and customers satisfied, but they expect them to pay the price when companies
struggle. They especially hate things done in secret. While much of the
bailout game was revealed in public, it took more than two years before the Federal Reserve acknowledged that it provided an additional
$1.2 trillion in bailout loans, including $100 billion to Citigroup.[12]

8. Joe Hagan, "The Most Powerless Powerful Man on Wall Street," Mar. 2009.
9. Rasmussen Reports, "51% Oppose Nationalization, Even of at Risk Banks," Feb. 2009.
10. Rasmussen Reports, "Americans Not Sure on Financial Reform Bill, but Don't Think Some Banks
    Are Too Big to Fail," June 2010.
11. Rasmussen Reports, "Only 28% Say Some Banks Are Too Big to Fail," Oct. 2009.
12. Mark Lewis, "Rubin Red-Faced over Enron? Not in the Times," Feb. 2002.

"These are all whopping numbers," said Robert Litan, a Brookings Institution scholar. The former Justice Department official added, "You're talking about the aristocracy of American finance going down the tubes without the federal money."

One of the benefits of belonging to "the aristocracy of American finance" is that you can always count on your friends in government to bail you out. Americans instinctively recognize that bailing out corporations sets a bad precedent that will come back to haunt the nation if we're not careful. One expert close to the situation made it clear that the people are right. "[TARP] has increased the potential need for future government bailouts by encouraging the 'too big to fail' financial institutions to become even bigger," according to Special United States Treasury Department Inspector General Neil M. Barofsky, appointed to oversee the Troubled Assets Relief Program (TARP). Barofsky pointed out, "These institutions and their leaders are incentivized to engage in precisely the sort of behavior that could trigger the next financial crisis, thus perpetuating a doomsday cycle of booms, busts, and bailouts."[13] As if the bailouts weren't bad enough by themselves, they set in motion a "doomsday cycle" to wreak havoc on the economy.

Apologists for the Political Class take a different view. A *Washington Post* editorial claimed that the Citigroup deal was profitable for taxpayers and that TARP was a "great deal for taxpayers."[14] However, Dean Baker of the *American Prospect* pointed out that the deal was profitable for taxpayers only if you forgot to subtract the cost of tens of billions of dollars of government subsidies that turned Citigroup around. "In short, anyone looking at the fuller picture would see that it is silly to claim that taxpayers made a profit in our investment in Citi." Baker figures that the taxpayer funding and guarantees helped put $90 billion into the pockets of Citi shareholders.[15] He wrote that even before the additional funding from the Fed had been disclosed.

---

13. Matthew Jaffe, "Bailout Watchdog Barofsky Sounds 'Too Big to Fail' Warning," Jan. 2011.
14. "No One Likes TARP, but It's Working," Apr. 2010.
15. Dean Baker, "Did We Make a Profit on Citigroup?" Apr. 2010.

Cato Institute senior fellow Dan Mitchell said:

As an economist, I should probably be most agitated about the economic consequences of TARP, such as moral hazard and capital malinvestment. But when I read stories about how political insiders (both in government and on Wall Street) manipulate the system for personal advantage, I get even more upset. Yes, TARP was economically misguided. But the bailout also was fundamentally corrupt, featuring special favors for the well-heeled. I don't like it when lower-income people use the political system to take money from upper-income people, but it is downright nauseating and disgusting when upper-income people use the coercive power of government to steal money from lower-income people.[16]

"Political connections play an important role in a firm's access to capital," according to Denis Sosyura, professor at the University of Michigan's Ross School of Business. He and a colleague, Ran Duchin, conducted a study that found unsurprising evidence of corruption: "U.S. banks that spent more money on lobbying were more likely to get government bailout money." Additionally, "banks whose executives served on Federal Reserve Boards were more likely to receive government bailout funds from the Troubled Asset Relief Program. . . . Political influence was most helpful for poorly performing banks."[17]

Voters continue to give the program a big thumbs-down. Even three years after the bailouts began, 61 percent thought it was a bad idea for the government to provide bailout funding for banks and other financial institutions. Only 24 percent thought it was a good idea.[18]

For the Political Class, however, it's a great ride, and the merry-go-round continues even after the bailouts are finished. As just one

16. Daniel J. Mitchell, "What Gets You Most Upset About the TARP Bailout, the Lying, the Corruption, or the Economic Damage?" Oct. 2010.

17. Ran Duchin and Denis Sosyura, "The Politics of Government Investment," Apr. 2011.

18. Rasmussen Reports, "68% Say Bank Bailout Money Went to Those Who Caused Meltdown," May 2011.

example of the ever-revolving door, Jacob Lew left Citigroup shortly after the bailouts to join the Obama administration. Just before returning to "public service" Mr. Lew received a $944,000 bonus from Citigroup.[19] That bonus, like all the bonuses for bailed-out executives, was made possible by the taxpayer funding provided by the Political Class. That revolving door plays an even bigger role than campaign contributions in cementing the alliance between government and Big Business. It's just the way the Political Class takes care of the family.

It wasn't just the bank bailouts that bothered voters. From the moment GM and Chrysler received bailouts, Ford became the best-liked car company in America.[20] Even after General Motors emerged from bankruptcy and paid back some of the government loans, most voters said the government bailout of the automaker was bad for the economy.[21] Partly, it's because 41 percent expected the quality of GM cars to get worse with the government in charge. Additionally, reflecting an underlying fear of corruption, 57 percent expected the government to pass laws and regulations giving GM an unfair advantage over other car companies.[22]

It's worth noting that opposition to the auto bailouts continued despite government and company hype about how GM had emerged from bankruptcy. Part of the reason may have been that the costs seemed of a greater magnitude than the benefits. Megan McArdle, a senior editor for the *Atlantic*, noted that the government gave GM four times what the company was worth in 2008. She said, "The question is whether it was worth it to the taxpayer to burn $10–20 billion in order to give the company another shot at life. To put that in perspective, GM had about 75,000 hourly workers before the bankruptcy. We could have given each of them a cool $250,000 and still come out well ahead."[23]

---

19.   Jim McElhatton, "Lew Earned $1.1M from Citigroup Before State Department Job," July 2010.

20.   Rasmussen Reports, "Ford Still the Favorite Among Big Three Automakers," June 2011.

21.   Rasmussen Reports, "Only 27% Have Positive View of Government Bailouts," Mar. 2011.

22.   Rasmussen Reports, "57% Expect Government Will Give GM, Chrysler Unfair Advantages," May 2009.

23.   Megan McArdle, "GM's Profits Are Still a Huge Net Loss for Taxpayers," May 2011.

Part of the concern with both the Wall Street and auto industry bailouts is that 68 percent of the nation's adults believe that most of the money went right to the people who created the economic crisis. When President Barack Obama forced General Motors to fire their CEO, Rick Wagoner left with a $20 million retirement package. "Under Wagoner's leadership," according to ABC News, "GM lost tens of billions of dollars, took billions in taxpayer-financed aid, and cut tens of thousands of jobs."[24] Without a government bailout, Wagoner would have gotten nothing.

As for the Wall Street bailout, only 22 percent thought the government was primarily interested in making the system work for everyone. Most (51%) think the politicians were more concerned with Wall Street than Main Street. None of this surprised anyone.[25] In October 2008, before the bailouts were even approved, voters expected the worst—63 percent said Wall Street would benefit more than the average taxpayer.[26] Just nine months later, after the bailouts were enacted, that figure jumped to 80 percent.[27]

The bailouts were splashy and too big to hide. Prior to the bailout era, corporate welfare payments tended to be more modest. Sometimes they cost "just" a few billion, such as the recent cash-for-clunkers program. Other times the costs are hard to measure, such as when politicians legislate a privileged position for some companies over their competitors. Almost always the deals are unpopular with voters, and the real cost is greater than the stated costs. An even bigger problem, however, is that corporate welfare programs have a corrosive impact on both the political system and free market competition. They lead Americans to believe that "government operates by the wrong values and rules, for the wrong

24. Michelle Leder and Justin Rood, "Payday: GM's Rick Wagoner Drives Away with $20M Retirement," Mar. 2009.

25. Rasmussen Reports, "64% Say Government Hasn't Been Tough Enough on Wall Street," May 2011.

26. Rasmussen Reports, "63% Say Wall Street, Not Taxpayers, Will Benefit from Bailout Plan," Oct. 2008.

27. Rasmussen Reports, "80% Say Wall Street, Not Taxpayers, Benefited More from Bailout as Goldman Sachs Announces Record Profit."

people and purposes," according to Democratic pollster Stanley Green-berg. He adds that the public perception is that "government rushes to help the irresponsible and does little for the responsible. Wall Street lobbyists govern, not Main Street voters."[28] That's why seven out of ten voters believe that government and Big Business operate together against the rest of us.

Corporate welfare programs have convinced most voters that our sys-tem of government has become a legalized extortion racket operated by the gang of Washington insiders. Fifty-nine percent of American adults believe that when members of Congress meet with regulators and other government officials, they do so to help their friends and hurt their po-litical opponents. Only 19 percent disagree.[29] Sixty percent believe most politicians will break the rules to help people who gave them large cam-paign contributions. The flip side is that the politicians could also break the rules to hurt those who don't contribute. In fact, 68 percent of all Americans say most business leaders contribute to political campaigns primarily because the government can do so much to help or hurt their business. Only 8 percent disagree.[30] Among business managers in the private sector, 83 percent say business leaders give primarily because of concern about what the government can do to their business.

Completing the loop in what most Americans view as a corrupt sys-tem, 57 percent believe political donors get more than their money back in favors from members of Congress.[31] These favors are not just concerts or Yankees tickets. Sixty-three percent think big businesses take advan-tage of the political process to hurt smaller competitors. Only 15 percent disagree.[32]

Many things that are normal in Washington are shocking to those who live just about anywhere else in the nation. Consider the case of

---

28.   Stanley B. Greenberg, "Turning Out the Democrats," July 2011.
29.   Rasmussen Reports, "Americans Agree Congress Doesn't Play by the Rules," Feb. 2009.
30.   Rasmussen Reports, "Most Say Political Donors Get More Than Their Money's Worth," Feb. 2009.
31.   Ibid.
32.   Rasmussen Reports, "Americans Agree Congress Doesn't Play by the Rules," Feb. 2009.

Meredith Attwell Baker, a former FCC member who voted in favor of a controversial merger allowing Comcast to acquire NBC Universal. Just a few months later, she went to work in a senior position at Comcast. The *New York Times* noted that her "rapid shift from regulator to lobbyist for the regulated will only add to Americans' cynicism about their government. The fact that it is legal and that she is just one of many doesn't make it better."[33] Fifty-nine percent believe some companies routinely hire regulators to get favorable treatment from the government, and nearly as many (53%) think companies that regularly hire former regulators get that special treatment.[34] Few disagree.

The corrupt relationship between government and Big Business has convinced many that capitalism as practiced in the United States is really nothing more than a form of "crony capitalism," a view that erodes confidence in the driving force of the nation's economy. Many voters have come to believe that free market competition has been replaced with a system where politically well-connected companies can keep the profits during good times and get bailed out when they mess up. The American people know the difference—just 35 percent now believe capitalism is the same as a free market economy.[35]

While the bailouts have grabbed headlines and cost far more than the usual corporate welfare programs, the federal government funds a number of more modest programs that are also unpopular with voters and have a corrupting influence on both government and free market competition.

- Just 37 percent of voters support the continuation of crop and farm subsidies, a program that costs taxpayers tens of billions of dollars annually. While the cost varies from year to year, support

---

33. "That Didn't Take Long," May 2011.
34. Rasmussen Reports, "51% Think It's Bribery When a Company Offers a Government Regulator a Job," May 2011.
35. Rasmussen Reports, "Just 35% Say Free Market Economy Is the Same as Capitalist Economy," May 2009.

for the program would probably be lower if voters knew that most of the subsidies went to agribusiness corporations.[36]

- By an overwhelming 70 to 15 percent margin, voters say it's time to stop providing funding for foreign countries to buy military weapons from US companies.[37]

- The federal government's Export-Import Bank provides billions of dollars in loans and loan guarantees to companies such as Boeing and General Electric. Its stated purpose is to sustain American jobs by financing US exports, but just 29 percent want to continue such funding.[38]

- Just 27 percent of voters favored spending $2 billion on federal tax credits for those who buy electric cars. Even though 55 percent opposed the plan, the government provides a $7,500 bonus to ease the sticker shock for buyers of cars such as GM's Chevy Volt.[39]

- Only 35 percent supported the cash-for-clunkers program, but Congress passed it despite 54 percent being opposed.[40]

- Only 39 percent supported the government plan to provide a credit for first-time home buyers.[41] It, too, was approved by Congress.

- By a 58 to 23 percent margin voters oppose the core program of the Small Business Administration (SBA)—government loan guarantees for those hoping to start small businesses but unable to find financing elsewhere.[42]

---

36. Rasmussen Reports, "Voters See These 'Corporate Welfare' Programs as a Good Place to Cut Government Spending," Aug. 2011.

37. Ibid.

38. Ibid.

39. Rasmussen Reports, "55% Express Sticker Shock over Tax Credits for Electric Cars," Aug. 2010.

40. Rasmussen Reports, "54% Oppose 'Cash for Clunkers' Plan to Spur Purchases of Greener Cars," June 2009.

41. Rasmussen Reports, "Most Like Tax Credits for First-Time Home Buyers, but 47% Oppose Continuing Them," Sep. 2009.

42. Tad Dehaven and Veronique de Rugy, "Terminating the Small Business Administration," Aug. 2011.

For all who believe that politicians can't cut spending because voters won't let them, the above list should be sobering. Americans overwhelmingly believe that reducing government regulations and taxes would help small businesses more than making loans available. Entrepreneurs themselves, by a 76 to 18 percent margin, agree.[43]

All of this also raises an important question: how does it happen? If corporate welfare has such a toxic impact on both democracy and free markets and voters don't even like the individual programs, how come we end up with so much of it?

The simple reason is that corporate welfare is consistent with the Political Class agenda and perspective. That worldview was popular in 1775, but was rejected by the American Revolution in 1776. When the king of England gave monopoly rights to the East India Tea Company, it was against the law for the colonists in America to buy their tea from anybody else. Then it was known as mercantilism. Some now call it state capitalism.

Ian Bremmer in his excellent book *The End of the Free Market: Who Wins the War Between States and Corporations?* describes state capitalism as "a system in which the state dominates markets primarily for political gain." Bremer adds that "state capitalists see markets primarily as a tool that serves national interests, or at least those of ruling elites, rather than as an engine of opportunity for the individual. State capitalists use markets to extend their own political and economic leverage—both within society and on the international stage."[44]

State capitalism, using all the tools of corporate welfare, reflects a worldview that puts government in charge rather than citizens and consumers, and it deludes elected politicians into believing that the government is the center of the universe. Vice President Joe Biden expressed this view nicely when he made the absurd claim that "every single great

43. Rasmussen Reports, "58% Want to End Small Business Administration Loan Guarantees," Aug. 2011.
44. Ian Bremmer, *The End of the Free Market: Who Wins the War Between States and Corporations?* (2010).

idea that has marked the twenty-first century, the twentieth century, and the nineteenth century has required government vision and government incentive."[45] If Biden's statement were true, voters all around the world would be begging to invest more tax dollars in corporate welfare projects. They aren't, because voters know that innovations from electricity and the lightbulb to Kindles and iPods have come from private investments, not government vision. Seventy-one percent believe that private sector companies and investors are better than government officials at determining the long-term benefits and potential of new technologies; only 11 percent believe that government officials have a better eye for the future of technology.[46]

While some politicians believe that government should direct resources to invest in new technologies that private investors overlook, voters take a dim view of that as well. When government provides funding for some new technology that private investors refuse to back, 64 percent believe it's likely that the government money will be wasted.[47] That's just one of the reasons that seven out of ten Americans prefer a free market economy over a government-managed economy.[48]

The differing perceptions between the Political Class and Mainstream Americans reflect that the Political Class wants to take us back to 1775, while the American people look forward to applying the promise of July 4, 1776, to the twenty-first century.

In rejecting rule by kings, the colonists who founded our nation also rejected mercantilism. They preferred a system where you didn't need permission from the king to sell tea to your neighbors. In the United States, belief in free markets has worked well for more than two hundred

45. Celeste Katz, "VPOTUS Joe Biden: Dems Will 'Keep the Senate and Win the House,'" Oct. 2010.

46. Rasmussen Reports, "71% Think Private Sector Better Than Government at Measuring Technology Potential," Aug. 2011.

47. Ibid.

48. Rasmussen Reports, "72% Favor Free Market Economy over One Managed by the Government," July 2011.

years, but Bremmer warns, "State capitalism represents a direct challenge to that belief." He adds a chilling bit of reality to the challenge facing America today:

> As with mercantilism, state capitalists use markets to build state power. Forced to choose between protection of the rights of the individual, economic productivity, and the principle of consumer choice, on the one hand, and the achievement of political goals, on the other, state capitalists will choose the latter every time.

Among the Political Class, the notion that the economy could work without the government leading the way is beyond the realm of possibility. John Judis, a senior editor for the *New Republic*, says that a real recovery from the current economic doldrums is possible only with "a huge infusion of government spending."[49] Voters don't see it that way. Sixty-four percent believe that job creation is more likely to come from decisions made by business leaders focused on growing their own businesses rather than from political leaders.[50] It's likely that a serious effort to eliminate the massive federal debt would do more to restore economic confidence than any new government spending initiative.

The Political Class preference for political goals over "the rights of the individual, economic productivity, and the principle of consumer choice" is precisely what leads to the worst abuses of corporate welfare programs. For politicians what matters is that *they* are in charge and can help their friends. Voters, on the other hand, see the government as one institution among many that help make society work. Government plays an important role, but not the lead role; individuals take the lead in charting a course for their own lives. As they pursue their own dreams and relationships, they also help build a stronger community and nation.

The problem with putting politics first is ideally illustrated in the

---

49.   John B. Judis, "New Republic: A Lesson from the Great Depression," Aug. 2011.
50.   Rasmussen Reports, "60% Trust Business Leaders More Than Government to Create Jobs," Jan. 2011.

saga of Fannie Mae, a supposedly private company pretending to provide a public service. According to company spin, its mission was to help citizens realize the American Dream of homeownership. In reality, it simply milked a special relationship with the government—the government guaranteed all the money that Fannie Mae borrowed. That let the company borrow money at extraordinarily low rates, then loan it out at higher rates by purchasing home mortgages. The details of the story are sordid enough to warrant reading a detailed accounting in a great book, mentioned earlier, *Reckless Endangerment*, but the short version is that the company passed on only a bit of its interest subsidy to the homeowners it claimed to champion. The remainder—two-thirds of the total subsidy—was siphoned off the top to pay shareholders and officers, as well as to cover the cost of a vast political patronage program.

It is staggering to read just how many politicians held press conferences announcing a new homeowner initiative in their district or somehow got a friend or relative on the Fannie payroll. The man who made it all happen, Jim Johnson, took home $5.1 million in 1995 alone.[51] After he left Fannie, he ended up at Goldman Sachs, a company that seemed to find itself in the middle of countless corporate welfare situations and also needed a bailout. When all was said and done, Fannie Mae collapsed and left taxpayers on the hook to pay off approximately $317 billion in loan guarantees. That's more than $1,000 for every man, woman, and child in America today.

The Political Class belief in state capitalism, and their use of corporate welfare to buy influence, is one reason that most Americans today have come to believe that the federal government is more of a threat to individual rights than a protector of those rights. While politicians may justify their intervention by claiming a need to manage the economy, just 28 percent of voters believe that promoting economic growth is a more important function than protecting individual rights.[52] But most

---

51.   Gretchen Morgenson and Joshua Rosner, *Reckless Endangerment: How Outsized Ambition, Greed, and Corruption Led to Economic Endangerment* (May 2011).

52.   Rasmussen Reports, "53% View Government as Threat to Individual Rights," May 2011.

Americans don't want a government-managed economy.[53] Most say protecting individual rights is the more important function, again reflecting the values articulated in the Declaration of Independence. If individuals have the opportunity to pursue their own dreams, the economy will benefit.

Over the entire debate runs a reality that few in Washington want to admit: state capitalism requires voters to place their trust in government at a time when voters believe government is badly broken. Given a choice between trusting the government and trusting their own judgment, voters reject Washington every time. On economic matters 74 percent of voters trust their own judgment more than that of the average member of Congress. Only 13 percent take the opposite view. By a two-to-one margin, voters trust their own economic judgment more than that of the president of the United States.[54] Overall, just 23 percent are even somewhat confident that policymakers know what they are doing. It's hard to sell state capitalism when people don't trust the state.

To align government policy with voter preferences and basic American concepts of fairness, corporate welfare programs should be completely removed from the federal budget. This is not something that should be reduced, but something that should be utterly eliminated. A wall should be established between the government and corporations to prevent future abuses. The wall should be built along the lines of the separation of church and state. To align government policy with the voters there should be a complete separation between corporate America and federal government subsidies. This attitude extends to the tax code as well. Only 21 percent want the government to provide targeted tax breaks that help certain companies and industries. Sixty-six percent say it's better for the economy if the government simply treats all companies

---

53. Rasmussen Reports, "72% Favor Free Market Economy over One Managed by the Government," July 2011.
54. Rasmussen Reports, "23% Confident Policymakers Know What They Are Doing About the Economy," July 2011.

and industries equally.[55] That may not be as much fun for the politicians, but it's what the voters want.

In the case of the separation of church and state, the Constitution of the United States established limits to protect the churches from the state. In the case of corporate welfare, ways will have to be found to protect the American people from the alliance between government and Big Business.

This is easier said than done.

Because corporate welfare is such an integral part of the way the Political Class works, resistance to reform will be fierce. The Political Class likes the system that gives them power and the right to spend other people's money. For the same reason, elimination of corporate welfare is essential to prevent the Political Class from undoing the American Revolution and taking us back to 1775. Congress will always look for ways to hide special favors in the back pages of absurdly complex legislation. Congress prefers a system where, as former House Speaker Nancy Pelosi said, you "have to pass the bill so that you can find out what's in it."[56] Voters prefer a sensible reform that would shine a light on legislation and let everyone in the nation have a chance to root out potential problems. With the sole exception of extreme emergencies, 82 percent want legislation posted online in final form and available for everyone to read *before* Congress votes on it.[57] Voters aren't talking about a mere three days for citizens to check out the fine print. That three-day limit is short enough that both Pelosi and her successor, John Boehner, were willing to promise it (a promise that both broke). Voters have something more serious in mind. Fifty-three percent of all voters nationwide want legislation posted online for two full weeks before a vote is taken. Another 24 percent think one week should be enough. Six percent could

55. Rasmussen Reports, "64% Favor Lower Tax Rates with Fewer Deductions," Aug. 2011.

56. David Freddoso, "Pelosi on Health Care: 'We Have to Pass the Bill So You Can Find Out What's in It,'" Mar. 2010.

57. Rasmussen Reports, "Most Think Congress Doesn't Read What It Votes On, Favor Putting Bills Online Well in Advance," Jan. 2011.

live with something shorter than a week, and an additional 6 percent think no requirement for posting online is needed. Posting items online won't prevent corporate welfare all by itself, but it makes it tougher for the politicians to get away with things.

Voters also want to completely shut down the revolving door. Seventy-four percent want to ban regulators from going to work for the companies they regulate. This includes 32 percent who favor a lifetime ban that would prohibit regulators from ever working for companies they once regulated. Another 42 percent think five years is a long enough cooling-down period before freeing regulators to work in the industry they oversaw. Seventy-four percent want retiring members of Congress to be banned from lobbying for five years. By a 48 to 21 percent margin, voters think that companies that offer jobs to regulators should be banned from doing business with the government.[58] That's because most, 51 percent, believe that when a company offers a government regulator a job, it's a form of a bribe.[59]

To reduce the potential for shenanigans by increasing transparency, most adults (55%) also want full disclosure of all meetings between members of Congress and regulators. While that may offend the Political Class, it's actually the middle ground in public perceptions. The more extreme view, held by 29 percent, is that such meetings should be prohibited entirely. Only 5 percent say that there is no need for disclosure, while 12 percent are not sure.[60]

One more step along the path to transparency is overwhelmingly supported by voters. Seventy-five percent believe that the Federal Reserve should be audited. Public clamor forced a preliminary audit in 2011, but more investigation and disclosure are required.

Requiring all bills to be posted online for at least a week, closing

---

58. Rasmussen Reports, "74% Favor Banning Regulators from Working for Those They Regulate for at Least Five Years," May 2011.

59. Rasmussen Reports, "51% Think It's Bribery When a Company Offers a Government Regulator a Job," May 2011.

60. Rasmussen Reports, "Obama Action on Lobbyist Disclosure Is a Step Most Americans Will Welcome," Mar. 2009.

the revolving door, eliminating secret meetings between members of Congress and regulators, and auditing the Fed could be first steps toward changing the culture in Washington. From a dollars-and-cents perspective, building that wall of separation between government subsidies and corporate America requires eliminating all direct payments, subsidies, loans, and loan guarantees to corporations. That would initially save about $50 billion a year on average, with the biggest savings coming from eliminating crop subsidies. As indicated in the bullet points above, voters are ready to cut spending on all of these items. The $50 billion annual savings might be a bit on the low side, but it's better to be cautious rather than extravagant when estimating savings. The Cato Institute estimates that corporate welfare payments currently total more than $100 billion a year, but some of these programs might better be classified as government investments (e.g., a subsidy for Amtrak looks like corporate welfare, but the rail company is 100 percent owned by the government).[61]

Regardless of the specific amounts, the really big payoffs from eliminating corporate welfare will come from preventing future bailouts. Americans are adamant on this point and have been making themselves heard. During 2010 several incumbent politicians were defeated in primaries largely because they had voted for bailouts. This outraged the *Washington Post* and others in the Political Class who thought the bailouts saved the world. The *Post* went so far as to call the politicians dumped by voters "TARP martyrs."[62] Unfortunately, opposition and outrage are exactly what you'd expect from the Political Class whenever voters assert their authority as the sovereign power in the land.

Voter opposition is the most important ingredient in preventing future bailouts. While the politicians ignored voters in the fall of 2008 on the subject, the response will make elected politicians think twice before doing so again.

Still, it may be wise for voters to seek protection from companies that

---

61.   Chris Edwards, "Special-Interest Spending," Apr. 2009.
62.   "The Political Price of Backing Invaluable TARP," July 2010.

want to demand protection because they are "too big to fail." It's important to note that voters didn't buy this argument during the bailouts of
2008 and 2009. Most said it would be okay to let the largest banks in the
country go out of business.[63]

But the regulators listened to Wall Street and not Main Street. So it
might be wise to take away some of the regulatory authority that let them
bail out their friends. And it is important to shift the focus of regulatory
efforts back to protecting the people who trusted the banks with their
money rather than protecting the banks and the bankers.

Only 17 percent favor breaking the larger banks up into smaller
banks. Another 29 percent think larger banks deserve stricter regulation than smaller banks. While that brings to a total of 46 percent those
who want action taken specifically on the biggest banks, a roughly equal
number (49%) say even the biggest of the banks should be treated like
all the others.[64]

Given those attitudes, and the strong desire to prevent future bailouts, a modest approach might focus on the Federal Deposit Insurance
Corporation (FDIC), one of the more popular New Deal legacies. Currently, the FDIC guarantees all bank deposits up to a total of $250,000
per account. Those limits are way more than enough to protect the vast
majority of Americans and small business owners. To avoid undue risk
to taxpayers from any single company, a limit could be placed on the
total amount of guarantees that could be provided to any one bank. This
has been suggested by Dr. Mark Calabria of the Cato Institute and others. Banks would be allowed to grow as large as they want, but taxpayers
would no longer provide unlimited guarantees. If a bank grew to the
point where it exceeded the total FDIC guarantee limit, it would have to
do so either by taking in accounts without federal guarantees, or perhaps
by limiting the amount guaranteed on all accounts in that bank. In prac-

---

63.   Rasmussen Reports, "Americans Not Sure on Financial Reform Bill, but Don't Think Some Banks
       Are Too Big To Fail," June 2010.
64.   Rasmussen Reports, "Only 28% Say Some Banks Are Too Big to Fail," Oct. 2009.

tical terms, this would have no impact on the vast majority of depositors, but it would limit the federal liability.

A related change might also require the FDIC to protect only the deposits that are insured when a bank fails. There is no need to protect wealthy people who knowingly put money into an unguaranteed account. Yes, this would increase the risk and exposure for those who have more than a quarter of a million dollars in a single account, but people with such cash reserves will have plenty of reasons to carefully consider the safety of their bank. A side benefit of these changes is that those wealthier depositors with more money at risk would be likely to monitor their bank's creditworthiness far more carefully than a government regulator. It is also consistent with the tendency of Americans to believe it would be better for the financial system to have more competition and less regulation.[65]

Dr. Calabria believes that other actions should also be taken to protect taxpayers from future bailouts by "limiting the ability of regulators to throw money at failing companies." He suggests "repealing Section 13-3 of the Federal Reserve Act, which allowed the AIG, Bear, and other Federal Reserve bailouts and repealing the Exchange Stabilization Fund, which allowed Treasury to bail out the mutual fund industry."

Regardless of the specifics, the objective must be to prevent future bailouts of failing companies. When the failing companies are banks, small and midsize depositors should be protected, but that's different from protecting the bank itself.

These steps are all part of constructing the necessary wall between corporate America and the state. Eventually the government will have to eliminate all direct payments, subsidies, loans, and loan guarantees from the federal government to corporations large and small. Doing so will save the American taxpayer $50 billion a year or more. As already discussed in chapter 6, ending corporate welfare will also require elimination of all preferential tax treatment for favored companies and indus-

---

65. Rasmussen Reports, "Americans Say Free Trade Good for Economy, but Costs Jobs," Nov. 2010.

tries. While the savings are not as big as the numbers from changes in national security, Social Security, and Medicare, they're still significant. But the bigger value from eliminating corporate welfare will come from eliminating the corruption of both the political process and free market competition.

Americans rejected state capitalism when they dumped tea into the Boston Harbor on December 16, 1773. They rejected government run by a self-selected elite on July 4, 1776. Those foundations led America to become a great economic power and a great role model of freedom and liberty. Those foundations are now at risk. Today, seven out of ten Americans believe that government and Big Business tend to work together against the rest of us. Corporate welfare is a big part of the reason why.

If government of the people, by the people, and for the people is to survive, corporate welfare must end.

9

———•———

Giving the People a
Return on Investments

You can learn a lot about people by listening carefully in casual settings. It's especially helpful to listen to people in settings where politics and government are the last things on their mind. After all, that's the way most Americans spend most of their time. Years ago, I was getting a bite to eat in a sports bar. Along with everybody else in the room I was cheering when the Yanks scored and grumbling when they struck out. Most of us went back to our own conversations during the commercials, until a political ad came on and the candidate mentioned "compassion." Some guy at the bar then snorted loudly, "That son of a b—— wants to raise my taxes." That got an even bigger cheer than the Yankees. I'm sure the political message about "compassion" sounded better to campaign consultants than to the cynics at the bar, but voters have become skilled at determining what politicians mean despite what they say.

This is why there is so little trust when politicians call for government investments in their favored projects. Politicians like to talk of investing rather than spending because Americans love investing in the future. Most voters own stocks, bonds, or mutual funds, and the overwhelming majority of those who don't expect to do so someday. Investing in a family home is often considered part of the American Dream, and many

Americans routinely talk of investing their time in a project or new business.

When people invest on their own, they expect to make money and know how to measure it. People buying stock in a company think the company will do well. They are hoping that the stock's value will go up and they'll eventually be able to make a profit. With some stocks, they might earn dividends along the way. Others might hope for a steadier return and place their money in a bank or a certificate of deposit to earn a little interest. Regardless of the strategy, Americans recognize the importance of deciding what you do with the money and measuring what kind of a return you get. When politicians talk about government investments, they talk only about the spending side of the equation. They talk about investing in the nation's future, in people, and in compassion, but don't make it clear how to measure the return. This is why guys in sports bars don't believe them and scream, "That son of a b—— just wants to spend more of my money." Voters are all too familiar with bridges to nowhere and other such boondoggles.

As a result, when politicians talk about investing in, say, job creation, many voters roll their eyes. By a 68 to 18 percent margin, Americans believe that a billion dollars invested by companies to grow their own business will create more jobs than a billion dollars invested by the government on new highways.[1] With that perspective, a job-creation strategy that transfers money away from private businesses makes little sense.

Perhaps frustrated by voter skepticism, politicians sometimes go over-the-top and make ludicrous statements trying to tap into the American love for investments. Agriculture Secretary Tom Vilsack stated with a straight face that every dollar spent on food stamps returns an economic benefit of $1.84. He tried to claim that the food stamps program is a form of investment in economic growth.[2] If that were the case, Americans

---

1. Rasmussen Reports, "45% Say Government Should Reduce Spending on Roads and Highways Until Budget Is Balanced," Aug. 2011.
2. "Obama Ag Secretary Vilsack: Food Stamps Are a 'Stimulus,'" Aug. 2011.

wouldn't be concerned that it's too easy for people to get food stamps.[3] The government could simply issue more food stamps and our economic woes would be behind us. Those with even an ounce of common sense realize that's not the way reality works. Of course, some politicians claim that all government spending improves the economy, a view rejected soundly by the American people.[4]

Not all claims for generating a return on government spending sound as tone-deaf as those made by Vilsack. President Obama mentioned government investments eight times in his 2011 State of the Union address. He argued for "investments—in innovation, education, and infrastructure—[that] will make America a better place to do business and create jobs."[5] That logic instinctively makes sense to many if the investments are wisely made.

But it's hard to have confidence about government investments in innovation when, as mentioned earlier, only 11 percent believe that government officials are better than private investors at seeing potential benefits of technology. Seventy-one percent believe private investors will do a better job.[6]

Even the most famous and successful government innovation in technology was viewed skeptically by the American people. In the 1960s, President John F. Kennedy issued a national challenge, calling for "landing a man on the moon and returning him safely to the earth." To his credit, he did not attempt to minimize the cost and size of that investment, asking "Congress and the country" to make a commitment "which will last for many years and carry very heavy costs." He said that there was no middle ground: "If we are to go only halfway, or reduce our

3. Rasmussen Reports, "55% Say Those Who Receive Food Stamps Should Be Required to Work," Apr. 2011.

4. Rasmussen Reports, "55% Say Decreased Government Spending Good for the Economy," July 2011.

5. Barack H. Obama, "2011 State of the Union Address," Jan. 2011.

6. Rasmussen Reports, "71% Think Private Sector Better Than Government at Measuring Technology Potential," Aug. 2011.

sights in the face of difficulty, in my judgment it would be better not to go at all." While asking a lot, President Kennedy also made it clear that he saw potentially worthwhile returns. It was, according to the president, a key step in "the battle that is now going on around the world between freedom and tyranny." He added, "We go into space because whatever mankind must undertake, free men must fully share."[7]

Americans generally approved of the Apollo space program during the 1960s, but remained skeptical of the costs. Even while NASA mounted an unprecedented media campaign aided by stunning visuals, heroic astronauts, and live television coverage, roughly half the nation consistently wanted less money spent on the space program. Partly the public doubted the returns could be delivered. An early poll found roughly one-third thought the United States would get to the moon first, one-third thought it would be the Soviet Union, and one-third didn't know. Only once during the 1960s did a majority of Americans believe the race to the moon had been worth the cost, and that came in the summer of 1969 at the time of the first moon landing. Still, even when the government program delivered on its stated goal, only 53 percent believed it was worth the amount of money spent.[8]

Forty years later, the space program draws similar reviews. As the Space Shuttle program came to an end, a Rasmussen Reports survey found that just 50 percent of American adults believed it had been worth the expense to taxpayers. Prior to the hype surrounding the final mission, only 40 percent held that view. Even though space exploration has always been a government program, Americans are evenly divided as to whether future exploration should be funded by the government or the private sector.[9]

By a 63 to 27 percent margin, Americans now believe the government should cut its spending on space exploration at least until the bud-

7. John F. Kennedy, "Special Message to the Congress on Urgent National Needs," May 1961.

8. Roger D. Launius, "Public Opinion Polls and Perceptions of US Human Spaceflight," 2003.

9. Rasmussen Reports, "50% Say Space Shuttle Program Worth What It Cost Taxpayers," July 2011.

get is balanced.[10] Collectively, the data suggest a willingness of voters to put up with moderate amounts of government investment in space, but it is not a top priority. The amount invested should be adjusted in response to other budget realities, and private sector options should be considered. Government investment in innovation in other areas also draws tepid reviews.

If the public saw truly significant returns from government investments, they would overwhelmingly support them. If they thought all the money was wasted, the public would demand an end to such programs as many have clamored for an end to earmarks, but the reality of most government investments is somewhere in between, and so is the public response. It's a bit like a family trying to set aside money for retirement. It's tough and most are willing to do so, but they'll trim their investments during tough times rather than run up a credit card even further.

In his 2011 State of the Union address, President Obama didn't shoot for the moon—he kept his sights a little closer to home, calling for investments in education, a theme that most Americans heartily endorse. Sixty-one percent agree with another of President Obama's assertions: "A world-class education is the single most important factor in determining not just whether our kids can compete for the best jobs but whether America can outcompete countries around the world."[11] That is one reason public schools are able to spend more than $600 billion a year on K–12 education. The spending grows to more than $700 billion annually when private schools are included.[12]

But, while willing to spend enormous amounts on education and believing strongly in the importance of education, just 26 percent believe that our nation is currently providing a "world-class education" for our children.[13] Year in and year out, Gallup finds that a majority of Ameri-

10.   Rasmussen Reports, "45% Say Government Should Reduce Spending on Roads and Highways Until Budget Is Balanced," Aug. 2011.
11.   Rasmussen Reports. "26% Say US Public Schools Provide World-Class Education," Aug. 2011.
12.   Jeffrey M. Silber and Paul Condra, *BMO 2010 Education Industry Report*, Sep. 2010.
13.   Rasmussen Reports, "26% Say US Public Schools Provide World-Class Education," Aug. 2011.

cans are dissatisfied with the "quality of education children receive in kindergarten through grade twelve."[14] Rasmussen Reports polling finds that only 11 percent believe the nation is getting a good return on the average of more than $10,000 spent per child per year for K–12 education. Seventy-two percent disagree and say taxpayers are not getting their money's worth.[15]

When most politicians see data like that, they seem to always come back to a need for more money. To many of them, that's all there is to government investing. But just 34 percent of voters believe student performance will improve if more money is spent on funding for schools and education programs.[16] Only 29 percent of adults are willing to pay higher taxes so more money could be spent on schools.[17] It's not that voters oppose the concept of investing in education; it's just that they don't believe more money will provide adequate returns.

A similar response is found to the third item in the State of the Union wish list for investments—infrastructure programs. As mentioned in the first chapter, only 41 percent support the president's high-speed-rail plan; even that level of support came only after a major presidential speech and propaganda push.[18] While politicians envision taking credit for such projects, voters instinctively prepare for the inevitable cost overruns and diminishing returns. On the president's high-speed-rail plan, that has already happened: a portion of the track that was supposed to cost about $7 billion is now expected to cost $3–$7 billion more than anticipated.[19] Voters have learned over the years that the cost of government investments is typically higher than projected and that the promised returns often fail to materialize.

These gut instincts from voters have been validated by Oxford Uni-

14. Lydia Saad, "Americans Support Federal Involvement in Education: Democrats Want More Federal Involvement in Schools; Republicans Want Less," Sep. 2010.

15. Rasmussen Reports, "72% Say Taxpayers Not Getting Their Money's Worth from Public Schools," Apr. 2011.

16. Ibid.

17. Rasmussen Reports, "65% Oppose Four-Day School Week," Apr. 2010.

18. Rasmussen Reports, "41% Favor High-Speed Rail Plan, 46% Oppose," Feb. 2011.

19. Megan McArdle, "California High-Speed Rail Project to Cost More Than Expected," Aug. 2011.

versity's Bent Flyvbjerg, who wrote a book on such megaprojects. "It is becoming increasingly clear that such projects have strikingly poor performance records in terms of economy, environment, and public support. Cost over-runs and lower than predicted revenues frequently place project viability at risk and redefine projects that were initially promoted as effective vehicles to economic growth as possible obstacles to such growth."[20] This from a guy who has served as an adviser to "more than 40 public and private organizations, including the EU Commission, the United Nations, national and local government, auditors general, banks, and private companies. His work covers both developed and developing nations."

Michael Barone of the *Washington Examiner* notes that inexpensive bus service from the private sector with no government funding outperforms high-speed rail in providing inner-city transportation for many on a budget. "You can beat the proposed Minneapolis–Duluth line by going just slightly over the speed limit on I-35. The proposed line from the college town of Iowa City to Chicago would take longer than the currently operating bus service." Barone's conclusion: "So the private sector provides cheap intercity transportation while government struggles to waste $53 billion. Please remind me which is the wave of the future."[21]

In addition to stopping funding for the high-speed-rail project, voters are also ready to eliminate subsidies for Amtrak. In fact, most Americans are even open to the idea of selling Amtrak and getting the government completely out of the passenger rail business. Dropping the high-speed-rail proposal and ending Amtrak subsidies would reduce projected spending by more than a hundred billion dollars over the next decade.

It's not just railroad spending that makes voters uncomfortable. Only 40 percent of voters supported the president's call for a $50 billion federal jobs and infrastructure program. An even smaller number, 28 percent, believe that such a spending plan would do more for the economy

20.   Bent Flyvbjerg et al., *Megaprojects and Risk: An Anatomy of Ambition* (2010).
21.   Michael Barone, "Traveling Back to the Future on Intercity Buses," Aug. 2011.

than cutting government spending and reducing the deficit.[22] That ties back to the earlier showing that voters believe money invested by private companies pursuing their own interests will create more jobs than government investment in new highways.

As a result, a plurality of Americans (45%) say the federal government should cut spending on roads and highways at least until the federal budget is balanced.[23] It's interesting to note that highway projects are always touted by politicians as jobs programs rather than any analysis of how much spending is really needed on the highways.

The instinctive response of voters that government "investments" rarely deliver the promised payoff was also confirmed by three professors at Harvard Business School—Lauren Cohen, Joshua Coval, and Christopher Malloy. They examined decades of data to measure the benefit a district received when its representative became an important committee chairman. The view from Washington is that a powerful legislator can steer federal money to the folks back home and they'll be much better off. However, the Harvard researchers learned that exactly the opposite was true. "It was an enormous surprise, at least to us, to learn that the average firm in the chairman's state did not benefit at all from the increase in spending," says Coval. "Indeed, the firms significantly cut physical and R&D spending, reduced employment, and experienced lower sales." So when the government increases "investment" in an area, the private sector cuts back. "Fiscal spending shocks appear to significantly dampen corporate sector investment and employment activity."[24]

Despite plenty of experience, many elected politicians, lobbyists, and others continue to talk as if government investment in just about anything provides an obvious benefit. From the view of the Political Class, the only challenge is getting voters to set aside enough money. Voters, as

---

22. Rasmussen Reports, "61% Say Cutting Spending Will Create More Jobs Than Obama's New $50 Billion Program," Sep. 2010.

23. Rasmussen Reports, "45% Say Government Should Reduce Spending on Roads and Highways Until Budget Is Balanced," Aug. 2011.

24. Lauren Cohen et al., "Do Powerful Politicians Cause Corporate Downsizing?," Mar. 2010.

is typical in the early twenty-first century, see things entirely differently. They don't want to set aside the money unless they believe the returns will be worth the cost and the risk. Given the current lack of trust in the political process, it's a tall order to convince the voters of the potential for a return.

Consider, for example, a US Department of Transportation "analysis" that claimed that $1 billion of new transportation spending would create forty-seven thousand new jobs. It was believed that every extra billion spent would create another forty-seven thousand jobs.[25] If that were true, solving the unemployment challenges facing the nation would be easy. In fact, if that were true, President Obama's stimulus plan would have solved the nation's economic challenges in 2009. But it's not true, and one reason is that the billion to pay for the highways would have to come from somewhere else and would cost jobs somewhere else. A Congressional Research Service (CRS) study put it this way:

> To the extent that financing new highways by reducing expenditures on other programs or by deficit finance and its impact on private consumption and investment, the net impact on the economy of highway construction in terms of both output and employment could be nullified or even negative.[26]

One 1996 study by the Federal Highway Administration presented the concept of investing in highways as an investment with diminishing returns. They provided a better return when the system was first being built and the major highways had a big impact on transportation routes. Later on, once the system was more complete, the returns for each dollar invested declined or disappeared. That intuitively makes sense.

The Heritage Foundation's Dr. Ronald Utt summarizes the available research by noting, "Claims that highway spending can quickly create

---

25.   Ronald Utt, "More Transportation Spending: False Promises of Prosperity and Job Creation," Apr. 2008.

26.   Ibid.

jobs and spur the economy are highly questionable given the mixed findings of decades of independent academic studies on the relationship between federal spending programs and job creation."[27]

Results from other government investments is equally discouraging, perhaps more so. Roughly 50 million children attend elementary schools, middle schools, or high schools, and another million or so are in pre-K programs. Roughly one hundred thousand public schools and more than thirty thousand private schools are drawing upon the talents of nearly 4 million teachers. This is a massive commitment to the future of the nation, and voters recognize the significance. Seventy-three percent consider teaching one of the most important jobs in the nation.[28]

Americans think highly of teachers and the value of education, but not so highly of the results. Despite dramatic increases in government spending per student over several decades, test scores for students have not improved,[29] and American students lag behind those of other nations in many areas.[30] Most Americans believe textbooks are more interested in political correctness than accuracy.[31] They also believe discipline in schools is lacking today.[32]

As for higher education, the costs of college have been soaring while students are spending only half as much time studying as they did a few decades ago. "Nearly half of the nation's undergraduates show almost no gains in learning in their first two years of college," reported *USA Today*, summarizing a book, *Academically Adrift: Limited Learning on College Campuses*. Research showed that more than a third of all traditional college students have no significant improvements in learning even after *four full years* of college. That's a staggering assessment. After spending four years of life and tens or hundreds of thousands of dollars in tuition

27. Ibid.

28. Rasmussen Reports, "73% Say Being a Teacher Is One of the Most Important Jobs," May 2010.

29. John E. Chubb and Terry M. Moe, *Liberating Learning: Technology, Politics, and the Future of American Education* (2009).

30. Joel Klein, "The Failure of American Schools," June 2011.

31. Rasmussen Reports, "60% Say Their Kids' Textbooks Place Political Correctness over Accuracy," Mar. 2010.

32. Rasmussen Reports, "68% Say School Discipline Is Too Easy These Days," July 2011.

and housing, one out of three students didn't learn anything. You don't have to have a college degree to recognize that's a bad investment.

And the three thousand students in this study received good grades on average. Still, in a typical semester, half never had a class where they had to write "more than 20 pages a week," and a third never had to read "more than 40 pages per week."[33] Another study found that a third of seniors who frequently skipped homework and class preparation still got A's for their effort.

Defenders of the status quo point to studies showing that college is still a great investment. Those who go to college earn more than those who don't. But that's a little bit like the claim that highway projects create lots of jobs if you ignore other things that could have been done with the same money. Richard Vedder, author of *Going Broke by Degree: Why College Costs Too Much*, points out that people who go to college already had an advantage because "they did better in high school."[34] In other words, they would have earned more even if they had not gone to college.

Whether the issue is innovation and space programs, infrastructure and highways, or any educational programs and financial aid, voters appreciate the goals of potential government investments but are skeptical about the competence of the government to deliver tangible returns. When reports circulate of job-creation programs that cost $2 million per job or other projects that flop, the underlying skepticism is reinforced. In the current political environment, aligning government policy with voter attitudes requires focusing more on getting a good return for the money taxpayers are already investing rather than calling for more investments. The ideal solution would be something along the lines of reducing spending by, say, 10 percent but improving the rate of return by 20 percent or more. The bigger those numbers get on both sides of the equation, the better.

In the area of innovation, the best way to do this is to end all corpo-

33. Mary Beth Marklein, "Report: First Two Years of College Shows Small Gains," Jan. 2011.
34. Ibid.

rate welfare payments, as discussed in the previous chapter. If private investors and businesses are better at identifying the benefits of new technologies, let them do it and let them pay for it. Nobody likes it when government officials try to pick winners and losers in the private sector.

With infrastructure projects and education projects, the challenge is different. It's defining the objectives more clearly and ensuring that the public dollars invested go for the highest-priority projects. Ultimately, like most other solutions to the federal budget debacle, the answer lies in shifting decision-making authority away from government officials and into the hands of private citizens.

Consider highway projects in the context of data from *The 2008 Status of the Nation's Highways, Bridges, and Transit: Conditions and Performance*, published by the US Department of Transportation. The United States has more than 4 million miles of roads and highways, most of which are traveled relatively little. The vast majority of these roads (76%) are under the jurisdiction of local governments. Twenty percent are state controlled, and about 4 percent are the responsibility of the federal government. The 165,000 miles of the Interstate Highway System may be just a small portion of the road mileage, but they account for about 44 percent of all traffic in the United States.

While improvements could always be made, the roads are in pretty good shape. Ninety-three percent of traffic travels on roads officially defined as adequate or better, including 57 percent whose condition is rated good. Both figures have gotten better in recent years. Not surprisingly, rural roads tend to be in better shape than the heavily trafficked urban roads. These figures are consistent with the public's assessment. Forty-eight percent say the highways they drive on are in good or excellent shape, 42 percent say fair, and just 9 percent rate the highways as poor.

Most of the system's six hundred thousand bridges are inspected every two years, and most are in good shape. The federal government owns about 1.5 percent of these bridges. Out of the six hundred thousand bridges from coast to coast, only two of the major bridges have collapsed over the past decade. That is two too many, but it's not a sign of a systemic problem.

Federal, state, and local governments combined spend more than $160 billion a year on highways. About half of that is spent on capital projects such as building new roads or rehabbing and upgrading older highways. Roughly a quarter is spent on maintenance, and the rest goes to a variety of administrative, finance, law enforcement, and safety functions. The federal government pays for nearly half of all capital expenditures on highways. Clearly the system is not on the brink of collapse, and slight increases or decreases over a short time are not going to have a major impact on the highway system. Longer term, however, spending patterns could have a significant impact.

With such a sprawling and massive operation, the only way for voters to demand a better return on this major national investment is with an approach that lets those who benefit from the spending bear the cost. The Department of Transportation has done a whole range of calculations about how much various levels of spending on highways would theoretically reduce the wear and tear on cars. Those who would do the most driving would save the most. They are also the best positioned to determine whether the estimates of savings from better roads are as big in the real world as they are on paper.

So, the federal government has a chance to regain some credibility by restoring the integrity of the federal Highway Trust Fund. Seventy-three percent of voters think all federal gas taxes should be paid into that fund and used only to pay for building, maintaining, and repairing highways (with perhaps a bit set aside for mass transit). Most also think some additional money should be contributed from the general fund, perhaps in the belief that the highways provide some general benefit to society beyond the personal benefits.[35] That's okay so long as it's done on a matching basis so that highway spending goes up only when drivers are

---

35. Rasmussen Reports, "53% Oppose Gas Tax Hike, Even If Dedicated Only to Interstate Highways," July 2011.

willing to pay more. Currently, for every $4 paid from the Highway Trust Fund, about $1 is contributed from the overall operating budget. That seems reasonable. With a formula like this in place, federal highway funding would no longer be determined by politicians seeking earmarks; spending levels would be determined by how much motorists are willing to pay in taxes on gasoline at the pump.

Once limits are placed on spending, government officials will have to prioritize projects and get creative rather than asking for as much money as they can get. Solutions to some other problems may also be found by aligning costs and benefits. For example, one of the big challenges in some areas is traffic congestion, especially during rush hours. Congestion pricing plans have been suggested for years so that if someone drives in rush hour, they pay a slightly higher toll. Those with more flexible plans might consider driving at another time. A limit on spending for new highways might spark more interest in such experimentation.

But, much as the linkage between the gas tax would change the behavior of politicians, it would also affect drivers in their role as voters. If voters could trust where the money was going, they would evaluate the trade-offs much differently. Polling shows just how big a difference this could make. Currently, when the money from the gas tax goes into a big pot for the politicians to divvy up, hardly anybody supports an increase in the gas tax.[36] In fact, a plurality favors eliminating the federal gasoline tax until prices at the pump come down. But if the tax revenue is tied directly to more spending on highways, support for raising the gas tax jumps to 33 percent. So there's not yet support for raising taxes to support more highway spending, but the linkage of gas taxes to highway spending suggests voters will respond differently if the quality of highway driving deteriorates. And, along the way, that linkage will prevent politicians from spending more than is appropriate. The same logic could apply to state and local road-building projects as well.

When it comes to education, a similar approach is needed: it's important to identify whom the federal policy is intended to benefit. The

---

36.   Ibid.

stakes, however, are much higher. While the nation spends more than $160 billion annually on highways and roads, spending for education at all levels tops $1.2 trillion. Imagine if that money could produce better returns! If our system can be fixed to deliver a world-class education, lives will be changed for the better, the number of people living in poverty will decline, and the long-term foundations of the economy will give our nation a competitive edge over every other nation in the world.

The good news is that the tools for such a revival are at hand. The Internet and handheld digital communications are already working to change education every bit as much as the emergence of television changed radio; as much as the emergence of cable television changed regular television; and as much as the Internet has changed everything about television. Even for those of us who grew up in the era when three television networks ruled the land, it's become normal to watch "TV" shows on an iPad and get news on our phone.

The potential for transformational change is so great that even some in the world of traditional education have started to take notice. "Stanford University, George Washington University, Indiana University, and the University of Missouri have all launched online, diploma-granting high school programs over the past few years, and several other four-year universities offer online classes to high school students."[37]

The Bill & Melinda Gates Foundation is donating more than $20 million to create online courses in forty-two states.[38] But if the changes in education are anything like the changes in other industries, many of the most profound innovations will come from newcomers to the field.

The exciting possibilities for the field of education are well beyond the scope of this book. The question to address here is how these issues affect federal spending. Consider the current state of higher education. The federal government has invested heavily in making sure that just about anyone can go to college if he or she wants. It currently holds nearly a trillion dollars in student loans and provides grants to 8 million

37.   Jason Koebler, "Universities Begin to Offer Online High School Diplomas," Aug. 2011.
38.   Jason Koebler, "Gates Foundation Donates $20 Million for Online Courses," Apr. 2011.

students that never have to be repaid. Most Americans believe that any qualified student who wants to get a loan for college can do so, and just 31 percent now believe it is too hard to get a college loan.[39] A bigger problem is that the rising cost of college leaves many students with a debt burden that takes far too long to repay.

Not surprisingly, a flood of federal money intended to help students has had the unintended consequence of dramatically raising the cost of going to college. Those increased costs aren't going to help the students. An analysis by *Investor's Business Daily* (IBD) found that from 1989 to 2009, the number of college students grew by 51 percent while the number of faculty members grew by 75 percent. The number of administrators grew by 84 percent during that same time. The *IBD* analysis was based upon figures from the National Center for Education Statistics.[40]

In a normal business setting, the economies of scale would kick in and the number of administrators per customer would decline. Exactly the opposite has happened in the world of higher education. While the bureaucracy is growing, just 57 percent of students at four-year colleges graduate within six years! Despite all the extra administrators, just 30 percent believe colleges and universities do enough to monitor students' behavior. Most believe that they are not doing enough to stop underage drinking on campus. Only 43 percent believe the schools do enough to ensure the safety of their students.[41]

Perhaps the best way to highlight the growing costs associated with higher education is by examining a relatively new phenomenon — for-profit colleges. These schools are regulated just like not-for-profit private and public colleges. They are also subjected to an additional level of regulatory scrutiny due to their profit motive. Even though many Americans have never heard of them, roughly 10 percent of college students attend a for-profit college. Some of these schools have been leaders

39.   Rasmussen Reports, "31% Say It's Too Hard to Get a Student Loan," June 2010.
40.   David Hogberg, "Pop Quiz: Why Are Tuitions So High?," Aug. 2011.
41.   Rasmussen Reports, "46% Say Colleges Don't Monitor Student Behavior Enough," Aug. 2009.

in adapting new Internet technologies to higher education, and they are currently more likely to serve lower-income students with greater needs.

Tuitions at for-profit colleges are similar to those at other schools. However, tuition and fees provide about 90 percent of the revenue at for-profit schools. At public schools, the tuition and fees make up only about 16 percent of the revenue. At private not-for-profit schools, the comparable figure is 26 percent. What this means is that a public college or university spends four or five times as much per student as a for-profit college. The tuitions are about the same, but taxpayer subsidies make up the difference at the public universities.[42] At private not-for-profit schools, the difference is made up by a combination of government funding, alumni contributions, and endowments.

Part of the difference reflects that public universities engage in a lot more research and devote more of their energies to things other than teaching students, but public support is for helping students get an education rather than building up prestigious institutions. In fact, it's similar to the dynamic of guaranteeing bank deposits: Americans think the federal government should have been concerned about protecting depositors rather than bailing out banks. In education, Americans want the federal government to provide financing for students, not to subsidize the faculty lounge. Unfortunately, at a majority of colleges, the tuition paid by students subsidizes research projects and other non-teaching-related activities.[43]

As you might suspect, the way to address this concern is to align federal policies with underlying public attitudes. Voters overwhelmingly support providing college loans for all academically qualified poor and middle-class students, but they are not supportive of an expensive giveaway. In fact, the public is evenly divided as to whether it is more important to make sure everyone who wants to attend college can get a loan or whether the top priority should be making sure that all college loans

---

42. Jeffrey M. Silber and Paul Condra, *BMO 2010 Education Industry Report*, Sep. 2010.

43. Andrew Gillen et al., "Who Subsidizes Whom?," Apr. 2011.

are repaid.[44] That suggests a tightening of standards or that collection procedures may be in order.

Voters are also evenly divided on whether grants that don't have to be repaid should be provided for low-income students. Most oppose providing such grants to middle-class students. At a time when Pell Grants have grown from helping 2 million students a year to 8 million within a decade, these public attitudes suggest a little tightening of standards might be in order. Those at the bottom end of the income ladder should be protected, but those a bit better off could receive loans rather than grants. Since Pell Grants currently cost the federal government about $30 billion annually, converting half of these to loans could result in significant savings.

The bigger issue relates to the high costs of elite schools. Just 28 percent believe the government should provide student loans and grants to help cover the cost of attending the most expensive colleges.[45] From an economic perspective, that makes sense since only 3 percent think those who attend Ivy League schools are better workers than those who go to other schools.[46] On the jobs front, an overwhelming 81 percent of Americans believe that people learn more practical skills through life experiences and work after college rather than *in* college.[47]

From a policy perspective, the overall attitudes suggest support for something like a program that limits the total amount of government grants and loans to the tuition costs for an average university. If Harvard or Yale wants to provide extra assistance for their students, let them fund it from their endowments. If their schools are as good as they claim, they should have no trouble getting the loans repaid, but there's no need for the federal government to get involved.

If the total amount of grants and loans is restricted to the cost of an av-

---

44. Rasmussen Reports, "Voters Like Government Student Loans, Frown on Pell Grants That Don't Have to Be Repaid," Aug. 2011.

45. Rasmussen Reports, "31% Say It's Too Hard to Get a Student Loan," June 2010.

46. Rasmussen Reports, "3% Say Ivy League Schools Produce Better Workers," Mar. 2011.

47. Rasmussen Reports, "81% Say People Learn More Outside the Classroom Than Inside," Mar. 2010.

erage tuition, it will still meet the needs of the vast majority of students. It will also provide pricing pressure on universities that charge more. An added bonus is that students would have a lower debt burden when they leave school. A key to making all of this work, however, is that the students get to choose the school. To help spur the needed innovations, the government will have to resist the natural Political Class temptation to prop up the government-subsidized universities and let the students select the schools that best meet their needs. Funding of university research centers should be done separately rather than by pretending the money is going to help students.

A similar process is needed for K–12 schooling, but the federal government pays only about 8 percent of the total tab of K–12 education. Forty-eight percent comes from the states, and 40 percent from local governments, with the rest coming from parents in the form of private or parochial school tuition.[48] Changes are desperately needed in a system that devours vast amounts of money but often fails to deliver value. Testing of 2011 high school graduates showed that just 52 percent met college-readiness standards in reading. Only 45 percent met such standards in math.[49] In a society where the vast majority of high school graduates plan on attending college, it is unacceptable for them not to be ready to do so.

Given the federal government's minimal role in funding, the drive for improvement and innovation will naturally come from the states, local government, and the private sector. That's as it should be. It's impossible to know what the world of education will look like in a decade or so, but we can be confident things will get much better so long as voters demand a better return on investment and policymakers focus on helping students rather than defending the status quo.

That's the real message for all government investments. The United States invests a lot of money in government projects—more than a tril-

---

48.   Jeffrey M. Silber and Paul Condra, *BMO 2010 Education Industry Report*, Sep. 2010.

49.   John E. Chubb and Terry M. Moe, *Liberating Learning: Technology, Politics, and the Future of American Education* (2009).

lion dollars every year in education, more than $160 billion in highways, nearly $20 billion in our space program, and more. Certainly, ways exist to reduce costs a bit at the federal level, but the real benefit will come from getting a better return on what we already spend. So when a politician starts talking about the need to spend more on government investments, voters need to resist the temptation to say, "That son of a b—— just wants to spend more of my money." Instead, voters need to challenge those politicians to stop spending and focus more on the other side of the investing equation.

10

———•———

Tightening the Belt
of the Beltway

Talk to most voters for any length of time and discussions about the federal budget crisis will move to the topics of federal payrolls and trimming fat from federal spending.

Americans overwhelmingly believe that government employees in general do not work as hard as those in the private sector. It's also believed that government workers are paid more than comparable workers in the private sector and have more job security and better benefits.[1] These general attitudes are supported by the fact that government employees report their personal finances are in better shape than their private sector counterparts.[2]

At the same time, it's important to recognize that American voters are not seeking to throw government workers "under the bus." They just want all men and all women to be treated equal. That's why 71 percent believe that the goal should be for government employees to receive

1. Rasmussen Reports, "Most Americans Still Think Those in Private Sector Work Harder, Earn Less Than Government Employees," Aug. 2011.
2. Rasmussen Reports, "Two Economies: Government Workers Optimistic, Private Sector Not," Dec. 2009.

pay, perks, and benefits comparable to those in the private sector. Only 14 percent believe they should be paid less.[3]

Rather than engage in a rational discussion on the topic, both political parties play up stereotypes that support their point of view. Those who defend the government employees talk about the incredible work done at enormous personal risk by police, firefighters, and the US military. They play up stories of dedicated schoolteachers who not only work hard, but pay for school supplies out of their own pocket. Those on the other side point to stories of government employees who play solitaire on the computer all day, receive outrageous pensions, or make $200,000 a year as lifeguards (with the added bonus of early retirement).

Enough truth is out there for both stereotypes to gain traction, but the American people have a much more rational perspective on the situation. They know the federal workforce includes both extremes as well as many people who simply go to work every day, do their best, and go home. They recognize that the private sector workforce has gone through significant contraction in recent years, while government workers were largely protected for most of the recession. In fact, during 2009, government workers grew more optimistic about their personal finances and the overall economy, while those in the private sector became more pessimistic.[4]

This dynamic has played out dramatically in some state budget battles, most notably in Wisconsin, where Democratic state senators fled the state to try to prevent the legislature from acting on proposals for reducing payroll costs and taking away collective bargaining rights for public employee unions. After the legislation passed, Democratic activists tried to defeat a state Supreme Court justice who supported the measures and also tried to recall several Republican state senators. The state was flooded with money, protests, extreme rhetoric, and unavoidable campaign ads during the first half of 2011, during what should have been a quiet time on the political calendar.

---

3. Rasmussen Reports, "46% Say Government Workers Are Paid More Than Comparable Private Sector Workers," June 2010.
4. Rasmussen Reports, "Two Economies: Government Workers Optimistic, Private Sector Not," Dec. 2009.

In the heated standoff between Republican governor Scott Walker and public employee unions, voters tended to side with the unions on the issue of collective bargaining rights.[5] However, on the underlying economic issues they sided with the governor. This was documented not only by polling data, but by the tactical decision of the unions to accept all the economic concessions proposed by Governor Walker while choosing to fight over the issue of collective bargaining rights.

Americans may want to avoid the extreme political activity that spilled out in Wisconsin, but they are supportive of more modest efforts to bring the federal payroll under control. Sixty-six percent of voters nationwide favor cutting the federal payroll by 10 percent over the coming decade. Only 22 percent are opposed.[6] There are many feasible ways of reducing the payroll by 1 percent annually for ten years. Some of the savings could come from attrition, simply not replacing those who retire or take another job. In other cases, there might be pay freezes, other cost-saving measures, or, unfortunately, occasional layoffs. In practical terms, every agency of the federal government would have to make its own decisions as to the best possible way to reduce its own payroll by at least 1 percent a year for ten years.

The potential impact of a steady reduction of the federal payroll is enormous. The federal government currently has approximately 1.4 million employees outside the military (cutbacks in the military payroll were already discussed in chapter 3). A 10 percent reduction in federal payroll costs would lead to direct annual savings of approximately $25 billion a year. However, if no change is made, the federal payroll would continue to grow by approximately $65 billion over the coming decade.

So the combination of direct savings and elimination of expected increases would reduce the federal payroll by about $90 billion annually compared to currently projected levels. Additional saving would likely be generated because a smaller workforce would by necessity lead to

5.   Rasmussen Reports, "Wisconsin Voters Oppose Weakening Collective Bargaining Rights in General, but Strongly Support Specific Changes," Mar. 2011.

6.   Rasmussen Reports, "Two-Thirds Favor Cutting Federal Payroll by 10%," Nov. 2010.

the elimination or reduction of some government programs. After all, if you have a tight budget and just enough employees to do the work, it's hard to dream up new ways for government to get involved in the lives of the American people. On top of that, a smaller workforce also would require less spending on supplies, training, and support. These numbers aren't as big as the savings from national security, Social Security, and Medicare, but $90 billion a year is real money, even to the federal government.

Support also exists for similar payroll reductions in state and local governments. This sort of thing is often forgotten in the focus on Big Government, but the savings to the nation from such an effort would be even bigger than the reduction of the federal payroll. Eleven times as many people work at the state and local level as at the federal level. Implementation of such a plan at the state and local level would also have to be done in a manner that is respectful to the employees.

It's important to keep in mind that the growth of the government workforce means the nation now has just over six private sector workers for each government employee. That means average private sector workers are contributing more than 15 percent of their pay for the average government employee. Anything that can reduce that burden will be a plus for the nation.

As part of the overall payroll reduction, one fertile area for reform is federal pension benefits. Currently, military retirees can receive retirement benefits after twenty years of service and more substantial benefits after thirty years of service. This allows some personnel to retire as early as their late thirties with a pension and health care for life. If you enter the military at age eighteen, you can retire after twenty years with a lifetime pension at age thirty-eight. Those who stay for thirty years can receive a lifetime pension equal to 75 percent of their highest salary along with lifetime health insurance benefits. It all starts as early as age forty-eight. Other federal employees also participate in a pension plan with a low minimum retirement age — fifty-seven.

Voters don't have a problem providing pensions for government employees. But 71 percent believe that government pension benefits are better than those in the private sector. If a government worker has put in enough time to collect a pension, six out of ten voters believe that they should find another job and wait until they retire at around age sixty-five to receive the full pension benefits.[7] If people completed their military service at age forty-eight, they would still be eligible to receive a full lifetime benefit, but the payments wouldn't begin until they reached age sixty-five. In most cases, such individuals would find another job until their benefits kicked in, and many would earn a second pension along the way. Changes such as this cannot be made unilaterally for current military personnel and other federal employees, but they could be implemented going forward (with perhaps a phase-in period). Some of the savings from the reduced benefit promises could be used to reduce the $4 trillion in currently unfunded liabilities in the federal pension system. The rest could be used to help federal agencies reach the goal of reducing payroll by 1 percent per year for a decade.

It's important to highlight the inclusion of all benefits rather than just salaries in the calculation to reduce payrolls.

Asking every agency of the federal government to reduce its payroll costs by 1 percent a year is a reasonable target, since every agency can trim a little here and there. Nobody likes cutting his own budget, but it can be done. Corporate America has been cutting back over the past several years as the nation's economy has wobbled, and for many Americans it's simple decency for the government to do the same. It's also common sense to refrain from asking agencies to take on significant new assignments as their payroll is reduced. If a new task must be addressed, an older expense needs to be trimmed first. Those who support a balanced budget need to refrain from calling on the government to do new things. For most voters that's not a problem, but it's something to keep in mind.

Just lowering the federal payroll, even by 10 percent, won't be enough. Uncle Sam must tighten his belt in other ways. Voters also complain about wasteful spending, and plenty of stories support their perception.

---

7. Rasmussen Reports, "71% Believe Government Workers Get Better Pensions Than Those in Private Sector," Mar. 2011.

It's painfully easy to find stories about such things as a $615,000 grant to "digitize Grateful Dead photographs, tickets, backstage passes, flyers, shirts, and other memorabilia."[8] There are also stories about the Defense Department buying hundreds of thousands of airline tickets and never using them, the Department of Education providing student funding for students—and a school—that doesn't exist,[9] and the Department of Veterans Affairs spending money to maintain buildings it doesn't use. It's also easy to find stories about federal funding for a "critter crossing" in Vermont and overpriced hammers and screwdrivers in the military budget.

While mentioning such projects is good for a laugh or to confirm the worst fears of some, identifying these items won't solve the problem. There will always be mistakes and waste and silliness in any organization—public or private—spending trillions of dollars. Anybody serious about restraining federal spending will focus on bigger and more structural solutions to minimize it rather than just pointing fingers. It's a little bit like someone who wants to go on a diet and lose weight. It's easy to see that a brownie sundae deluxe should be avoided, but skipping one dessert won't accomplish the goal. A serious dieter will set up a plan with goals and probably some exercise routine and will need discipline to keep working toward those goals, even when extra effort is required. In addition to skipping the brownie sundae deluxe, it may be necessary to cut back on even healthy foods a bit.

The same concepts apply to solving the federal government's fiscal crisis. It's not enough to just say federal government spending should be restrained. Targets for spending limits should be established and policy changes made to reach those targets (such as those suggested in previous chapters). Once the major policy changes get us close to the targets, a little extra effort may be required. The spending limits will help

8. Tina Korbe, "Updated—Worst of the Waste: The 100 Outrageous Government Spending Projects of 2010," Dec. 2010.
9. Brian Riedl, "Top 10 Examples of Government Waste," Apr. 2005.

squeeze the cringe-worthy research projects and overpriced hammers out of the mix.

Fifty-six percent of voters favor a law that limits the growth of US government spending each year to how much the population has grown plus inflation. Just 21 percent are opposed. It's also interesting to note that a third of those who are opposed to such limits want a stricter spending limit. Only 4 percent of all voters want no spending limits. This desire for limits reflects that voters recognize the problem. Seventy-four percent understand that government spending over the past ten years has grown by more than the growth of the population plus inflation. Only 4 percent mistakenly believe it has grown at a slower pace.[10]

This spending framework, not surprisingly, is a middle ground between those who want to slash spending dramatically and those who want the government to keep growing faster than the economy, but it would dramatically slow the projected growth of federal spending over the next decade.

Is that type of spending restraint attainable? Certainly! Most of the steps toward achieving that goal have already been addressed earlier in the book. A military strategy to Protect America First would save money that we currently spend to defend other nations. Other savings would come from reducing corporate welfare, demanding a better return on government investments, and consolidating welfare expenditures in the budget. Over time, federal government spending would consume a smaller and smaller share of the economy.

Of course, setting those goals for putting the federal government on a diet is one thing, and making it happen is something else. Some frustrated fiscal conservatives dream of writing strict legislation that will force spending reductions to be made according to some formula. That's just wrong. No diet plan in the world can help someone who insists on that brownie sundae deluxe at every meal, and no budget formula and

---

10. Rasmussen Reports, "56% Favor Spending Cap Tied to Population Growth and Inflation," May 2011.

no budget plans can implement themselves. The targets are useful only in trimming the last bits of savings after the big steps (such as those in earlier chapters) have already been taken. Ultimately, though, leadership is needed, and it is currently lacking in Washington today.

Finding leaders worthy of trust is essential for all who would like to see the government downsized. Let me repeat that point. Those who want to see government downsized need to work on restoring trust in our system of politics and government. When I say that while giving speeches around the country, conservative and libertarian activists are often shocked. Many of them have devoted all their energy to showing how government programs rarely work as promised and always cost more than expected. Others tap into the deep wellsprings of skepticism about politicians to raise doubts about government in general. Their concerns are legitimate, but if changes are to be made, organizations need to be entrusted with the moral authority to bring about change. For big issues, such as Social Security, Medicare, and taxes, voter approval can be obtained directly, but to handle smaller budgetary issues and the details of the budget, elected politicians who will consistently implement the public's desires are needed.

John Maxwell is a leadership expert who speaks to Fortune 500 companies, international government leaders, and organizations as diverse as the United States Military Academy at West Point and the National Football League. He has spent a lifetime leading people, studying leaders, and teaching people how to become successful leaders. Corporations and other organizations pay top dollar for his presentations, and his books have sold 19 million copies, enough to earn him a slot in the Amazon.com Hall of Fame. Along the way, Maxwell has observed, "There is a common misperception among people who aren't leaders that leadership is all about the position, perks, and power that come from rising in an organization."[11] This misperception is understandable after watching corporate officers drive companies such as General Motors

---

11.   John C. Maxwell, *The 21 Irrefutable Laws of Leadership: Follow Them and People Will Follow You* (2009).

into bankruptcy while taking tens of millions of dollars for themselves. When executives for failed companies that had to be bailed out by taxpayers take home seven-figure salaries, it's hard to think of leadership in any other way. Those corporate chieftains took shareholders and taxpayers for a ride and walked away with outlandish amounts of money.

That's just the private sector. Voters are more concerned about elected politicians and other "public servants" who seem to share the view that "leadership is all about the position, perks, and power that come from rising in an organization." Forty-six percent of voters believe *most* members of Congress are corrupt, and 85 percent believe those in office put their own careers ahead of helping others.[12] As was mentioned earlier, most also believe that members of Congress will use the power of their office to help those who contribute to their campaigns and hurt those who won't.[13] Voters overwhelmingly believe the game in Washington is a form of legalized extortion and that businesspeople give money to politicians because they're afraid of what will happen if they don't.[14]

Maxwell acknowledges, "In recent years, we've observed more than our share of leaders who used and abused their organizations for their personal benefit," but he still maintains, "The heart of leadership is putting others ahead of yourself. It's doing what's best for the team." Those who seek first the perks of the job are bureaucrats, not leaders. By that standard, there are few leaders in official Washington these days. Unfortunately, there are lots of elected politicians.

To solve our nation's fiscal crisis will require true leadership, politicians who will put the preferences of voters ahead of their own dreams and their own careers. Listening to the voters on topics such as national security, Social Security, Medicare, and taxes is a good start. Any elected politician who wants to be a sacrificial leader, however, must also go further and display leadership among the federal workforce. The public mood is demanding cuts in the federal payroll and the reduction or elim-

---

12.   Rasmussen Reports, "New High: 46% Think Most in Congress Are Corrupt," July 2011.
13.   Rasmussen Reports, "Americans Agree Congress Doesn't Play by the Rules," Feb. 2009.
14.   Rasmussen Reports, "Most Say Political Donors Get More Than Their Money's Worth," Feb. 2009.

ination of many programs. Implementing these changes in a thoughtful manner will require leadership that can win credibility and trust among both taxpayers and government employees.

A simple starting point would be for the president of the United States to cut his own pay in half and call upon Congress to cut their own pay by 25 percent at least until the federal budget is balanced. The pensions for both the president and Congress should be eliminated. These are the types of steps leaders should take before asking anybody else in the federal workforce to sacrifice. They are also popular with voters. Eighty-two percent support the 25 percent pay cut for members of Congress, and a plurality (48%) support a 50 percent pay cut for the commander in chief. Fifty-nine percent of voters don't think members of Congress should receive government pensions when they leave office, and 52 percent want to cut or eliminate the presidential pension of nearly $200,000 per year.[15] This doesn't even require legislation. Any member of Congress or candidate for Congress could instantly cut his or her own pay and pension benefits.

Most voters would like to go even further and see a 25 percent cut in the White House and congressional staffing. While the Political Class may consider such suggestions outrageous, most others would probably consider such steps to be leading by example. All of these proposals together don't add up to much direct dollar savings in a nation that is more than $100 trillion in debt, but they do begin to establish credibility for leaders who will have to deal with the downsizing of government.

These should be considered starter steps and nothing more. As mentioned earlier, politicians should also give up any appearance of special privileges by letting any American buy the same health care coverage that members of Congress and other federal officials enjoy. Other steps will be needed to clean up the reputation that DC politicians have earned over the years. The objective is not to impose a vow of poverty on politi-

---

15. Rasmussen Reports, "Voters Favor Pay Cuts for Congress, President Until Budget Is Balanced," Aug. 2011.

cians, but to have leaders show that they are willing to make sacrifices in their own finances and staff support before they ask others to do so.

When asking agencies to trim their payroll by 1 percent a year, leaders who have made sacrifices in their own pay and benefits will be able to honestly say they tried other options first. They will have demonstrated the necessity of the restraints they demand by living it out themselves. They will be in a stronger position to demand enforcement of restraints to keep spending growth within limits.

For any of this to work, voters will need to find a group of politicians who will become leaders by representing the American people in the budget battles. No matter what systems and budgetary targets are put into place, the only way that government spending will be cut is if a group of elected politicians maintain a disciplined commitment to achieving those goals year in and year out. People in positions of power are needed to restrain the Political Class desire to bust the budget and increase spending.

To take just one example, the US Postal Service announced that it may have to lay off 120,000 workers and cut their benefits unless the federal government is willing to cover its losses. Most voters say no to such spending. In fact, 75 percent would rather cut mail delivery back to three or four days a week rather than have federal subsidies cover the losses.[16] Plenty of people in the Political Class will be ready to protect the Postal Service, but who will protect the voters?

Establishing workable targets to achieve these desired results requires careful consideration. Again, just like a diet, it's important to know what you're looking to accomplish. For a diabetic, keeping weight off is important, but the real objective is keeping blood sugar under control. So even if you reach your desired weight, more changes may be required if your blood sugar is still too high.

In budgeting, the objective is to provide tools that will help keep the

---

16. Rasmussen Reports, "75% Favor Big Cuts in Mail Delivery Rather Than Give More Money to Postal Service," Aug. 2011.

government trim, rather than spending money on the financial equivalent of brownie deluxe sundaes. This probably means the best approach
is to enforce a spending cap equal to current expenses plus population
growth and inflation on the government's operating budget. Programs
such as Social Security, Medicare, and unemployment insurance would
be exempt because they operate through trust funds instead of through
the budget. Despite what the government wants to believe, those funds
belong to those who paid them and can be used only for the designated
purposes.

Interest on the federal debt should also be exempt from the spending that is included in the population-growth-plus-inflation spending
formula. That's partly because the best way to control interest costs is to
reduce the debt, but it's also because the volatility of interest rates could
have a distorting impact on other spending decisions. In a year when
interest rates fell a point or two, the declining interest costs would go
down so much that it might provide an excuse for politicians to increase
other spending. On the other hand, if interest rates went up in a year,
the total cost of interest payments would go up dramatically. In that case,
the required cuts to stay within the overall spending limits would be so
severe that it would be hard to implement them. Regardless of the specific numbers, it would be a policy nightmare as spending increased or
decreased in response to interest-rate swings.

The proposals already mentioned in this book would reduce the
growth of spending enough to stay within these spending targets. Looking to the future, establishing an overall restraint will provide an important benchmark to ensure that spending never again gets so far out of
control.

Those who want to restrain the growth of federal spending should also
be looking for large and systemic savings that can be found throughout
the budget. As always, the best solutions will be those that improve the
services for Americans while reducing the cost. Additionally, proposals
that bring the government into line with public opinion do more than
just help with the budget; they help restore confidence in our system of
governance.

One example of this could be the nation's system of unemployment insurance. This was originally part of the New Deal Social Security program, and it's a joint federal-state effort. The program is broadly popular and a key part of the nation's safety net. Most of the funds are collected by the federal government, but distributed to the states for distribution. The tax, paid by the employer, is currently 6 percent on the first $7,000 in pay each year for each worker. It's not a huge amount (up to $420 for a worker in 2011), but the program can be made to work better for workers by recognizing that the twenty-first century is vastly different from the 1930s.

Borrowing from ideas mentioned earlier, workers could be given a choice between staying with the government unemployment program and selecting a private sector option. As with health insurance, the tax money paid by the employer could be used by the workers for any plan. If the workers find something that can save money, they can keep the change. As with Social Security and Medicare, giving workers more choice is likely to be popular with voters.

This would open the field for workers to consider a variety of options beyond just a weekly unemployment check. Some might prefer to buy a package that would cover their mortgage payment or other bills during a time of unemployment. Others might want to seek options that provide higher weekly payments or funds for retraining. Still others might like to spend less for the insurance up front and receive their unemployment benefits as a loan. The real power of the idea is that it gives workers a chance to make the decisions for themselves. If the government program is the best option, they will take it. If not, they will choose a different option on their own without having to get involved with the political process.

To make something like this work would require a bit of creativity. Some minimal guidelines for the private insurance might need to be enacted (e.g., perhaps a requirement for some level of cash support during the first months of unemployment). There might also be a need to have a tiny portion of the tax from each worker put into a general fund to protect all workers and maintain the solvency of the government's portion of the program.

Regardless of the specifics, the dollars involved are significant. During 2011, the federal government spent about $135 billion on unemployment benefits. If a significant number of workers select private insurance options, the government costs would come way down while workers would receive a better service. Most of the changes would result in savings for the Unemployment Insurance Trust Fund, but such reforms could also reduce the need for federal workers. That, in turn, could make it easier for the Department of Labor to reduce its payroll by 1 percent a year.

Just to drive home the point, enacting a reform on unemployment insurance is far more effective in terms of resolving the budget crisis than railing against NPR. NPR doesn't take enough government funding to be a reasonable target for spending cuts, but it comes under fire because it suits the ideologies of some self-proclaimed budget crusaders. Politicians who present cutting NPR as a solution to the budget crisis aren't really interested in cutting the budget. They're just interested in using the budget argument to drive their own political agenda. They pretend they're battling the budget because it enables them to sell a more popular story to voters. Voters support balancing the budget; they don't support petty partisan squabbles.

That's why a reform such as the unemployment proposal works best; it puts decision-making authority in the hands of individual Americans rather than politicians and bureaucrats. It offers a variety of options for workers so they can choose the one that works best for them. From a budgetary perspective, it reduces government spending in a big way and it helps a government agency reduce its payroll.

As mentioned earlier, trimming agency payrolls and limiting the growth of federal spending to population growth plus inflation are possible only with a commitment to avoid giving the agencies more work to do. Even better are changes that reduce the workload for federal agencies.

One way to accomplish this is through regulatory reform. Americans recognize the need for some basic regulations, but also tend to think that more competition will produce better results for consumers than more regulation.

Voters recognize that companies have a vested interest in serving consumers well and treating workers well. Still, a delicate balance is needed in the regulatory arena. Some regulations are needed, but excessive regulation has a devastating effect on consumers, companies, and the US economy. As discussed in the chapter on health care, one way to address this balance is to let the states compete to find the right mix of regulation and competition to hold companies accountable. Large corporations dislike the state-by-state approach, but that's hardly a reason to drop the idea. Up until the 1980s, most banks operated within state lines and were regulated by state authorities. Then, pushed by some who claimed we needed bigger banks, the state system was overturned. Just a few years ago those bigger banks collapsed, demanding hundreds of billions of dollars from taxpayers to stay afloat.

At the federal level, three systemic reforms could help find the right balance. One would simply require that every time an agency proposes a new regulation, it must drop an old regulation.

A second would require all regulations to be approved by Congress before implementation. This sounds like common sense, but Congress is often out of the loop, and unelected bureaucrats can impose massive regulatory burdens without any appropriate checks and balances. Every now and then, the regulators do things so off-the-wall that the excesses become apparent. A recent example came when the Food and Drug Administration claimed Cheerios should be regulated as a drug. Only 4 percent of voters nationwide agreed with the FDA, while 87 percent disagreed and opposed such regulation. On the broader question of government regulation of cereal, just 13 percent believe more regulation is needed while 69 percent disagree.[17] Applying checks and balances won't eliminate all the excesses, but it will restore an important level of accountability for the regulators.

It's important to note that the elimination of checks and balances for regulators was not an accident, but intentional. A central desire of the Political Class is to move decision making as far as possible away from

---

17.   Rasmussen Reports, "Cheerios 87, FDA 4," June 2009.

control by voters. President Herbert Hoover embraced this approach to governing as he led the nation into the Great Depression, and President Barack Obama shared the same mind-set when promoting his health care plan. A report in *Investor's Business Daily* noted the nation now has more federal regulators than the total number of employees working for McDonald's, Ford, Disney, and Boeing combined.[18]

A third reform of the regulatory process would build upon the estimates that the Congressional Budget Office provides on the cost of regulations. If the budget objective is to hold the growth of spending to population growth plus inflation, a similar limit should be placed on the growth of regulatory costs.

All three of these regulatory reforms are conceptually popular with voters. Nothing like this has ever been implemented before, so plenty of details need to be worked out. In working out those details, it will be important to honor the underlying voter desire to hold companies accountable with the right mix of regulation and competition. Voters generally have more faith in competition, but as was discussed in the chapter on health care, sometimes it takes a lot of work to create a situation where competition can flourish.

Many voters want to go beyond the proposals already mentioned in the chapter and see a Balanced Budget Amendment added to the US Constitution. Fifty-six percent of voters support this proposal and just 22 percent are opposed.[19] Given the recent history of the federal government, it's easy to understand why. Any effort to align the federal government with voter preferences must eventually lead to the passage of a Balanced Budget Amendment (BBA).

Having said that, it's important to note that such an amendment is not a silver bullet to solve the budget crisis. It would make sense to pass a BBA only *after* major reforms such as those outlined in this book have been implemented. That's because structural solutions such as a BBA

---

18.   John Merline, "Regulation Business, Jobs Booming Under Obama," Aug. 2011.
19.   Rasmussen Reports, "56% Favor Balanced Budget Amendment," Sep. 2011.

THE PEOPLE'S MONEY   233

can work only so long as they are realistic, supported by the nation's leaders, and most important, supported by the American people. Unfortunately, some people place undue faith in structural solutions as a tool for forcing people to do what they don't really want to do. However, no matter what rules are put in place, if the American people want to find a way around them, they can. If a Balanced Budget Amendment were in effect right now, it would require massive and immediate cuts in Social Security and Medicare. The American people would rebel, a loophole would be found, and the BBA would be rendered meaningless. As *National Review*'s Rich Lowry has noted, every proposed version of the Balanced Budget Amendment has an exception for when the nation is at war. He concludes, "As a plot to get Nancy Pelosi to declare war on Switzerland or another handy inoffensive country, this is brilliant. Otherwise, it's wholly inadequate."[20]

Given that reality, the BBA should be viewed more as a tool to help keep spending under control, rather than a tool to get there in the first place. This is still vitally important. As every dieter knows, keeping the weight off is often harder than losing it in the first place. Those who dream the BBA could be used to force unpopular decisions on an unwilling public simply misunderstand the process, but those who understand it could be used to lock in the victories earned from implementing fundamental reforms realize what a powerful tool it could be.

The BBA should come after other reforms are implemented for a couple of other reasons. One is that the accounting issues discussed in the first chapter need to be resolved before a BBA can even be accurately defined. A second is that current renditions of the BBA might allow government spending to continue at higher levels than necessary. Rushing a symbolic amendment ahead of its time could end up doing more harm than good.

In summary, even after the reforms outlined earlier in the book are implemented, voters are supportive of efforts to reduce the federal payroll and encourage other belt-tightening. These include:

---

20.   Rich Lowry, "Against the Balanced Budget Amendment," July 2011.

1. Reducing the federal payroll by 1 percent a year for ten years.
2. Requiring all federal employees to wait until age sixty-five to receive full pension benefits.
3. Limiting the growth of federal spending to the growth of population plus inflation.
4. Pay cuts for members of Congress and the president.
5. Elimination of congressional and presidential pensions.
6. A 25 percent reduction of congressional staff.
7. Letting workers use their unemployment insurance taxes for either the government unemployment program or a private sector option.
8. Regulatory reform to reduce the federal workload. Require all agencies to drop one regulation for each new regulation, requiring congressional approval for all final regulations before implementation, and limiting the growth of regulatory costs to the growth of population plus inflation.
9. Passage of a Balanced Budget Amendment *after* other reforms have been implemented to bring the budget in balance.

Plenty of other changes are possible as well. But for all of the structural changes that can be implemented, all efforts to instill budgetary discipline require getting leaders in office who will represent voters rather than politicians who serve the Political Class. Elected politicians who want to become leaders need to make sacrifices to earn the trust of voters. They need to remember Maxwell's view that "the heart of leadership is putting others ahead of yourself. It's doing what's best for the team."

11

---•---

Adding It All Up

Over the past eight chapters, I have outlined a number of policy changes that would align government policy with popular opinion and fundamentally alter the federal budget. Yet many readers may feel that those proposals don't measure up to the "tough choices" that are needed to balance the budget. What about the pain that politicians and pundits say will be inflicted by cutting the government? Some advocates of extreme spending cuts speak of the need to wipe out whole agencies—get rid of the Department of Education, the Department of Energy, or some other bureaucracy. On the other side of the aisle, countless members of the Political Class dream of the day when the American people will finally accept the need for massive tax hikes to fund the status quo. Like George Grenville, the British prime minister who long ago implemented the Stamp Act, they complain about the "ungrateful people of America" and whine about how Americans want more government than they are willing to pay for.

If you're looking for that type of slash-and-burn or make-'em-pay approach to the nation's fiscal crisis, this book has surely disappointed. That's because it's focused on where the American people want to go and what it will take to align government policy with that direction. The American people have good, sound, positive instincts and are far more interested in moving the nation forward rather than settling old scores. The Political Class's belief that tough choices are needed says more about how the Political Class disagrees with the American people than anything else. The Political Class wants a government powerful enough to rule a nation. The American people want to govern themselves.

Following those instincts, the American people's gut reactions lead to a budget that offends just about everyone in Washington because it is based upon common sense and pragmatism rather than ideology. Still, the question remains, can relatively inoffensive concepts—such as cutting back on the US role as world policeman, allowing people to select their own retirement age, and demanding a better return on government investments—really make much of a dent in the federal budget?

The answer is yes.

• Following the ideas described in this book, which are broadly supported by the American people, federal spending in the operating budget alone would be reduced by $10 trillion over the coming decade ($35.9 trillion compared to $45.7 trillion under current policies).

Total Federal Spending 2012–2021

(In Trillions of Dollars)

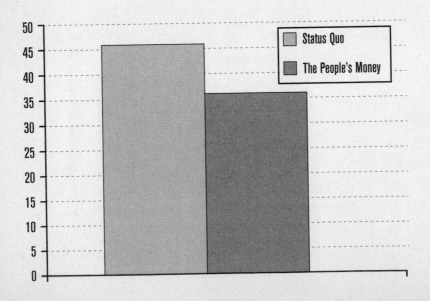

- Cumulative operating deficits over the next decade would be reduced from a current projected total of $9.7 trillion to $2.9 trillion.

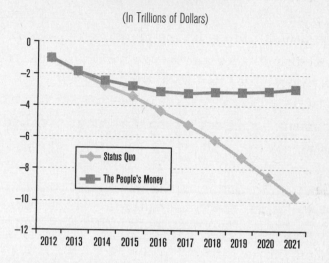

Cumulative Operating Deficit

(In Trillions of Dollars)

- Taxes would be cut by $3 trillion over the full decade.

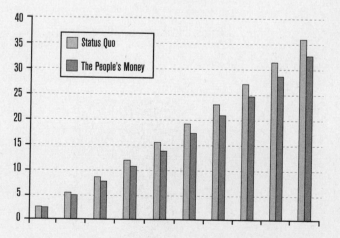

Cumulative Federal Tax Revenue

(In Trillions of Dollars)

- Federal spending in 2021 will be 24 percent of GDP if current policies are pursued. However, with the reforms proposed in this book, spending would be just 16.8 percent of GDP in 2021. That would be the lowest since 1956.

Projected Government Expenditures as Percent of US GDP

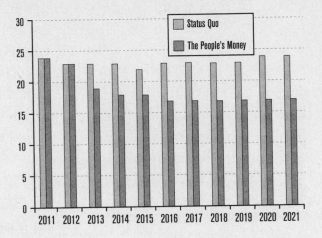

- The federal budget, as currently measured, would be balanced by 2018 (following the status quo approach, there would still be a $952 billion deficit in that year). Ten years from now, the budget would have a $138 billion surplus (as compared to a $1.3 trillion deficit under current policies).

Federal Deficit in Billions

(Numbers > 0 Reflect Surplus)

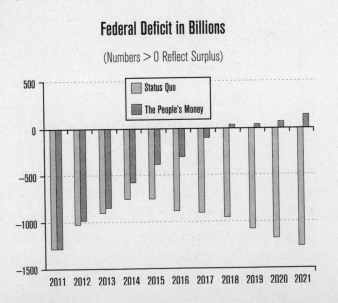

- Under current policies, the federal deficit is projected to get worse in every year from 2015 to 2021. With the reforms outlined in this book, the deficit would get better in every year from 2012 to 2021.

The biggest impact of all would be found by taking into account the long-term unfunded liabilities in the Social Security and Medicare trust funds. As noted in chapter 2, the real debt of the US government is approximately $120,000,000,000,000 ($120 trillion). In addition to the annual operating deficit, this figure grows by about $3 trillion a year. If the current policies are followed, the government will be approximately $160 trillion in debt ten years down the road. That's a $40 trillion increase in the debt burden. However, if the commonsense reforms supported by voters are implemented, the total debt will fall dramatically from $120 trillion today to $18 trillion in 2021.

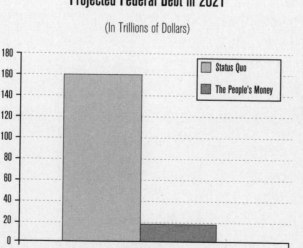

Projected Federal Debt in 2021

(In Trillions of Dollars)

What this means is that the Social Security trust fund would be balanced for the long term. The Medicare trust fund would be in balance. The operating budget would be showing a surplus, and the budget would be on track to repay the entire federal debt during the 2020s. No debt, no unfunded liabilities, no unconscionable burden to pass on to future generations.

Projected Federal Debt

(In Trillions of Dollars)

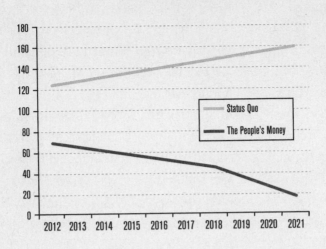

Another huge bonus would result from aligning government policy with voter preferences. The elimination of the debt burden would have an enormously positive impact on the US economy. Voters believe that reducing the debt, reducing government spending, and reducing taxes are all good for the economy.[1] The approach in this book would accomplish all three. That the government actually listened to the people rather than the Political Class would add to the level of consumer confidence.

Following the lead of the American people would reduce the total federal debt by more than $100 trillion over the next decade and leave the nation $142 trillion better off than the status quo. That's the kind of debt relief that can stimulate significant economic growth.

It is widely recognized that an improving economy also improves government finances. Tax revenues go up during good economic times, means-tested spending goes down, and deficits decline. If the budget is already balanced when that economic boost appears, surpluses will

---

1.   Rasmussen Reports, "Most Voters Still Think Tax Cuts, Spending Decreases Benefit Economy," June 2011.

grow. That will lead to a political firestorm about what to do with the surplus—some will want to use the "extra" money to fund new government programs, while others will say it should be used to enable tax cuts. Voters, however, have a different idea. Eighty percent say that any surpluses should be used to pay down the federal debt accumulated in earlier times.[2] So, until the federal debt is paid off, there would be no new spending and no new tax cuts.

All of this sounds good, but it's important to take some time to see where the numbers come from. Unfortunately, that requires digging step-by-step through an array of federal documents and reference points. A cynic, upon studying the budget documents provided from official sources, might conclude that the Political Class didn't want the American people to find out how the federal government was spending their money!

So, where did these numbers come from?

The starting point for all serious budget projections should be the work of the Congressional Budget Office (CBO). The CBO provides some of the best and most impartial research in all of Washington, DC. Their reports on budget projections, updated regularly, provide reams of useful information for budget junkies. To see if the proposals in this book will lead to a balanced budget, the place to start is with the CBO projections of the status quo. However, for the layperson, a bit of decoding is often needed because of restrictions placed upon the CBO by the politicians in Congress.

As already mentioned in chapter 2, one of the challenges of reading CBO numbers is that the agency is required to report budget updates in terms of changes to projected spending. That basic concept skews the entire debate. Imagine the government spending $10 on something today and expecting spending to reach $12 next year. If spending grows only to $11, it's reported as a spending cut. This creates all manner of confusion in budgetary discussions. What passes for spending cuts to the

---

2.   Rasmussen Reports, "80% Think Any Budget Surplus Should Go to Paying Down the Debt," July 2011.

nation's politicians are considered reductions in spending growth to any-body else. That said, the CBO publishes the raw numbers, which allow us to find out what's really going on.

In August of 2011, the CBO published its last update before this book went to press. Other updates will come over the years, and the specific numbers will change a bit from time to time. But the essentials of the debate will remain unchanged unless major policy changes are imple-mented. And voters don't expect that to happen anytime soon. Two-thirds expect nothing will be done until after election 2012.[3]

The August 2011 CBO update showed long-term projections based upon the so-called spending cuts that Congress had agreed to as part of their deal to raise the debt ceiling. In that deal, Congress allegedly cut spending by a trillion dollars over the coming decade and set in place a mechanism to support another trillion and a half dollars in cuts. So what happens to federal spending with all those cuts? As shown below, it grows from $3.6 trillion in 2011 to at least $5.2 trillion in 2021!

Summary of Projected Baseline Federal Budget Outlays

(All Figures in Trillions of Dollars)

2011	2012	2013	2014	2015	2016	2017	2018	2019	2020	2021
3.597	3.609	3.579	3.688	3.870	4.125	4.317	4.496	4.767	5.007	5.248

Source: CBO, Table I, page xi, author's calculations

Assumes all unspecified deficit reduction comes from reductions in projected spending rather than revenue increases.

Keep in mind that the spending growth outlined in the table above assumes that Congress will carry through on its effort to reduce the growth of spending by finding more than a trillion dollars in unspecified cuts. It also assumes that Congress will actually deliver on the trillion dollars in "cuts" allegedly agreed to in the debt-ceiling deal. Most voters nationwide believe it is unlikely that those "cuts" will ever materialize.

---

3.   Rasmussen Reports, "Just 38% Think Major Spending Cuts by Congress Likely in the Next Year," Jan. 2011.

But the CBO is required to report what the current law says, regardless of how likely the law is to be implemented.

Despite the enormous growth in government spending projected for the next decade, the CBO projects significant deficit reduction because federal tax and other revenues are projected to grow from $2.3 trillion in 2011 to $5.0 trillion in 2021. That these tax and spend numbers can grow so rapidly, despite political talk of budget cutting, highlights the need for one reform mentioned in chapter 2. Budget projections and reports should focus on real dollar changes rather than changes from a mythical current services budget. Think how different the tone of a story might be if the official documents noted the truth. Even if you assume that Congress will reduce the growth of spending over the next decade by the promised $2.2 trillion, annual spending will increase from $3.6 trillion this year to $5.2 trillion in a decade! Of that $1.6 trillion in spending growth, $0.7 trillion is required to offset the impact of inflation.

Because it is required to base its projections upon whatever current law is on the books, the CBO shows that deficit spending is heading down dramatically over the coming years. Its official baseline projections show the following:

Summary of Official Projected Baseline Deficits

(All Figures in Billions of Dollars)

2011	2012	2013	2014	2015	2016	2017	2018	2019	2020	2021
-1,284	-973	-510	-265	-205	-278	-231	-211	-259	-277	-279

Source: CBO, Table I, page xi

If that table reflected reality, I would not have needed to write this book. While the CBO's work to develop those numbers is impeccable, the result is pretty meaningless. The data is based upon a series of faulty assumptions that reflect the way Congress pretends to see the budget world, and the CBO is required to process the data. The CBO report puts it this way: "If some of the changes currently specified in current law did not occur and current policies were continued instead, much larger deficits and much greater debt could result."[4] The numbers are staggering. Fortunately, the CBO provides the raw data to come up with some figures that are a bit closer to reality. Those show the official federal debt growing by nearly $10 trillion over the next decade rather than the official projection of $3.5 trillion. Remember, that doesn't even include the growth in unfunded liabilities.

On a single-year basis, the numbers are also depressing. Taking out the unrealistic policy expectations, the CBO numbers show an annual deficit in 2021 of $1.3 trillion, more than four times larger than the official projection. That's little changed from the 2011 deficit, which is the third largest in history (the only two larger deficits were in 2009 and 2010). Not only that, the adjusted numbers show the deficit increasing for seven consecutive years, 2015–21. As if this weren't bad enough, the CBO reports, "Beyond the 10-year projection period, further increases in debt relative to the nation's output almost surely lie ahead if certain policies remain in place."

The difference between the official deficit projections and the more reality-based numbers, highlighted in the table below, comes down to five policies:

1. The official numbers assume Congress will really deliver on the promised trillion dollars plus of unspecified reductions in spending growth.
2. The official numbers assume that Congress will stick to the so-called discretionary spending caps agreed to in the 2011 debt-ceiling deal. Given the recent track record of Congress, that's hard to believe.
3. Under current law, the already low Medicare reimbursement rates paid to doctors are projected to be cut dramatically. That's not going to happen.

---

4.   Congressional Budget Office, *Budget and Economic Outlook: An Update*, Aug. 2011.

4. The official projections assume that the Bush administration tax cuts will be allowed to expire in 2012. Nobody is seriously suggesting such a huge middle-class tax hike.

5. Current law shows that indexing for the Alternative Minimum Tax (AMT) for inflation will end in 2012. Originally, this tax was designed to prevent the very wealthy from using loopholes to completely avoid taxation. Now roughly 4 million people pay this tax.

Adjusting the Official Projected Baseline Deficits for Likely Policy Changes

(All Figures in Billions of Dollars)

	2011	2012	2013	2014	2015	2016	2017	2018	2019	2020	2021
Official Projection	−1,284	−973	−510	−265	−205	−278	−231	−211	−259	−277	−279
Adjustments	0	−51	−385	−482	−545	−606	−672	−742	−816	−897	−985
Revised Projection	−1,284	−1,024	−895	−747	−750	−884	−903	−953	−1,075	−1,174	−1,264

Source: CBO, Table I, page xi, and Table 1–8, page 26, author's calculations
Adjustments include extra debt service costs from additional interest on federal debt.

With these adjustments, the projected revenue and outlay numbers are summarized below:

Revised Revenue and Outlay Projections

(All Figures in Billions of Dollars)

	2011	2012	2013	2014	2015	2016	2017	2018	2019	2020	2021
Revenue	2,314	3,559	3,469	3,652	3,793	3,893	4,044	4,151	4,275	4,389	4,511
Outlays	3,597	4,583	4,364	4,399	4,543	4,777	4,947	5,104	5,351	5,563	5,775
Deficit	−1,284	−1,024	−895	−747	−750	−884	−903	−953	−1,075	−1,174	−1,264

Of course all these numbers will fluctuate a bit over time, even if no policy changes are implemented. If the economy gets a bit better than projected, the deficit numbers will look a bit less depressing. On the other hand, if the economy doesn't do quite as well as projected, the deficit numbers will get a bit worse. But these are reasonable targets to use as a starting point.

As described in chapter 2, these deficit projections do not come close to properly measuring progress toward what voters mean by a balanced budget. We'll take a look at the numbers using a more meaningful measure of balance later in this chapter, but there is some value in seeing how the numbers stack up using the faulty accounting systems of the Political Class. That's the standard used in the current debate, so options need to be framed in that manner as well. If nothing else, reviewing the numbers in this manner will reassure those who fear that a new accounting approach might merely be a gimmick to hide ongoing deficits.

Using the CBO numbers as a starting point, the table on page 247 shows how the budget looks in 2011, how the status quo budget would look in 2021, and how the budget aligned with voter preferences would look in 2021. It's worth noting that even after restraining the growth of spending with the reforms mentioned earlier in this book, federal spending will still be higher in 2021 than it is today. Looking at the details, spending will be higher in five of the six budget categories than it is today. Only a politician could call the increase in spending from $3.6 trillion in 2011 to $4.0 trillion in 2021 a spending cut!

At the same time, however, in all six categories, spending will be lower than it would have been in the status quo budget. Overall, spending will be 30 percent lower by implementing these reforms.

The short answer in terms of the difference between the Status Quo approach and the People's Money approach is that it's the difference between following the Political Class or listening carefully to the American people. Numerically, the difference comes from implementing the reforms mentioned earlier in this book—instituting a Protect America First military strategy, giving people the option to choose their own Social Security and Medicare retirement age, giving individuals more control over their health care spending, eliminating corporate welfare,

Comparison of Current Federal Revenue, Spending, and Deficits
2011 vs. 2021 Status Quo and 2021 with Reforms

(All Figures in Billions of Dollars)

Year	2011	2021 Status Quo	2021 People's Money
Revenue	2,314	4,511	4,178
National Security	853	1,093	651
Social Security	734	1,281	973
Medicare	494	847	602
Means Tested	695	1,022	745
Other	600	663	449
Interest	221	869	619
Total Outlays	3,597	5,775	4,040
Surplus/(Deficit)	(1,283)	(1,264)	138

demanding a return on investments, tightening up a bit on eligibility standards for welfare, and trimming the federal payroll.

Over the next decade, the People's Money approach would generate cumulative deficits of $6.8 trillion less than the status quo. Of that total, $2.3 trillion would come from the military budget, $1.2 trillion from Social Security and Medicare savings, $900 billion from means-tested programs, $770 billion from reduced interest payments, $690 billion from the elimination of corporate welfare payments, and $447 billion from reduction in government payrolls.

Keep in mind that those changes are merely reductions in savings from the status quo and projected spending. Even with all of these changes, the federal budget would still grow from $3.6 trillion in 2011 to $4.0 trillion in 2021. However, that's much slower growth than the rate of population growth plus inflation, and it's a low enough rate of growth to lead to a balanced budget within seven years.

Even more important, though, are the long-term savings that would eliminate the massive unfunded liabilities in Social Security and Medicare.

Measuring the Savings

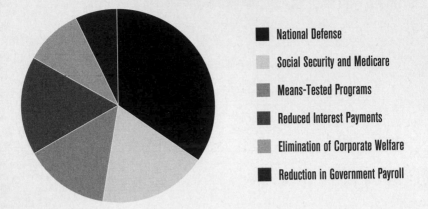

- National Defense
- Social Security and Medicare
- Means-Tested Programs
- Reduced Interest Payments
- Elimination of Corporate Welfare
- Reduction in Government Payroll

A more detailed answer is provided in the table below and the explanatory notes that follow.

Year	2011	2012	2013	2014	2015	2016	2017	2018	2019	2020	2021
Traditional Measurement	-1,284	-1,024	-895	-747	-750	-884	-903	-953	-1,075	-1,174	-1,264
National Defense Cuts	0	0	0	0	0	0	0	0	0	0	0
Savings from Ending Wars		0	0	0	67	120	172	174	179	182	186
Savings from Not Defending Others		0	13	42	71	99	130	162	192	224	256
Social Security Tax Cut	0	0	-301	-319	-337	-360	-378	-398	-418	-436	-457
Social Security Benefit Cuts	0	0	0	0	0	0	0	0	0	0	0
Social Security Other Revenue	0	0	302	306	309	314	314	313	311	305	301
Social Security Voluntary Change	0	0	0	0	0	0	0	0	1	3	6
Medicare Tax Hike	0	0	-109	-77	-39	5	53	107	113	118	124
Medicare Other Revenue	0	0	76	106	135	166	194	222	221	217	214
Medicare Benefit Cuts	0	0	0	0	0	0	0	0	0	0	0
Medicare Voluntary Change	0	0	0	0	0	0	0	1	2	4	30
Medicare 5–Year Adjustment	0	0	0	0	0	0	0	0	0	0	0
Corporate Welfare	0	20	40	50	60	70	80	85	90	95	100
Government Payroll	0	10	17	25	32	40	48	56	64	73	81
Ground Transportation	0	7	4	13	14	19	17	19	21	22	23
NASA	0	2	3	4	4	4	4	4	4	4	5

Year	2011	2012	2013	2014	2015	2016	2017	2018	2019	2020	2021
Education	0	15	16	17	17	18	19	20	21	22	23
Foreign Aid	0	2	2	3	3	3	3	3	4	4	4
Other Means-Tested Programs	0	-15	-16	3	26	62	90	122	166	208	254
White House/Congress Cuts, Other Savings	0	1	1	1	1	1	1	1	1	1	1
Interest Savings		0	1	2	8	26	57	94	140	192	250
Revised Update	-1,284	-982	-846	-572	-379	-297	-99	34	38	66	138
Deficit Reduction	0	42	49	175	371	587	804	987	1,113	1,240	1,402
Cumulative, Deficit Reduction		42	91	266	637	1,224	2,028	3,015	4,128	5,368	6,770

National Defense Cuts—No reductions in spending growth or cuts in spending are projected in programs or personnel defending the vital interests of the United States.

Savings from Ending Wars—The CBO projections show spending for "Overseas Contingency Operations" ranging from $165 billion to $186 billion every single year from 2011 to 2021. This funding is above and beyond the baseline military spending and is used to pay for wars in Afghanistan, Iraq, and Libya. There is no public support for continuing these operations through the next decade. The projected savings in the table above assume that this spending on wars is held steady from 2012 to 2014 and then phased out entirely by 2017. People may argue about whether that is too fast or too slow, and the real answer may ultimately be determined by the situation on the ground. Regardless, American voters are ready to zero out this spending as soon as possible, and certainly within five more years. If there is a need to leave troops in Iraq or Afghanistan for a lengthy period, it should be folded into the larger military budget rather than being an add-on. It should, of course, be noted that there is limited public support for troops to remain in those countries for more than a modest time.

Savings from Not Defending Others—The American people are not isolationists, but they have no desire to be the world's policeman and are ready to remove troops from Western Europe, Japan, and other places. Few recognize that the United States spends six times as much on the military as any other country in the world, and most don't even support spending three times as much. This suggests a strategy that relies more on Dwight Eisenhower's and Ronald Reagan's view that use of military forces abroad should be more restrained than it has been since the Cold War ended. Strategically, the objective would be to defend the vital interests of the United States, rather than seeking to maintain order in the rest of the world. Numerically, the projections show baseline spending inching up a bit in 2012, holding steady in 2013, and then gradually working to a target level described in chapter 3. That target would show military spending in 2021 equal to where it was in 2001, along with changes only to match the growth of population and inflation. Under this approach, the military baseline spending would decline from $546 billion in 2011 to $449 billion in 2021. Spending on veterans' affairs would increase from $142 billion to $202 billion during the same time. In later years, the cost of veterans' affairs would decline due to a smaller number of military personnel and a smaller number of injuries from military operations. The United States would still be spending three times as much on defense as any other nation in the world. Obviously, spending could change from the baseline if strategic conditions shift.

Social Security Tax Cut—Under current law, 12.4 percent of most wage compensation is paid in Social Security taxes. Half is paid by the employer and half by the employee. As described in chapter 4, however, that would be increased to 14.6 percent, but the employee portion would be made optional. Those who wanted to maintain their current retirement age could pay it, while those who wanted to pay less in taxes could do so in exchange for delaying retirement benefits. The effect of these changes is to reduce the mandatory Social Security tax from the current 12.4 percent to 7.3 percent (half of 14.6 percent). The projections are made on a static-analysis basis, meaning that no economic growth is assumed from this tax reduction.

Social Security Benefit Cuts—Absolutely no Social Security benefit cuts are proposed in this book or included in these projections.

Social Security Other Revenue—This reflects the revenue from those people who voluntarily pay more to Social Security in exchange for a lower retirement age. The particular numbers depend heavily upon how many people decide to choose a higher retirement age and lower taxes. The projections here assume that 30 percent of workers opt for the higher retirement age in 2013 and that the share grows to 54 percent by 2021. It also assumes that all who choose this option choose to pay none of the voluntary taxes and accept the highest-possible retirement age. Given polling, these numbers are as good a starting point as any, but there is no way to provide a more precise estimate. If more people opt for the higher retirement age, this revenue total would be a bit smaller, but there would be no impact on the long-term balance of the Social Security program. Short-term revenues would be a bit higher if fewer people select the higher retirement age. The way that federal accounting works, these revenues do not count as additional taxes since they are voluntary. Instead, they count as offsets against Social Security outlays (benefit payments) and reduce the net Social Security spending reported in budget totals.

Social Security Voluntary Change—If voters are given the right to select a higher retirement age beginning in 2013, a small number of people in their late fifties would likely accept that option. By 2019–21, the effects would be seen on the spending side of the equation as they would begin collecting benefits a few years later than originally scheduled. For purposes of this projection, it is assumed that one-tenth of 1 percent fewer people would receive benefits in 2019, growing to half a percent in 2021. These numbers are relatively meaningless in the larger budget debate but point to a trend that will grow over time. Within a generation or so, the voluntary trade-offs for a higher retirement age could cut the required benefit payments in half.

Medicare Tax Hike—Medicare taxes are projected to grow for most workers from 2.9 percent currently to 3.9 percent in 2014, then increase a point a year until the total is 7.9 percent, as discussed in chapter 5. As with Social Security, half of the tax is currently paid by the employee and half by the employer. And as with Social Security, the employee half would be made optional. That results in a lower mandatory tax rate in 2013 (1.45%), 2014 (1.95%), and 2015 (2.45%). After that, the mandatory rate would be higher than it is today, peaking at 3.95 percent in 2018 and beyond. So the projections show a reduction in projected Medicare tax receipts for 2013 to 2015 and an increase in revenue from 2016 to 2021. It's important to note that the mandatory tax for Social Security and Medicare combined will drop from 15.3 percent today to 11.25 percent in 2021.

Medicare Other Revenue—As with Social Security, this revenue is from those who voluntarily pay more to keep a lower retirement age. And as with the Social Security revenue, it is technically counted as a reduction in Medicare outlays (along with other Medicare premium payments). It is assumed that 30 percent of workers opt for the higher retirement age in 2013 and that the share grows to 54 percent by 2021. It is important to note that this approach will strengthen the Medicare trust fund in the short term. However, if more people opt for the higher retirement age, the amount of short-term benefit will be reduced. At the same time, if more people opt for the higher retirement age, the long-term prospects for the Medicare trust fund will improve.

Medicare Benefit Cuts—Absolutely no Medicare benefit cuts are proposed in this book or included in these projections.

Medicare Voluntary Change—If voters are given the right to select a higher retirement age beginning in 2013, a small number of people in their late fifties would likely accept that option. By 2019–21, the effects would be seen on the spending side of the equation as they would begin collecting benefits a few years later than originally scheduled. For purposes of this projection, it is assumed that one-tenth of 1 percent fewer people would receive benefits in 2019, growing to half a percent in 2021. In the earliest days of this reform, some people may simply want to stay on their private insurance plan a little bit longer. These numbers are relatively meaningless in the larger budget debate but point to a trend that will grow over time. Within a generation or so, the voluntary trade-offs for a higher retirement age could significantly cut the required benefit payments.

Medicare Five-Year Adjustment—As the new Medicare plan is implemented, trustees will monitor the progress to see how many people are opting for higher retirement ages, how the market forces are reducing the cost of health care, and how the tax changes are affecting the short- and long-term solvency of the trust fund. Further changes might be needed, but none are projected at this time since it is assumed that Medicare will be in long-term balance by 2021.

Corporate Welfare—Ending corporate welfare is enormously popular, and the projections are consistent with the discussion in chapter 8, with savings starting at $20 billion and reaching $100 billion a year.

Government Payroll—The federal government employed 1,345,000 in 2011 outside the military and the postal service. That is up 24 percent from a decade earlier and projected to grow to 1,368,000 in 2012. The average compensation package for a federal worker in 2009 was reported to be $123,049, including health care, pension, and other benefits. Compensation growth with the status quo model is projected at 3 percent per year. Voters support a cut in total compensation of 1 percent per year for a decade. That would reduce the government payroll from $175.6 billion in 2011 to $158.8 billion in 2021. However, without the savings, payroll costs are projected to reach $240.0 billion in 2021. It is assumed that the military payroll will be reduced by an equal or larger share as troops are brought home from Europe and Japan. Those savings are not included in this line item because they have already been built into the military budget discussion.

Ground Transportation—Projections assume that spending on ground transportation is held steady for a decade. This could be achieved by ending the president's high-speed-rail plan, ending Amtrak subsidies, and slowing the growth in spending on highways. If additional highway spending is needed, it should be funded by increases in the gasoline tax.

NASA—Figures project a general decline in spending on the space program, consistent with voter attitudes and the end of the Space Shuttle program.

Education—As described in chapter 9, this reflects a reduction in the number of grants provided for higher education and replacing them with loans. Also, it assumes placing limits on the amount of loans available so that the program supports those who want to attend college rather than supporting elite universities.

Foreign Aid—While not addressed earlier in this book, polls have consistently shown a desire to cut foreign aid. Most recently, voters expressed a desire to eliminate all foreign aid to every Middle Eastern country except Israel.[5]

Other Means-Tested Programs—Projections assume a cap on means-tested spending. While it is assumed that means-tested spending should decline after the recession, government projections show it continuing to rise. The projections in this estimate show means-tested spending growing at the current levels for 2012 and 2013. Then, spending growth is slowed to reach a spending target by the year 2021. That target would show means-tested spending in 2021 equal to where it was in 2008 along with increases equal to the growth of population and inflation. Despite the reduction in spending growth, means-tested spending would grow from $695 billion in 2011 to $745 billion in 2021.

White House/Congress Cuts—As noted earlier, little in the way of monetary savings is to be achieved by cutting the White House and congressional payrolls and staffs, but it's important for those at the top to lead the way, and the changes are projected to reduce currently anticipated spending by about a billion dollars a year.

Interest Savings—These savings result from reduction in the cumulative debt and are based upon interest rates assumed for other CBO projections.

As has been noted, the current system of budgets and accounting does not reflect a balanced budget in the way that the American people understand the term. Under current rules, the federal government treats trust fund money as if it's owned by the government and can be used according to the whims of Congress. The government borrows the money from the trust funds to pay for programs in the operating budget. However, most Americans don't see it that way.

If the government measured the balanced budget in a way that respected the trust funds and the American people, the short-term num-

---

5.   Rasmussen Reports, "Most Americans Favor End of the US Foreign Aid to Middle East Except Israel," Feb. 2011.

bers would look a bit different, but the trends would be similar. Every year for the next decade, the federal government is projected to borrow between $115 and $232 billion from the various trust funds. Adding in that borrowing, the reported deficit would be higher each year. However, over the same time, the federal government is projected to pay between and $208 and $389 billion toward Medicare. Those funds would now be paid out of the Medicare trust fund and reduce the reported operating deficit. A rough summary of how all this might look in 2021 is presented below:

Proper Accounting Estimate	2021
In billions of dollars	
Revenue	4,178
National Security	851
Social Security	655
Medicare	466
Means Tested	745
Other	717
Interest	925
Total Outlays	4,158
Surplus/(Deficit)	20

Author's calculations

One thing that jumps out right away in this summary is that the highest category of spending is interest on the federal debt. That's because, when the trust funds are treated as separate entities, the government interest payments to those funds become apparent. According to the president's budget documents, the government is expected to pay between $113 and $161 billion in interest every year to the Social Security trust fund. Interest paid to other trust funds will range from $65 to $145 billion annually.

Trust Fund Balance

It's important to remember that the numbers above refer to the year-to-year operating budget. While that's important, the larger problems facing the nation today are the unfunded liabilities highlighted in chapter 2. Projections showing these liabilities topping $100 trillion give a reliable sense of scale and correctly indicate that the unfunded liabilities are much bigger than the official debt. But while they give a healthy sense of scale, they should not be considered precise. If long-term economic growth is assumed to be a bit higher, the unfunded liabilities will come down. If long-term economic growth is assumed to be a bit lower, the unfunded liabilities will move higher.

Still, whether the number is over or under $100 trillion, the steps outlined in this book will completely eliminate those unfunded liabilities. The Social Security reforms will instantly balance that trust fund. The Medicare reforms will take a bit longer, but they will eliminate that program's $89 trillion long-term liability within a decade. Taking these factors into account, the difference between trusting the Political Class and trusting the American people is summarized succinctly by noting that, after ten years, the Status Quo would leave the nation $160 trillion in debt. The People's Money approach would reduce the total government debt from $120 trillion today to $18 trillion. The remainder would be paid off in the following decade.

CONCLUSION

The End of the Political Class

———•◆•———

In May 1979, I learned one of the most important lessons of my life. We were trying to convince the Getty Oil Company to fund a crazy idea for a new sports network called ESPN. Getty was then one of the top thirty-five or so companies on the Fortune 500 list and had already advanced our company $5 million a few months earlier. This meeting was to decide if they would take the leap and provide enough funding to make ESPN a reality, a commitment that ultimately took more than $100 million.

The Getty officials did their best to intimidate us and held the meeting in a room with a boomerang-shaped table. My father and I were on the inside of the boomerang, and about eight Getty officials were arrayed on the outside. The Getty team included Harold Berg, chairman of the board, who had just stepped down as CEO, Sid Petersen, the new CEO and president, our divisional vice president, some attorneys, and others. We had one guy on the other side whom we considered a friend: George Conner. We still keep in touch with him to this day. George was the guy sent by Getty to handle the due diligence on their investment, but his role in this meeting was more of an interested observer than a participant.

At some point in the meeting, someone on the Getty team asked about our revenue projections for 1988. I got to handle the question because I had done the details of the projections. It's hard to believe, but with no PCs or laptops in those days, the early versions of the projections were all done by hand on thirteen-column analysis pads. Projecting revenues for 1988 in May of 1979 would have been a challenge under any circumstances, but it was especially iffy for a company and an industry that didn't yet exist. ESPN was just a few months away from being the first advertiser-supported twenty-four-hour cable network.

As a twenty-three-year-old, I answered in much the way an earnest young congressional staffer might answer a question about the federal budget. I explained all the underlying assumptions by pointing out that if the cable industry grew at this rate, *and* this percentage of cable systems picked up satellite coverage, *and* our network was carried by some other percentage, *and* our average audience share was X, *and* we sold Y number of commercials per hour, *and* our sales rate was such and such, *and* our ads sold for a conservatively estimated cost-per-thousand viewers, the answer was obvious. In other words, I gave a precisely accurate, but utterly meaningless, answer. I have long since forgotten the specific assumptions, but I will never forget the response of Getty CEO Sid Petersen:

> *He doesn't know any more than we do what the revenue will be in 1988. We need to look at his underlying assumptions. If cable systems will carry ESPN, if people will watch it, and if advertisers will sponsor such narrowcasting programs, we have a winner. If not, it will be a dry hole. We make decisions like this in the oil industry every day, let's decide.*

Petersen was, of course, right. Making the details of the columns add up didn't matter; the underlying assumptions were what were truly important. If the fundamentals were sound, the business would be, too. Petersen was looking at the big picture rather than the details. For what it's worth, my projections showed that ESPN would be in about 30 million households by the end of the 1980s, a seemingly outlandish number at a time when only about 13 million households in the nation had cable. My projection was way off; ESPN was in closer to 60 million households by the end of that decade. The underlying assumptions were certainly correct and the fundamentals were sound.

In the decades since that encounter, I have not always remembered Petersen's lesson as well as I should have. But that says more about my own missteps than it does about the wisdom of that lesson.

However, applying that lesson to all I have learned about the federal budget crisis leads to a terribly disconcerting conclusion. The key facts are fairly straightforward: American voters have, for the last four or five decades, consistently elected candidates who promised to reduce government taxes and spending. Despite that clear directive from voters, government spending has gone up every single year since 1954. Rather than address the problem, politicians relied upon accounting gimmicks to cover it up. Voters don't understand how things got so bad, but are understandably horrified by the massive budget deficit threatening to pass unconscionable burdens on to future generations.

Politicians, a group notably averse to accountability, have come up with a clever story to say that voters are to blame. They make the absurd claim that voters like spending cuts in theory, but oppose changes in specific programs. That claim is a lie. The Political Class wants government spending to go up, not the American people.

That's why we have a budget crisis. It's not about the numbers, and it's not about the policies. Those certainly have to be addressed, but the real issue is that the Political Class thinks they should be in charge and allowed to pursue their own agenda. They want to rule the nation, rather than play a support role in a self-governing society; they want to pick economic winners and losers, rather than letting consumers pick those who serve them best. They hate the notion of having to ask voters for approval of their plans. While most of us are looking to the future, the Political Class longs to take us back to 1775, when kings were kings and consent of the governed didn't matter.

That view has been prevalent in Washington and on Wall Street at least since the 1960s, and probably longer. Those who thought of themselves as our betters dismissed as quaint such notions as balancing the federal budget, requiring down payments from those who wished to buy a home, and protecting trust funds set aside to pay for an intended purpose. They had creative, new approaches that they thought would work better than traditional ideas built upon generations of experience and common sense. Initially, they probably just hoped voters wouldn't notice, and later they launched a cover-up using accounting gimmicks. But by continuing to grow the government while voters continued to demand a different approach, the Political Class provoked a fight with the American people. Perhaps they really believed the American people would eventually thank them, or perhaps they didn't care. Whatever the expectation, the fight spanned decades and frustration grew among the American people. Finally, it boiled over following the Wall Street bailouts.

Given a choice between serving the voters and bailing out their friends, America's politicians had little hesitation. They didn't even try to convince voters that the scheme made sense. With the bailouts, the Political Class declared war on the very idea of self-governance and moved into open rebellion against the nation.

That's the truly disconcerting part. It is hard for someone who grew up believing in the ideals of our nation and its great heritage to acknowledge that a clique based in Washington, DC, and Wall Street would rather rebel against the nation than do their duty, but I cannot come to any other conclusion. As skeptical as most Americans are today about politics and politicians, I am convinced that they would become even more skeptical if they had the time to get more involved and actually see the way our political process works.

At its core, the Political Class rebellion seeks to restore the notion that some people should naturally rule over others. The politicians believe that their whims and opinions are superior to those of the people, a view rejected entirely by the American Revolution and the American people today. The claim that "all men are created equal" did not contain the caveat "but some are created *more* equal." Voters understand this. As has been the case throughout American history, voters are decades ahead of the politicians. Today, voters instinctively understand that the solution to our national challenges is to shift responsibility and decision-making authority away from politicians and back to individual citizens. That will solve the budget crisis by spending the People's Money as the people see fit. It will also solve the larger problem of the Political Class rebellion by reminding everyone that the American people are the sovereign authority of the land.

Sometimes, of course, people get discouraged. It is hard to feel optimistic when the economy is struggling and the political discourse is so toxic. Sometimes, too, the Political Class disinformation causes doubts—what if it's true? What if voters really are the problem? What if there's no way out short of a major tax hike? Or what if there's just no way out?

Voters are the solution, not the problem. There is a way out of the fiscal crisis: their way. It's a path that the Political Class won't want to take, but voters shouldn't be too concerned with what the politicians want. If every member of Congress gave up in disgust and quit tomorrow, it wouldn't be hard to fill the members' shoes. Even if every congressional staffer and lobbyist went with them, the country would do just fine.

A deeper cause for optimism comes from recognizing that the American people still believe deeply in the founding principles, principles that the Political Class has discarded. Voters look forward to seeing our nation move closer to the dream expressed so eloquently by Dr. Martin Luther King Jr. We want the United States to "rise up and live out the true meaning of its creed." That creed is a powerful affirmation of the nation's founding ideals.

Americans today overwhelmingly believe that all of us were created equal. We believe that all of us have been "endowed by our Creator with certain unalienable rights" including the right to "Life, Liberty, and the Pursuit of Happiness."

Americans still believe that governments derive their only just authority from the consent of the governed. When the United States is living up to its ideals, we believe we are a shining city on a hill, a beacon of hope and liberty, and the last best hope of mankind. Today, we also recognize that our nation needs the same thing that was needed at the end of the most famous presidential address of all time. The United States once again needs "a new birth of freedom" so "that government of the people, by the people, for the people, shall not perish from the earth."

Our challenge today is to make those timeless ideals work for the twenty-first century.

ACKNOWLEDGMENTS

————•◆•————

A book like this is a team effort, and for me the team begins with my wife of nearly twenty-five years, Laura. She was always available when I needed to bounce ideas off her and always patient with me when the stress of deadlines neared.

My oldest son, Andy, played an invaluable role, helping me organize the earliest drafts and doing a preliminary edit so I could submit something presentable to the publisher. It's at the same time humbling and gratifying to know that my son has grown up to be a better writer and editor than me.

I would also like to thank Louise Burke and Anthony Ziccardi at Simon and Schuster for believing in the project. Mitchell Ivers was a delight to meet and is an amazing editor. Natasha Simons provided valuable support work to keep the entire process flowing.

At Rasmussen Reports, my chief operating officer, Mike Boniello, deserves special thanks, as do Fran Coombs, Gina Jannone, Beth Chunn, and Alex Napoliello. It's also important to thank the millions of Americans who took part in Rasmussen Reports' surveys over the years to help me gain a better understanding of the public mood.

The chance to speak around the country and receive direct feedback from a wide variety of audiences gave me the chance to try out new ideas and ways to explain them. This was made possible by Premiere Speakers Bureau. Duane Ward, Shawn Hanks, and Brian Lord sent me to more places than I can remember, but every event was a learning experience.

On the policy front, I am deeply indebted to scores of scholars, analysts, and advocates whose writing about policy gave me a framework for translating public attitudes into a policy direction. Some took time to speak with me or review portions of the book, and I have tried to acknowledge their efforts in the text itself.

And, finally, this book would not have happened without the guidance, counsel, and efforts of my agent, Frank Breeden, at Premiere Authors Literary Agency.

BIBLIOGRAPHY

———•◆•———

"Ala. still collecting tax for Confederate vets." CBS News, 20 Jul. 2010. Web: 4 Sep. 2011.

America's Newsroom with Bill Hemmer & Martha MacCallum. FOX News, 17 Mar. 2011. Web: 30 Aug. 2011.

Andrews, Edmund L. "Vast Bailout by US Proposed in Bid to Stem Financial Crisis." *New York Times*, 18 Sep. 2008. Web: 9 Aug. 2011. http://www.nytimes.com/2008/09/19/business/19fed.html.

Andrews, Edmund L., and Peter Baker. "AIG Planning Huge Bonuses After $170 Billion Bailout." *New York Times*, 14 Mar. 2009. Web: 30 Aug. 2011.

Angrisano, Carlos, et al. *Accounting for the Cost of Health Care in the United States.* McKinsey and Company, 2007. Web: 30 Aug. 2011.

"Bailout Sparks Anger." *The Real News.* Real News Network, 28 Sep. 2008. Web: 9 Aug. 2011. http://therealnews.com/t2/index.php ?option=com_content&task=view&id=31&Itemid=74&jumival =2422.

Baker, Dean. "Did We Make a Profit on Citigroup?" *Michael Moore*, 2 Apr. 2010. Web: 30 Aug. 2011.

Ball, Robert M. "The Role of Social Insurance in Preventing Economic Dependency." National Conference on the Churches & Social Welfare, Cleveland, OH, 24 Oct. 1961. Social Security Online. Web: 9 Aug. 2011. http://www.ssa.gov/history/churches.html.

Barnes, James A. "Six of Ten Political Insiders Believe Public Is Ill-Informed." *National Journal*. Atlantic Media, 24 Mar. 2011. Web: 9 Aug. 2011. http://www.nationaljournal.com/politics/six-of-ten-political-insiders-believe-public-is-ill-informed-20110324.

Barone, Michael. "Traveling Back to the Future on Intercity Buses." *Real Clear Politics*, 25 Aug. 2011. Web: 31 Aug. 2011.

——. "Will College Bubble Burst from Public Subsidies?" *Washington Examiner*, 19 July 2011. Web: 30 Aug. 2011.

Bartlett, Dwight K., III. "Measures of Actuarial Status for Social Security: Retrospect and Prospect." *Transactions of Society of Actuaries* 33 (1983): 541–64. Web: 9 Aug. 2011. http://www.soa.org/.

Batkins, Sam, and Douglas Holtz-Eakin. "Toll in 'Temporary' Taxes: $1.4 Trillion." *Investor's Business Daily*, 14 July 2010. Web: 5 Sep. 2011.

Bensinger, Ken, and Carolyn Cole. "Masses Aren't Buying Bailout: Indignant Americans Stage Protests, Deluge Congressional Offices." *Los Angeles Times*, 26 Sep. 2008. Web: 9 Aug. 2011. http://articles.latimes.com/2008/sep/26/business/fi-voxpop26.

Bremmer, Ian. *The End of the Free Market: Who Wins the War Between States and Corporations?* New York: Penguin Group, 2010.

Bryan, William Jennings, ed. *The World's Famous Orations*. New York: Funk and Wagnalls, 1906; repr., New York: Bartleby.com, 2003. Web: 5 Sep. 2011.

Calmes, Jackie, and Dalia Sussman. "Poll Finds Wariness About Cutting Entitlements." *New York Times*, 20 Jan. 2011. Web: 9 Aug. 2011. http://www.nytimes.com/2011/01/21/us/politics/21poll.html?_r=2.

Carter, James E., Jr. "Human Rights and Foreign Policy." *Info USA*. Notre Dame University, June 1977. Web: 25 Aug. 2011.

——. "Remarks of the President at the Welcoming Ceremony." Civilian Terminal, Okecie International Airport, Warsaw, Poland, 29 Dec. 1977. The American Presidency Project. Web: 25 Aug. 2011.

Cho, David, and Neil Irwin. "Rubin, Paulson, Geithner, a Familiar Trio at Heart of Citigroup Bailout." *Washington Post*, 25 Nov. 2008. Web: 30 Aug. 2011.

Chubb, John E., and Terry M. Moe. *Liberating Learning: Technology, Politics, and the Future of American Education*. San Francisco: Jossey-Bass, 2009.

Clinton, William Jefferson. "1996 State of the Union Address." US Capitol, 23 Jan. 1996. *Welcome to the White House*. Web: 9 Aug. 2011. http://clinton4.nara.gov/WH/New/other/sotu.html.

CNN Wire Staff. "Mullen: Debt Is Top National Security Threat." *CNN US*. CNN, 27 Aug. 2010. Web: 25 Aug. 2011.

Cohen, Lauren, Joshua D. Coval, and Christopher J. Malloy. "Do Powerful Politicians Cause Corporate Downsizing?" *NBER Working Paper Series* w15839 (Mar. 2010). Available at SSRN: http://ssrn.com/abstract=1578677.

Cohn, Jonathan. "John Boehner Is Wrong: Bigger Government Goes with Bigger People. Just Ask the Dutch." *New Republic*, editorial, 25 July 2011. Web: 30 Aug. 2011.

Collins, James C., and Jerry I. Porras. *Built to Last: Successful Habits of Visionary Companies*. New York: Harper Collins, 1997.

Congressional Record. 14 Feb. 2011: H728–31. *Congressional Record Online*. Web: 24 Aug. 2011. http://www.gpo.gov.

Daly, Corbett B. "Obama Says He Cannot Guarantee Social Security Checks Will Go Out on Aug. 3." *CBS News*, 12 July 2011. Web: 30 Aug. 2011.

DeHaven, Tad, and Veronique de Rugy. "Terminating the Small Business Association." CATO Institute, Aug. 2011. Web: 4 Sep. 2011.

Dennis, Brady, and David Cho. "Rage at AIG Swells as Bonuses Go Out." *Washington Post*, 17 Mar. 2009. Web: 30 Aug. 2011.

Duchin, Ran, and Denis Sosyura. "The Politics of Government Investment" (Apr. 2011). Ross School of Business Paper No. 1127. Available at SSRN: http://ssrn.com/abstract=1426219.

Dueck, Colin. *Hard Line: The Republican Party and US Foreign Policy Since World War II*. Princeton: Princeton University Press, 2010.

Eberstadt, Nicholas. "Poverty Rate." *Milken Institute Review*, Fourth Quarter 2008, 41–49. Web: 6 Sep. 2011.

"The Economy in 2011." *New York Times*, 1 Jan. 2011. Web: 6 Sep. 2011.

Edwards, Chris. "Special-Interest Spending." CATO Institute, Apr. 2009. Web: 6 Sep. 2011.

Eisenhower, Dwight D. "First Inaugural Address." US Congress, Capitol, 20 Jan. 1953. Yale Law School: The Avalon Project. Web: 25 Aug. 2011.

Esipova, Neli, and Julie Ray. "700 Million World Wide Desire to Migrate Permanently: US Tops Desired Destination Countries." Gallup, 2 Nov. 2009. Web: 31 Aug. 2011.

Fisher, Richard W. "Remarks before the Commonwealth Club of California." Commonwealth Club of California, San Francisco, 28 May 2008. Federal Reserve Bank of Dallas. Web: 30 Aug. 2011.

Flemming v. Nestor. 363 U.S. 603. Supreme Court of the US. 1960. FindLaw.com. Thomson Reuters, 2011. Web: 23 Aug. 2011.

Flyvbjerg, Bent, et al. *Megaprojects and Risk: An Anatomy of Ambition*. New York: Cambridge University Press, 2010.

Freddoso, David. "Pelosi on Health Care: 'We Have to Pass the Bill So You Can Find Out What's in It.'" *Beltway Confidential*, 9 Mar. 2010. Web: 30 Aug. 2011.

Friedman, Milton. *Capitalism and Freedom: Fortieth Anniversary Edition*. Chicago: University of Chicago Press, 2002.

Galbraith, John Kenneth. *The New Industrial State*. Princeton: Princeton University Press, 2007.

Gallup Poll. "Timeline of Polling History: Events That Shaped the United States, and the World." 2011. Web: 24 Oct. 2011.

Gates, Robert M. "Remarks on the Role of the Modern Navy." Navy League Sea-Air-Space Exposition, Gaylord Convention Center, National Harbor, MD, 3 May 2010. US Department of Defense. Web: 25 Aug. 2011.

Gillen, Andrew, Matthew Denhart, and Jonathan Robe. "Who Subsidizes Whom? An Analysis of Education Costs and Revenues." Center for College Affordability and Productivity, Apr. 2011. Web. 5 Nov. 2011.

Giving USA Foundation. *Giving USA 2011: The Annual Report on Philanthropy for the Year 2010.* 2011. Retrieved from www.giving usareports.org.

Greenberg, Stanley B. "Tuning Out the Democrats." *New York Times,* editorial, 30 July 2011. Web: 30 Aug. 2011.

Hagan, Joe. "The Most Powerless Powerful Man on Wall Street." *New York,* 1 Mar. 2009. Web: 30 Aug. 2011.

Harvey, Philip. "The Right to Work and Basic Income Guarantees: Competing or Complementary Goals?" Philip Harvey, Rutgers University. Web: 31 Aug. 2011.

Haskins, Ron. "Fighting Poverty the American Way." Brookings Institution, June 2011. Web: 31 Aug. 2011.

Hayward, Steven F. *The Age of Reagan: The Fall of the Old Liberal Order.* New York: Prima Publishing, 2001.

Hogberg, David. "Pop Quiz: Why Are Tuitions So High?" *Investor's Business Daily,* 9 Aug. 2011. Web: 31 Aug. 2011.

Howard, Zach. "Vermont Single-Payer Health Care Law Signed by Governor." *Huffington Post,* 26 May 2011. Web: 4 Sep. 2011.

Huth, Mary M. "US Suffrage Movement Timeline, 1792–Present." Susan B. Anthony Center for Women's Leadership, University of Rochester, 2006. Web: 9 Aug. 2011. http://www.rochester.edu/sba/ suffragetimeline.html.

Immelt, Jeffrey R. "A Blueprint for Keeping America Competitive." *Washington Post*, editorial, 21 Jan. 2011. Web: 30 Aug. 2011.

Jaffe, Matthew. "Bailout Watchdog Barofsky Sounds 'Too Big to Fail' Warning." *ABC News*, 25 Jan. 2011. Web: 30 Aug. 2011.

Johnson, Rachel, et al. *Why Some Tax Units Pay No Income Tax*. Urban-Brookings Tax Policy Center, 2011. Web: 30 Aug. 2011.

Judis, John B. "New Republic: A Lesson from the Great Depression." NPR, editorial, 8 Aug. 2011. Web: 30 Aug. 2011.

Kahn, Joseph, and Alessandra Stanley. "Enron's Many Strands: Dual Role; Rubin Relishes Role of Banker as Public Man." *New York Times*, 11 Feb. 2002. Web: 30 Aug. 2011.

Kaiser Family Foundation and Health Research & Educational Trust. "Employer Health Benefits: 2010 Summary of Findings." Kaiser Family Foundation, 2 Sep. 2010. Web: 4 Sep. 2011.

Katz, Celeste. "VPOTUS Joe Biden: Dems Will 'Keep the Senate and Win the House.'" *New York Daily News*, 26 Oct. 2010. Web: 30 Aug. 2011.

Kennan, George. "The Sources of Soviet Conduct." *Foreign Affairs*, 1947. Web: 25 Aug. 2011.

Kennedy, John F. "Special Message to the Congress on Urgent National Needs." Congress of the United States, the Capitol, Washington, DC, 25 May 1961. JFK Library, 31 Aug. 2011.

King, Martin Luther, Jr. "I Have a Dream." Lincoln Memorial, Washington, DC, 28 Aug. 1963. American Rhetoric. Web: 9 Aug. 2011. http://www.americanrhetoric.com/speeches/mlkihaveadream.htm.

Klein, Ezra. "One Shot on Taxes: Don't Blow It, Democrats." *Washington Post*, editorial, 2 Aug. 2011. Web: 30 Aug. 2011.

Klein, Joel. "The Failure of the American Schools." *Atlantic*, June 2011. Web: 6 Sep. 2011.

Koebler, Jason. "Gates Foundation Donates $20 Million for Online Courses." *US News*, 29 Apr. 2011. Web: 31 Aug. 2011.

———. "Universities Begin to Offer Online High School Diplomas." *US News*, 8 Aug. 2011. Web: 31 Aug. 2011.

Korbe, Tina. "Updated—Worst of the Waste: The 100 Outrageous Government Spending Projects of 2010." *Foundry*, 28 Dec. 2010. Heritage Foundation. Web: 6 Sep. 2010.

Launius, Roger D. "Public Opinion Polls and Perceptions of US Human Spaceflight." *Space Policy* 19 (2003): 163–75. Science Direct. Web: 31 Aug. 2011.

Leder, Michelle, and Justin Rood. "Payday: GM's Rick Wagoner Drives Away with $20M Retirement." *ABC News*, 30 Mar. 2009. Web: 30 Aug. 2011.

Lew, Jacob. "Opposing View: Social Security Isn't the Problem." *USA Today*, editorial, 21 Feb. 2011. Web: 30 Aug. 2011.

Lewis, Mark. "Rubin Red-Faced over Enron? Not in the Times." *Forbes*, 11 Feb. 2002. Web: 6 Sep. 2011.

Lowry, Rich. "Against the Balanced Budget Amendment." *National Review Online*, editorial, 19 July 2011. Web: 5 Sep. 2011.

Lucas, Deborah. "The Budgetary Cost of Fannie Mae and Freddie Mac and Options for the Future Federal Role in the Secondary Mortgage Market." Congressional Budget Office, Testimony, 2 June 2011. Web: 24 Oct. 2011.

Madison, James. "The Federalist #51: The Structure of the Government Must Furnish the Proper Checks and Balances Between the Different Departments." *Independent Journal*, Feb. 1788. Constitution Society. Web: 9 Aug. 2011. http://www.constitution.org/fed/federa51.htm.

———. "James Madison to W. T. Barry." 1786. In *The Founders' Constitution*, ed. Philip B. Kurland and Ralph Kerner, 103–9. Vol. 1.

Chicago: University of Chicago, 2000. Web: 9 Aug. 2011. http://press-pubs.uchicago.edu/founders/documents/v1ch18s35.html.

Marklein, Mary Beth. "Report: First Two Years of College Show Small Gains." *USA Today*, 18 Jan. 2011. Web: 31 Aug. 2011.

Maxwell, John C. *The 21 Irrefutable Laws of Leadership: Follow Them and People Will Follow You.* Nashville: Thomas Nelson, 2007.

McArdle, Megan. "California High-Speed Rail Project to Cost More Than Expected." *Atlantic*, 11 Aug. 2011. Web: 31 Aug. 2011.

———. "GM's Profits Are Still a Huge Net Loss for Taxpayers." *Atlantic*, editorial, 12 May 2011. Web: 30 Aug. 2011.

McElhatton, Jim. "Lew Earned $1.1M from Citigroup Before State Department Job." *Washington Times*, 13 July 2010. Web: 30 Aug. 2011.

McGrane, Victoria, and Lisa Lerer. "Is Health Bill Too Complex to Grasp?" *Politico*, 30 July 2009. Web: 9 Aug. 2011. http://www.politico.com/news/stories/0709/25594.html.

Merline, John. "Regulation Business, Jobs Booming Under Obama." *Investor's Business Daily*, 15 Aug. 2011. Web: 6 Sep. 2011.

Mitchell, Daniel J. "What Gets You Most Upset About the TARP Bailout, the Lying, the Corruption, or the Economic Damage?" CATO at Liberty, 26 Oct. 2010. Web: 30 Aug. 2011.

Morgenson, Gretchen, and Joshua Rosner. *Reckless Endangerment: How Outsized Ambition, Greed, and Corruption Led to Economic Endangerment.* New York: Henry Hall, May 2011.

Myers, Robert J., and Francisco Bayo. "Hospital Insurance, Supplementary Medical Insurance, and Old-Age, Survivors, and Disability Insurance: Financing Basis Under the 1965 Amendments." SSA.gov., Feb. 1968. Web: 24 Oct. 2011.

Nixon, Richard M. "Radio Address on Older Americans." 30 Oct. 1972. Social Security Online. Web: 9 Aug. 2011. http://www.ssa.gov/history/nixstmts.html#radio.

———. "Statement on Signing the Social Security Amendments of 1972." 30 Oct. 1972. Social Security Online. Web: 9 Aug. 2011. http://www.ssa.gov/history/nixstmts.html#1972.

"No One Likes TARP, but It's Working." *Washington Post,* 1 Apr. 2010. Web: 30 Aug. 2011.

"Obama Ag Secretary Vilsack: Food Stamps Are A 'Stimulus,'" 16 Aug. 2011. http://www.realclearpolitics.com/video/2011/08/16/obama _ag_secretary_vilsack_food_stamps_are_a_stimulus.html.

Obama, Barack H. "2011 State of the Union Address." 112th Congress of the United States, Capitol, Washington, DC, 25 Jan. 2011. White House Online. Web: 31 Aug. 2011.

"OECD Health Data 2011—Frequently Requested Data." Organisation for Economic Co-operation and Development, 30 June 2011. Web: 4 Sep. 2011.

Orszag, Peter. "Too Much of a Good Thing: Why We Need Less Democracy." *New Republic,* 14 Sep. 2011. Web: 24 Oct. 2011.

Padgitt, Kail M. "Tax Freedom Day Arrives on April 12." *Special Report* 190 (2011): 1–8.

Paine, Thomas. "The American Crisis." Eds. Danny Barnhoon, George Welling, and Garry Wiersema. Department of Alfa-Information, University of Groningen, 20 May 1997. Web: 6 Sep. 2011.

Pew Research Center. "Section 3: The Deficit and Government Spending." *Fewer Want Spending to Grow, but Most Cuts Remain Unpopular: Changing Views of Federal Spending.* Pew Research Center, 10 Feb. 2011. Web: 9 Aug. 2011. http://people-press.org/ 2011/02/10/section-3-the-deficit-and-government-spending/.

"The Political Price of Backing Invaluable TARP." *Washington Post,* editorial, 5 July 2010. Web: 19 Aug. 2011. http://www.washingtonpost .com/wp-dyn/content/article/2010/07/04/AR2010070403831.html.

Preble, Christopher A. *The Power Problem.* Ithaca, NY: Cornell University Press, 2009.

Rampell, Catherine. "Many See the VAT Option as a Cure for Deficits." *New York Times*, 10 Dec. 2009. Web: 30 Aug. 2011.

Reagan, Ronald W. "Address to British Parliament." Parliament of the United Kingdom of Great Britain and Northern Ireland, Royal Gallery at the Palace of Westminster, London, 8 June 1982. American Rhetoric. Web: 25 Aug. 2011.

———. *An American Life*. New York: Simon and Schuster, 1990.

———. "Commencement Address at Notre Dame." University of Notre Dame, 17 May 1981. *National Review Online*. Web: 25 Aug. 2011.

———. "Radio Address to the Nation on Tax Reform." Camp David, MD, 12 June 1987. Tax Analysts. Web: 30 Aug. 2011.

Rector, Robert. "Uncovering the Hidden Welfare State: 69 Means-Tested Programs and \$940 Billion in Annual Spending." House Committee on Ways and Means, 5 Apr. 2011. Web: 31 Aug. 2011.

Rector, Robert, and Rachel Sheffield. "Understanding Poverty in the United States: Surprising Facts About America's Poor." Heritage Foundation, 13 Sep. 2011. Web: 24 Oct. 2011.

Rhee, Foon. "Push for Healthcare Reform Quotes Obama." *Political Intelligence*, 18 Nov. 2008. Web: 5 Nov. 2011.

Ribeiro, Ann Gonzalez. "'Temporary' Taxes That Stuck." Investopedia, 8 Feb. 2010. Web: 5 Sep. 2011.

Riedl, Brian. "Top 10 Examples of Government Waste." Heritage Foundation, 4 Apr. 2005. Web: 24 Oct. 2011.

Robinson, Thomas J. "Freedom Isn't Free: A Study of Compulsory Military Service in the United States Army." PhD diss., US Army Command and General Staff College, 2006. Web: 4 Sep. 2011.

Roosevelt, Franklin D. "Address to Advisory Council of the Committee on Economic Security on the Problems of Economic and Social Security." 14 Nov. 1934. Social Security Online. Web: 6 Sep. 2011.

———. "Message to Congress on Social Security." US Capitol, 17 Jan. 1935. Social Security Online. Web: 9 Aug. 2011. http://www.ssa .gov/history/fdrstmts.html#message2.

———. "1935 State of the Union Address." 25 Jan. 1935. University of Albany. Web: 31 Aug. 2011.

———. "Presidential Statement Signing the Social Security Act." 14 Aug. 1935. Social Security Online. Web: 30 Aug. 2011. http://www.ssa.gov/history/fdrstmts.html.

Saad, Lydia. "Americans Support Federal Involvement in Education: Democrats Want More Federal Involvement in Schools; Republicans Want Less." Gallup, 8 Sep. 2010. Web: 4 Sep. 2011.

Samuelson, Robert J. "Why We Must End Medicare 'As We Know It.'" *Washington Post*, editorial, 5 June 2011. Web: 30 Aug. 2011.

Schroeder, Steven A. "We Can Do Better—Improving the Health of the American People." *New England Journal of Medicine*, 20 Sep. 2007. Web: 24 Oct. 2011.

Sciolino, Elaine. "Madeleine Albright's Audition." *New York Times*, 22 Sep. 1996. Web: 29 Aug. 2011.

Sher, Lauren. "CNBC's Santelli Rants About Housing Bailout." *ABC News*, 19 Feb. 2009. Web: 6 Sep. 2011.

Sides, John. "Do Americans Really Want to Govern Themselves?" *Washington Post*, editorial, 23 Aug. 2010. Web: 9 Aug. 2011. http://voices.washingtonpost.com/ezra-klein/2010/08/do_americans _want_to_govern_th.html.

Silber, Jeffrey M., and Paul Condra. *BMO 2010 Education Industry Report*. BMO Capital Markets, Sep. 2010.

Sinclair, Gordon. "The Americans." 5 June 1973. American Rhetoric. Web: 29 Aug. 2011.

Smith, Ben. "Perdue: Cancel Congressional Elections." *Politico*, 27 Sep. 2011. Web: 24 Oct. 2011.

Smith, Jean Edward. *FDR*. New York: Random House Trade Paperbacks, 2008. Google Books. Web: 9 Aug. 2011.

Taft, Robert A. *A Foreign Policy for Americans*. Garden City, NY: Doubleday, 1951.

Tanner, Michael. "Bankrupt: Entitlements and the Federal Budget." *Policy Analysis* 623 (28 Mar. 2011). Web: 24 Oct. 2011.

Tax Policy Center. "Historical Payroll Tax vs. Income Tax." Urban Institute and Brookings Institute, 30 Apr. 2009. Web: 6 Sep. 2011.

"That Didn't Take Long." *New York Times*, editorial, 12 May 2011. Web: 30 Aug. 2011.

Truman, Harry S. "Statement by the President on the 10th Anniversary of the Social Security Act." 13 Aug. 1945. Social Security Online. Web: 30 Aug. 2011. http://www.ssa.gov/history/hststmts.html.

United States. Board of Trustees, Federal Old-Age and Survivors Insurance and Federal Disability Insurance Trust Funds. *The 2011 Annual Report of the Board of Trustees of the Federal Old-Age and Survivors Insurance and Federal Disability Insurance Trust Funds.* By Timothy F. Geithner et al. Washington: US Government Printing Office, 2011. Social Security Online. Web: 30 Aug. 2011. http://ssa.gov.

———. Census Bureau. "US Population Projections." 2008. Web: 6 Sep. 2011.

———. Congress. US House of Representatives. *Compilation of Patient Protection and Affordable Health Care Act.* 111th Congress, 2nd Sess. Washington: Office of the Legislative Counsel, 2010. Health Care. Web: 30 Aug. 2011. http://healthcare.gov.

———. Congressional Budget Office. *Budget and Economic Outlook: An Update.* Congressional Budget Outlook, Aug. 2011. Web: 6 Sep. 2011.

———. Council of Economic Advisors. *The Economic Report of the President.* 2008. FRASER. Web: 6 Sep. 2011.

———. Council of Economic Advisors. *The Economic Report of the President.* 2010. FRASER. Web: 6 Sep. 2011.

———. Department of Agriculture Economic Research Service. "Food Security in the US." 26 Aug. 2011. Web: 6 Sep. 2011.

———. Federal Highway Administration. "The Highway Trust Fund." US Department of Transportation, 6 Apr. 2011. Web: 9 Aug. 2011. http://www.fhwa.dot.gov/reports/financingfederalaid/fund.htm.

———. Federal Highway Administration. *2008 Conditions and Performance Report.* US Department of Transportation, 2008. Web: 31 Aug. 2011.

———. 1957–59 Advisory Council on Social Security. *Misunderstandings of Social Security Financing.* Social Security Online. Web: 23 Aug. 2011.

———. Office of Management and Budget. *Budget of the United States Government, Fiscal Year 2011.* White House. Web: 9 Aug. 2011. http://www.whitehouse.gov/omb/budget/Overview.

———. Office of Management and Budget. *Budget of the United States Government, Fiscal Year 2012.* Whitehouse.gov. Web: 9 Aug. 2011. http://www.whitehouse.gov/omb/budget/Overview.

———. Office of Management and Budget. *Historical Tables.* White House. Web: 9 Aug. 2011. http://www.whitehouse.gov/omb/budget/Historicals.

———. Social Security Administration. "Research Note #3: Details of Ida May Fuller's Payroll Tax Contributions." By Larry DeWitt. Social Security Online, July 1996. Web: 5 Sep. 2011.

———. Social Security Administration. "Research Note #20: The Social Security Trust Funds and the Federal Budget." By Larry DeWitt. Social Security Online, 17 June 2007. Web: 9 Aug. 2011.

———. *Social Security Amendments of 1972: Summary and Legislative History.* By Robert M. Ball. Social Security Online. Web: 23 Aug. 2011.

———. United States Navy. *Fact File: Amphibious Assault Ships.* 24 Jan. 2011. Web: 25 Aug. 2011.

———. United States Navy. *Status of the Navy.* 25 Aug. 2011. Web: 25 Aug. 2011.

USHistory.org. "Loyalists, Fence-Sitters, and Patriots." Independence Hall Association, 2011. Web: 24 Oct. 2011.

US Social Security Administration. Social Security Online. 26 Aug. 2011. Web: 30 Aug. 2011. http://ssa.gov.

Utt, Ronald. "More Transportation Spending: False Promises of Prosperity and Job Creation." Heritage Foundation, 2 Apr. 2008. Web: 31 Aug. 2011.

Washington, George. Letter to James Madison. 2 Mar. 1788. NYPL Digital Gallery. Web: 6 Sep. 2011.

Yager, Alicia. "Pundits Ponder Wisconsin Election Results at Society for Professional Journalists Forum." *Isthmus: The Daily Page*, 9 Nov. 2010. Web: 9 Aug. 2011. http://www.thedailypage.com/isthmus/article.php?article=31180.